BYFIELD

BYFIELD
Four Generations

The Descendants of
Abraham Byfield
and
Patience Corbin

By Paul W. Carpenter

BYFIELD
Four Generations

The Descendants of
Abraham Byfield
and
Patience Corbin

By Paul W. Carpenter

1 September 2015

Version 444

Table of Contents

Preface

Years ago, my parents gave me a folder containing family trees for both my father's and mother's families. The trees had been researched by my grandfather, Clyde Leslie Carpenter. Along with this folder I received a sword used in the Civil War by my great-great-grandfather, Oscar Fitzland Carpenter. The sword has been passed down to the eldest son through the generations. This was the beginning of my interest in genealogy and family history.

I've been following all the branches of my family tree for over 15 years. This is a project that can probably never be completed, but the research itself is rewarding. From my grandfather's sheaf of typewritten pages I've expanded the tree in all directions, adding ancestors extending to the beginnings of the settling of America.

My mother is a Byfield. In exploring the Byfield family I soon discovered that nearly every Byfield that I researched seemed to trace back to the same place - Abraham Byfield. At first this was just was just an impression, but as my research continued I became sure that I was related to just about every Byfield that I found. Finally, I made a list of every Byfield in the United States census of 1850. They all turned out to be descendants of Abraham Byfield.

A few years ago I decided that I would begin tracing all the descendants of Abraham Byfield and his wife, Patience Corbin. I wanted to see how much of the Byfield name in the United States started with that first family. My intent with this book is to enumerate at least the first four generations of the Abraham Byfield line. I also hope I can give a feel for who some of these people were and how they lived.

I have tried to be meticulous in my research. Each piece of information about a person needs to be proven by some record – a birth record, a census listing, a marriage record, a death certificate. Sometimes the pieces fit together easily and sometimes the connections are barely there. Some records no longer exist or never existed in the first place. Court houses burned or flooded, taking all the county records with them. The entire United States census for 1890 was destroyed by fire, leaving a big gap in the record. A girl might have been born just after 1880 and be married with a new surname by the time of the 1900 census. Is the fact that she gave a child the middle name of Byfield enough to connect her to a family of Byfields in the area?

Some connections aren't as sure as I would like, but I've done my best to only use what can be reasonably proven. In some cases I don't have proof for a fact but the information that I have is very likely to be true. In that case *the*

<u>*information will be presented in a different font and underlined like this*</u>. I'm sure there are errors. I hope that anyone reading this book that has better information will send me a note so that I can correct my records and update this book in the future. I would also love to have copies of photographs or family stories that I can include to give substance to the people and families recorded here.

About the Henry Numbering System

This book uses the Henry Numbering System. This system makes it easy to follow a family either backward or forward in time. From Wikipedia:

> The Henry System is a descending system created by **Reginald Buchanan Henry** for a genealogy of the families of the presidents of the United States that he wrote in 1935. It can be organized either by generation or not. The system begins with 1. The oldest child becomes 11, the next child is 12, and so on. The oldest child of 11 is 111, the next 112, and so on. The system allows one to derive an ancestor's relationship based on their number. For example, 621 is the first child of 62, who is the second child of 6, who is the sixth child of his parents.

Abraham H Byfield is designated "1" in this book.

The author of this book is "1541811".

About the Production of This Book

This book was created using Open Source software. I used *Linux Mint* as my operating system. My genealogy software is *Gramps* which is a great package available free for any operating system. Gramps includes a report tool that generates a detailed descendant report in a nearly print ready format. I used *LibreOffice Writer* to edit the files for the actual book using the Gramps report as a base point. LibreOffice is a free software package that is available on most operating systems. I used the free *Gimp* image processing software for editing images for print. Some of the graphics were created using the free *Inkscape* vector graphics editor.

BYFIELD ORIGINS

The Byfield name first appears in central England around Northamptonshire during the 11th century. Even by the 19th century, the Byfield name is most common in central England.

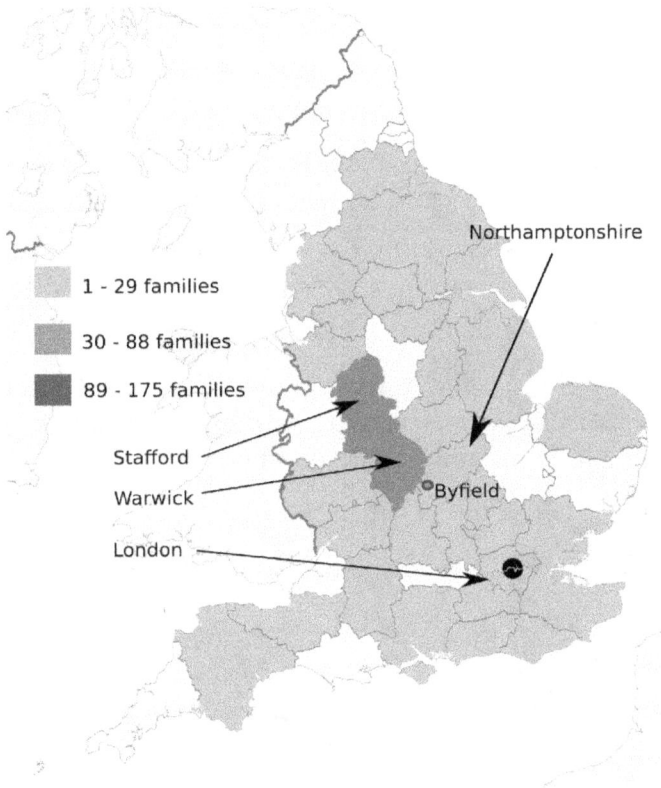

Based on England Map by Dr Greg with data from England 1891 census showing number of Byfield families in each county.

A town called Byfield is located in the southwestern corner of Northamptonshire county in England. The town probably grew up around the Byfield manor that is mentioned in the Doomsday Book (an early record of property in England).

The Byfield name is also found in Australia and in Jamaica. I speculate that the Australian Byfields are directly connected to the English Byfields. The Jamaican Byfields are possibly descended from slaves that were owned by an English Byfield. These are just my own hunches – I've not really researched the Byfields except in the United States.

Earliest Byfields in America.

There were very few Byfields in America prior to the appearance of the Abraham Byfield line around 1800.

The earliest Byfield known is Captain Nathaniel Byfield of the Boston area in the late 1600s. He was prominent in that area and is the person for whom the parish of Byfield near Cambridge is named. However, he had only daughters and so no Byfields are descended from him.

A few other Byfields appear in records prior to 1800 but I've found no evidence of their families so I can't tie them to the Abraham Byfield line:

- There were several Byfields that emigrated to Virginia, around Chesapeake Bay, in the mid 1600s. They were recorded in passenger lists as Bayfield, Bifield, Buffield, in addition to Byfield.

- A Thomas Byfield came to Maryland in 1774 and is probably the same one who enlisted as a substitute in the Revolutionary War. I've not determined if he had any family or where he settled.

- A Robert Byfield came to America in 1766.

- Another Thomas Byfield came to Maryland in 1778.

- There is a record of a Richard Byfield marriage to Elizabeth Roshton in New York in 1737.

- There is a will for William Byfield in New York in 1747 but no information about his family.

- A Thomas Byfield was a merchant in the Long Island area and is mentioned several times in town records there. He may be the same Thomas Byfield mentioned in the correspondence of William Penn who wrote about a lawsuit by Thomas Byfield against the estate of John King for some money owed.

None of the above Byfields are found in the 1850 Census – only Abraham and his family are enumerated. I take this to mean that any earlier Byfields must have returned to England or they had no sons that carried the Byfield name forward.

After 1850 a few Byfields came to the United States through Canada and these don't belong to Abraham's line.

Earliest records of the Abraham Byfield family

Abraham Byfield is the progenitor of most of the Byfield families in the United States. Although some other Byfields came to the country later, Abraham had a good 50 year head start. In the 1850 census, almost every Byfield listed (there are 75) is a descendant of Abraham.

Abraham came to this country in 1786 at the age of 21. The young nation was still operating under the Articles of Confederation. The Congress had just authorized the Silver Dollar and adopted the decimal system of currency. The Constitution and the United States' first President were still a few years away. Even calling the colonies "The United States" wouldn't happen for another year.

Abraham is remembered as coming from Ireland, but was likely a first generation Irishman. The Byfield name is not recorded in Ireland during the 1700s but is quite common in England. My guess is that Abraham's family came to Ireland from England before he was born or while he was very young.

In 1788 Abraham was described as "aged about 30 years, about 5 feet 10 or 11 inches high, has long dark brown hair, gray eyes, a fleshy bottle nose, is pretty much pitted in the face with the small-pox, his left thumb is crooked and much smaller than the other".

Five Pounds Reward.

RAN AWAY, from the subscriber, living in the upper part of Ann-Arundel County, on the 12th instant, *an Irish indented Servant Man*, named ABRAHAM BYFIELD, aged about 30 years; about 5 feet 10 or 11 inches high, has long dark brown hair, gray eyes, a fleshy bottle nose, is pretty much pitted in the face with the small-pox, his left thumb is crooked, and much smaller than the other; had on a brown Russia linen shirt, and oznaburg trousers (and carried others with him) an old small felt hat, a pair of old patched country-made shoes with one round silver plated buckle; he also carried with him, a coarse brown drab cloth coat and waistcoat with white metal buttons on them; the coat ragged under the arms, and a pair of blue German serge breeches with white metal buttons, and patched on each knee; he has other clothes with him; he acted as a School Master for me a short time, and for his bad behaviour I turned him to plantation work. I expect he will forge a pass, and a discharge from me; he pretended to be free, but by his indenture, which I have, he has a year to serve yet. It appears that he has correspondence with a *Robert Brett*, in Baltimore-Town, or Fell's-Point—I expect he will be harboured and assisted by him to make his escape. I will give a reward of *Thirty Shillings* for taking up and bringing home to me the said Servant, if 10 miles from home; if 40 miles, *Forty Shillings*; if 60 miles, *Three Pounds*; and if 100 miles, the above reward, with reasonable charges. I forewarn all persons from harbouring or employing the said Servant; and all masters of vessels, and others, are forbid carrying him off at their peril.

REUBEN MERIWEATHER.

July 16, 1788.

Advertisement posted by Reuben Meriweather in the Maryland Journal, 5 August 1788

To REUBEN MERRIWEATHER, of Ann-Arundel County.
SIR,

OBSERVING in the Maryland Journal, of the 18th inst. your advertisement of a certain Abraham Byfield, a Servant runaway, in which you are pleased to say " it appears he has a correspondence with me, and you expect he will by me be harboured and assisted to make his escape,"—to prevent unfavourable impressions from your affection in this way, I acquaint you and the Public, that in July, 1786, I was summoned on an inquest on board the Brig Greyhound, from Ireland, where asking questions among the people, found this man had come from the part of Ireland I did---As I knew several of his friends, the 4 h of February last, I received a letter from him (which is at your and the Public's inspection at any time) requesting me to forward a letter enclosed to a shipmate of his, called Timothy Lanahan, in some part of Virginia. This, Sir, is all my knowledge and correspondence, returning him for answer, I would when opportunity answered. How far this will justify your illiberal assertion, the candid Public will judge—I request for your own safety, in future, you will be more tender in making free with the name of any reputable citizen on such occasions, as no man that regards his character will be defamed, without cause, with impunity by any, however consequential in their own esteem. I know as little of him (save what is here inserted) as I either do or wish to know of you.

I am, the Public's obedient servant,
ROBERT BRETT.

Fell's-Point, July 21, 1788.

Robert Brett's response to Reuben Merriweather posted in the Maryland Journal, 5 August 1788

Abraham came to America as an indentured servant as did most immigrants during this time. The cost of passage from England to America was in the range of 15 to 20 pounds. The average agricultural worker in the late 1700s could earn 8-10 pounds per year, so it would be very difficult to save enough

"Brig Niagara full sail" by Lance Woodworth

for passage. Since there was a shortage of workers in the colonies, wealthy merchants or land owners were willing to pay for a person's passage in return for several years of that person's labor. By the late 1700s, an indenture contract for an adult man was 3 or 4 years.

Abraham Byfield arrived in America in mid-1786 aboard the brig Greyhound. The *brig* was a sailing ship with two main masts and square sails. It's possible that this is the same Greyhound that was involved in the "Greenwich Tea Burning" of 1774. This was a Tea Party type affair that happened in Greenwich, New Jersey.

It would have taken it six to eight weeks to make the passage. Conditions during the voyage would have been difficult. The food was bad and heavily salted. The drinking water was bad. Sickness was commonplace among the passengers and it was not unknown for deaths to occur. The Greyhound would have put into the docks at Baltimore, in Chesapeake Bay, either directly from Dublin or after making other stops along the Atlantic coast.

Once the passengers with contracts for indenture arrived, they could not leave the ship until their indenture was purchased. The ships master would advertise that he had indentured servants available and wealthy men would come from miles away to buy the contracts from the ship's master.

Abraham's contract was purchased by Reuben Meriweather. Meriweather owned a large plantation in Ann Arundel County, Maryland. The 1790 census showed him having 37 slaves, but actual slaves and indentured servants were counted the same on the census. Abraham must have been an educated man as Mr. Meriweather initially had him serving as a school master.

From the advertisement that Meriweather posted in 1788, it seems that he was displeased with Abraham and (probably as punishment) had sent him to work in the fields. This apparently upset Abraham to the point that he took his few belongings and left. Since Meriweather was still owed another year of service he took the usual step of advertising for his servant's return.[1]

There is no record, but we can assume that Abraham returned and completed his service to Meriweather as he was still in the area a few years later when he met and married Patience Corbin.

Patience Corbin

Patience Corbin was born in Maryland Colony, probably in the town of Baltimore, in 1775. The Corbin family had been in the Baltimore area for a hundred years – Patience is descended from Nicholas Corbin, who came to Maryland from England in 1671. Patience was the the daughter of Venson Corbin and his wife, Mary. The first census of the United States, in 1790, records that she had three brothers and three sisters, but very little else is known about her immediate family.

Marriage of Abraham and Patience

Abraham and Patience married in Baltimore in 1793, just as George Washington was beginning his second term as President of the United States. She would have been about 18 years old when she married Abraham, who was about 10 years older. They were married by the Reverend Lewis Richards at the First Baptist Church of Baltimore.

---

1 Robert Brett responded to Reuben Meriweather's advertisement in the same newspaper. From his response it appears that Mr. Brett was from the same area in Ireland as Abraham and they may have had some acquaintances in common. It would be interesting to research this Robert Brett to see were he came from in Ireland as a way to locate Abraham's family there. There is also mention of a Timothy Lanahan, thought to reside in Virginia, that may also be a clue to Abraham's origins in Ireland.

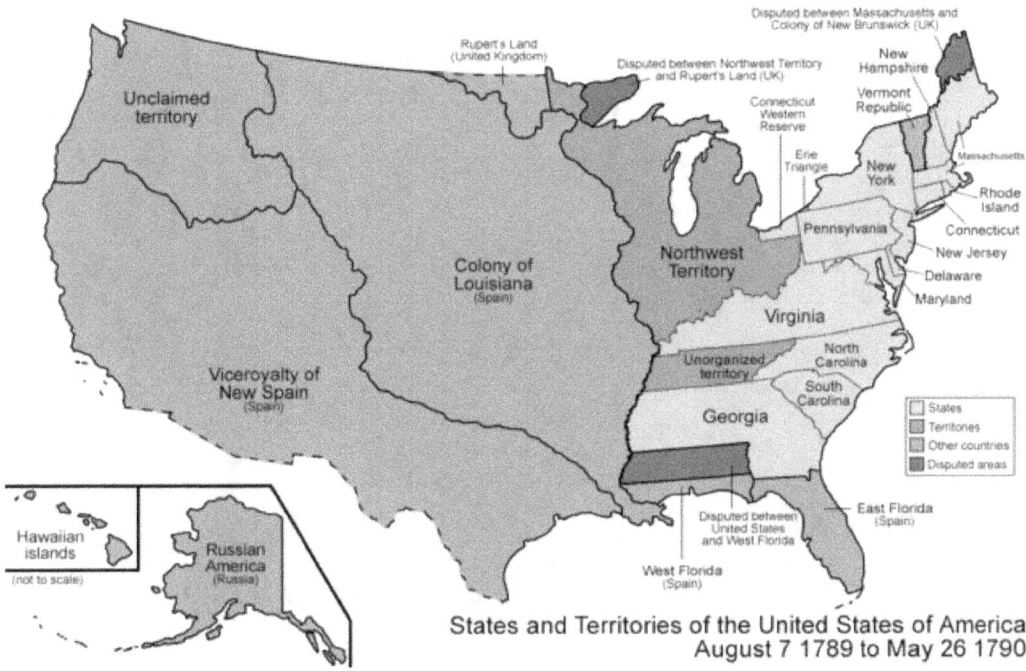

States and Territories of the United States of America
August 7 1789 to May 26 1790

Wikimedia Comons - Golbez

Migration to Pennsylvania and Ohio

Soon after their marriage, Abraham and Patience began their journey westward. It's unclear whether they intended to move to Pennsylvania and then decided later to continue westward or if they just made the move in stages.

It appears they spent some time in western Pennsylvania before continuing on to Ohio. There are rumors of at least one of the children being born in Somerset, Pennsylvania, but I've not been able find any proof. In 1811 there is a record of the postmaster at West Middleton, Pennsylvania, holding a letter for Abraham Byfield. We know that by then he had already been in Ohio for a few years.

The route from Baltimore to West Middleton would have followed the old Braddock's Road from Cumberland, Maryland, through the Allegheny Mountains and into western Pennsylvania. Current day U.S. Highway 40 follows the route of the old Braddock's Road very closely. This 260 mile journey would have taken several weeks. In the 1750s General Braddock had cleared a 12 foot wide swath from the wooded hills of Maryland and Pennsylvania to make a route to the fork where the Monongahela and

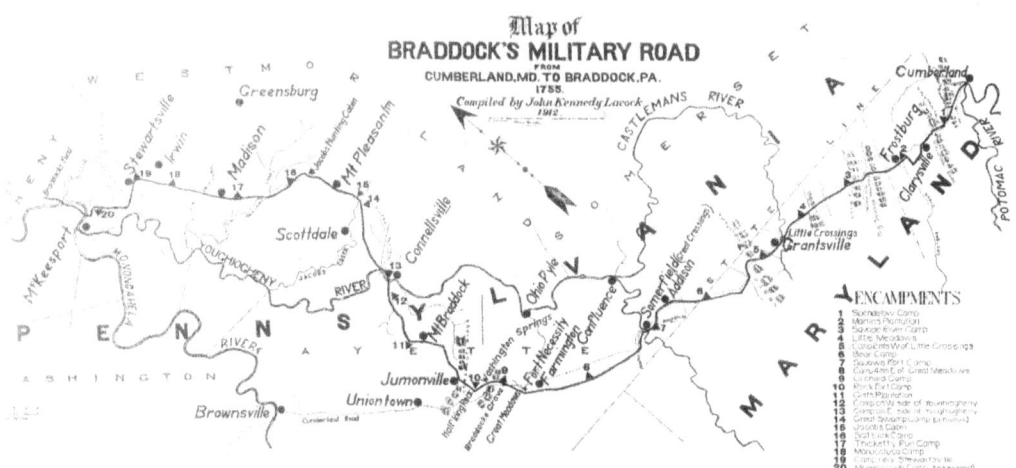

Map showing the path of Braddock's Road

Allegheny rivers fed into the westward curving river that the Mohawk Indians called "O-he-yo".

George Washington returned to Braddock's Road in 1784, traveling on horseback with his nephew, his friend Dr. James Craik, Craik's son, and several servants. Washington saw the need for a road West to "make a smooth way for the Produce of that Country to pass to our Markets." His return visit to the Alleghenies was in part for the purpose of inspecting property he owned there, but it also allowed him to evaluate the old road's suitability for future East-West travel. The road had been used very little during the Revolutionary War and in the years thereafter. But even though the wilderness was creeping back, Washington found it less primitive than on his first trip. He saw taverns here and there and landmarks which were becoming familiar to travelers. He recorded his impressions in a journal. ". . . Dined at Mr. Thomas Gists at the Foot of Laurel [Hill], distant from the Meadows 12 Miles, and arrived at Gilbert Simpsons' [on Braddock's Road, north of Uniontown] about 5 oclock 12 Miles further. Crossing the Mountains, I found tedious and fatieguing, . . . in all parts of the Road that would admit it I endeavoured to ride my usual traveling gate of 5 Miles an hour."

No Byfield appears in any census in 1800, but an Ohio census taken 1808 lists Abraham in Sprig Township, Adams County. From western Pennsylvania the new family would have taken a flatboat down the Ohio River to their destination. They settled in Adams County just west of Manchester along the southern border of Ohio. Manchester (originally Massie Station) was the first white settlement within the Virginia Military District along the Ohio River. It was first settled in 1790.

The birthplaces of Abraham's children are a little unclear but it appears that one or two of the eldest children were born in Maryland and then one or two in Pennsylvania during the family's migration to Ohio. The earliest evidence of the family in Ohio is an 1808 census however Abraham's son, Massia, claims to be born in Ohio around 1805.

A Flatboat on the Ohio River – From a woodcut print by artist Alfred R. Waud

The family stayed in Adams County, Ohio at least until Abraham's death around 1815. By 1817 the family was in Hamilton County, about 65 miles west of Adams County along the Ohio River, and the eldest son, George, is listed as the head of the family. They were in the Columbia Township, just east of the town of Cincinnati.

GENERATION ONE

1. **Byfield, Abraham H**

Abraham H was born in 1765, probably in Ireland. He died between 1815 and 1817 in Hamilton County, Ohio at the age of 50 years. He married Patience Corbin April 7, 1793 in Baltimore, Baltimore County, Maryland.

Adams County, Ohio. Newspaper mention. Scioto Gazette and Chillicothe Advertiser, Volume VIII, Wednesday, 24 January 1810, No. 475 :

> *George Caley, in New Market township, Highland County, reports that Henry ___? and Frederick Saum have appraised a horse found by Abraham H. Byfield.[2]*

Spouse: Corbin, Patience.

Patience was born about 1775 in _____. She died 14 April 1838 in Lancaster Township, Jefferson County, Indiana at the age of 63 years. She was buried in Byfield Cemetery, Lancaster Township, Jefferson County, Indiana. She was the daughter of Vincent Corbin and Mary. She married Abraham H Byfield on 7 April 1793 in Baltimore, Baltimore County, Maryland.

Children of Patience Corbin and Abraham H Byfield

+ 11 i.   George Washington Byfield. George Washington was born in 1795 probably in Maryland. He died on 3 June 1845 in Johnson Township, Scott County, Indiana.

+ 12 ii.   Horatio Byfield. Horatio was born on 29 August 1796 in Maryland. He died on 20 August 1859 in Dupont, Jefferson County, Indiana.

+ 13 iii.   Stella Harriet Byfield. Stella was born on 27 August 1798 in Ohio. She died on 13 October 1859 in Goodhue County, Minnesota.

+ 14 iv.   Holmes Byfield. Holmes was born in 1801 in Pennsylvania. He died on 5 June 1874 in Goliad, Goliad County, Texas.

---

2   This newspaper mention is the only record I have found that gives Abraham's middle initial. Speculation is that his middle name was Horatio since his second son was named Horatio.

+ 15 v.	Massia Byfield. Massia was born about 1805 in Adams County, Ohio. He died in 1880 in Leroy, Coffey County, Kansas.

+ 16 vi.	Andrew G Byfield. Andrew G was born on 6 May 1808 in Adams County, Ohio. He died on 2 March 1882 in Jennings County, Indiana.

+ 17 vii.	Vincent Byfield. Vincent was born in 1810 in Adams County, Ohio. He died before 1860, probably in Ohio.

+ 18 viii.	Eliza Ann Byfield. Eliza Ann was born about 1813 in Ohio. She died in _____ in _____.

Byfields in Indiana

It appears that the Byfield sons were already in the process of moving the family to Indiana by 1820. There is a record of the first Byfield land patent in Indiana filed by George and Horatio in 1820. In addition, one of Horatio's grandsons mentions stories of Horatio grading some early roads in 1818 or 1819. As George was listed as the head of the family in the 1820 census, it could be that Horatio had gone ahead to secure some land in Indiana and set things up for the family.

Over the next 20 years the Byfields purchased land and settled over several counties in southeastern Indiana. The only exception is Holmes who, by 1830, had migrated to Illinois on his way to eventually settling in the Republic of Texas.

All three of the Byfield families in the 1840 census for Indiana belong to the Abraham Byfield line. The one Byfield family in Ohio and one in New England at this time are recent emigrants from England that are not connected to Abraham. Of the 75 Byfields listed ten years later, in the 1850 census, all are descendants of Abraham and Patience except four. Three are a small family in Ohio that came from England. One is in California and claims to have been born in Illinois about 1805.

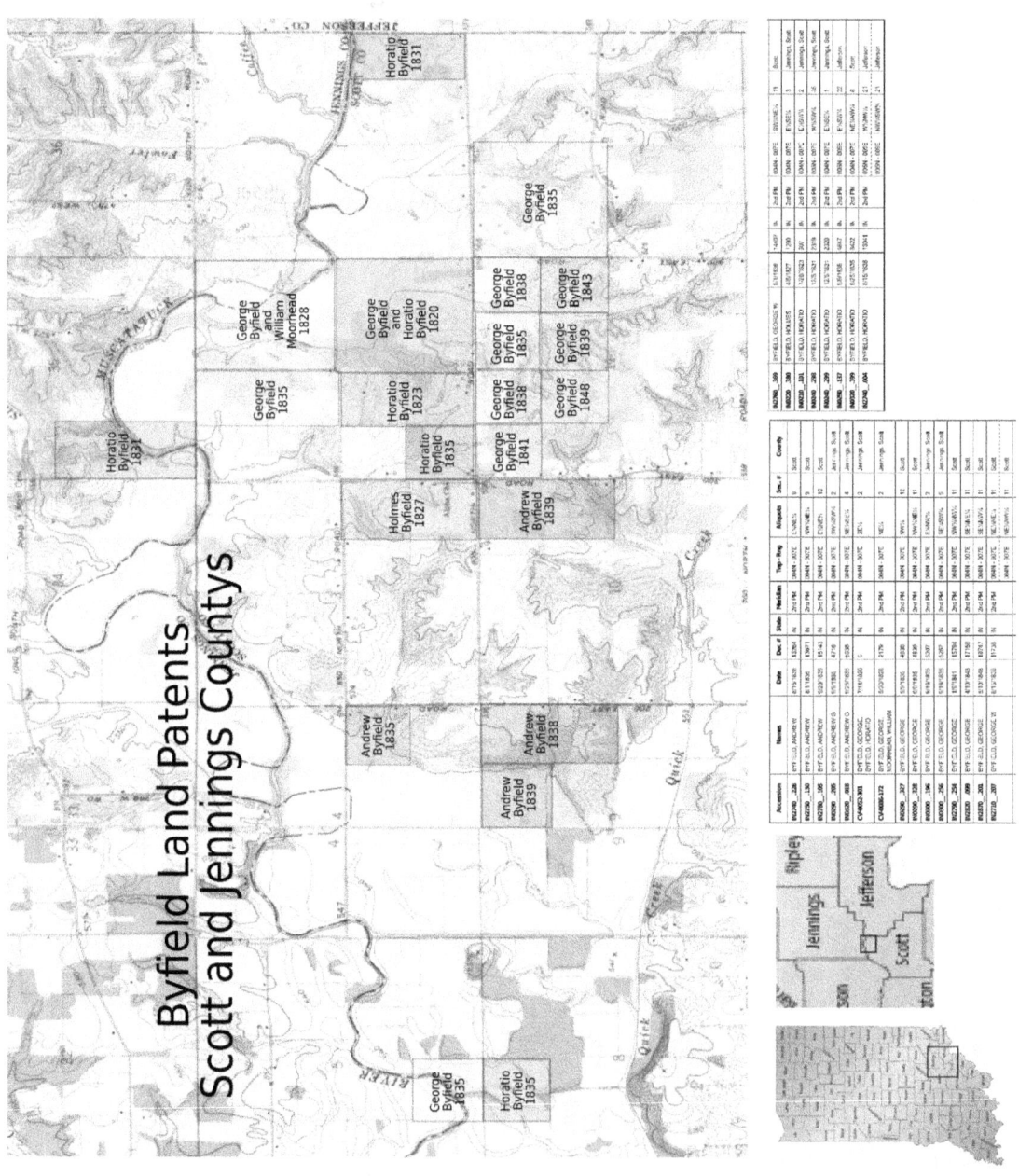

Land purchased from the government. The Byfields also purchased many tracts of land from earlier settlers.

GENERATION TWO

The second generation of Byfields firmly established the family in Indiana. Several of the children of Abraham and Patience set down roots and stayed in Indiana, but some moved farther west. By the late 1800s, in addition to the many Byfield families in Indiana, there would be Byfield families established throughout the Midwest. Stella and her husband settled in Minnesota, Massia lived in Illinois and then settled in eastern Kansas, Holmes went to Illinois and then to the Republic of Texas.

The westward migration would be continued by several of the third generation Indiana Byfield families. This next generation would spread Byfield cousins into Missouri, Iowa, Oklahoma, and additional areas of Kansas.

11.   **George Washington Byfield.** (Abraham H Byfield-1)

George Washington was born in 1795, probably in Maryland. He died on 3 June 1845 in Johnson Township, Scott County, Indiana at the age of 50 years, 5 months. He was the son of Abraham H Byfield and Patience Corbin. He married Magdalena Simonson on 21 May 1820 in Hamilton County, Ohio.

By 1815 George, his mother, Patience, and all of his brothers and sisters were living together in Hamilton County, Ohio. They were in the Columbia township, a few miles east of Cincinnati. In 1820 George married Magdelana and she is with the Byfield family in the 1820 census. Around this time, George's brother, Horatio, was already scouting land in southeastern Indiana. The first of many purchases of land from the government was made jointly by George and Horatio in mid-1820.

Around 1822 the Byfields loaded all their possessions onto a flatboat and traveled down the Ohio 88 miles to the little river town of Madison, Indiana. From there they made their way north and west to the new farms. Initially they probably set up on the land that Horatio had purchased from Jesse Spann in Jennings County, just west of the present-day town of Lancaster. Later they would spread out over the northern parts of neighboring Scott County.

The George Byfield homestead was located in northern Scott County along the Muscatatuck river. In 1834 George and others in the area petitioned the state to clear obstacles from the river so that it could be more easily used for travel and shipping. At that time, roads were few and were likely useless during wet weather. Before 1830, the Muscatatuck River was navigable, with local settlers being able to ship pork down the river to eventually reach New Orleans. However, around 1830, the river became no longer navigable, as dirt fill accumulated along the river bed.

George stayed in Scott County for the remainder of his life, making land purchases from the government frequently. By the time of his death, he owned hundreds of acres in the county and was able to leave a sizable tract to each of his children.

Most of George and Magdelana's children remained in Indiana. Sons George Washington and Charles Carel moved to different parts of Kansas in the late 1800s. Their son, Francis Marion, died in the Civil War.

Spouse: Magdalena Simonson.

Magdalena was born about 1800 in Ohio. She died in August 1846 in Jennings County, Indiana at the age of about 46 years, 7 months. She married George Washington Byfield on 21 May 1820 in Hamilton County, Ohio.

Children of Magdalena Simonson and George Washington Byfield

+ 111 i.   George Washington Byfield. George Washington was born on 11 August 1821 in Hamilton County, Ohio. He died on 2 April 1895 in Haddam, Washington County, Kansas.

+ 112 ii.   Harriet Byfield. Harriet was born in 1823 in Indiana. She died in 1845 in Jennings County, Indiana.

+ 113 iii.   Lewis Freeman Byfield. Lewis Freeman was born on 21 January 1825 in Jennings County, Indiana. He died on 10 January 1849 in Jennings County, Indiana.

+ 114 iv.   Mariah Byfield. Mariah was born on 17 May 1828 in Indiana. She died in May 1899 in Scott County, Indiana.

+ 115 v.   Ida Byfield. Ida was born in 1831 in Indiana. She died on 30 March 1852 in Graham, Jefferson County, Indiana.

+ 116 vi.   Albert Byfield. Albert was born December 20, 1833 in Indiana. He died July 23, 1888 in Codey's Bluff, Nowata County, Oklahoma.

+ 117 vii.   Francis Marion Byfield. Francis Marion was born on 8 November 1836 in Scott County, Indiana. He died on 2 March 1865 in Texaha, South Carolina.

+ 118 viii.   Charles Carel Byfield. Charles Carel was born on 17 March 1840 in Wabash County, Indiana. He died on 10 March 1899 in Costello, Kansas.

12.   **Horatio Byfield.** (Abraham H Byfield-1)

Horatio was born on 29 August 1796 in Baltimore, Maryland. He died on 20 August 1859 in Dupont, Jefferson County, Indiana at the age of 62 years, 11 months. He was buried in Byfield Cemetery, Lancaster Township, Jefferson County, Indiana. He was the son of Abraham H Byfield and Patience Corbin. He married Jennet Griffith on 23 November 1822 in Scott County, Indiana.

Records list a Horatio Byfield serving in the War of 1812 in Captain Luther Leonard's Company of Ohio Volunteers. As Horatio would have been just 16 years old in 1812, it's possible that this record is for his father. It's thought that Abraham's middle name was Horatio. Either way, this is the first record of a Horatio Byfield.

Shortly after the Byfields moved to Hamilton County, Ohio, Horatio went to Indiana. The first Byfield land purchase made from the government was not until 1820 but Horatio had probably already bought other property in

View of the Byfield Farm from the Road. Photo courtesy Indiana Historic Sites and Structures Inventory, Indiana DNR – Division of Historic Preservation & Archeology.

Jefferson County, Indiana, by 1817. His farm was located on the east side of Big Creek, just north of the present day town of Lancaster.

The Byfield farm on Big Creek was on land originally owned by Jesse Spann. Spann was a Revolutionary War soldier from South Carolina. He came to Indiana in 1816 by way of Garrard County, Kentucky[3]. He purchased 320 acres of land along Big Creek from the government. In 1825, Jesse Span buried a daughter, Elizabeth, in what would later become the Byfield Cemetery.

---

3   From *Early Settlers of Upper Big Creek* by Agnes Wilson.

Horatio saw that a good road was needed from his area south to the town of Madison. He built a large wooden plow and proceeded to make the road himself. That road probably was along the same route as present day Highway 7. This was done around 1817. The plow sat in his barn for many years before being discovered by William Wesley Woolen, who was a prominent man in early Indianapolis government and a close friend of the Byfield family. Mr. Woolen gave the plow to the State Museum where it was displayed for many years. In 1893 the plow was sent to be part of the Indiana display at the Chicago Worlds Fair.

By 1830 Horatio had built a handsome two story brick house on his property. This house would have been one room deep and several rooms wide with a full second story. The sills and lintels were stone with "9 over 6" windows in the Federal

View of the Horatio Byfield house. Photo courtesy Indiana Historic Sites and Structures Inventory, Indiana DNR – Division of Historic Preservation & Archeology.

style. This house was still standing in the late 1980s, but it, the barn, and even the large stone gateposts are now gone.

There is a very similar house, built around the same time, on the west side of Big Creek. This house was also built by Horatio but was probably for another family member. This house is still standing and looks like it is still in use. It has had a large addition put on the back of the house but the front view, less the paint on the brick, probably looks much as it did around 1830. However, the house on the east side of the creek was the homestead where it appears that Horatio and Jennet lived.

The farm on the east side of Big Creek, where Horatio and Jennet lived, also holds the Byfield family cemetery. The cemetery is located atop a little hill near the creek. Most of the cemetery is now gone but the large monument still remained in 1989 when the Indiana Division of Historic Preservation surveyed the site.

Another Byfield House on the West Side of Big Creek

James Hays had built the first mill dam on Big Creek and then sold his property along with the mill to Horatio Byfield. James Burns, one of the original settlers in the area, remembered that for many years farmers in the area had their corn ground at Horace's mill. Although the mill is gone, the mill stones probably still lay along the banks of Big Creek.

The Byfield Family Cemetery

The slavery issue had been a controversy since the founding of the republic, but was beginning to really heat up by the mid 1800s. Among those that were against slavery there were several schools of thought about how the abolition of slavery should be handled. We have a record of Horatio's position from this article in *The Emancipator* published in September of 1839:

A friend has sent us the Daily Courier, published at Madison, Ind., dated August 16, which gives us what the editor delicately calls "the proceedings of a respectable portion of the citizens of this county in opposition to the workings of a few lazy scamps who are endeavoring to breed disturbance by agitating the subject of abolition." The article appears as a report and resolutions presented by a committee and adopted at "a respectable meeting of citizens, held at Wirt, in Jefferson county, on the 10th of August." The names of the Committee are Thomas Bland, B. F. Whitson, Samuel Tinical, James Burns and Horatio Byfield. G. W. Hensley and Milton George were secretaries. In their report, this "bland" committee say,

"We do not wish to be understood as being friends to slavery, but, having nothing to do with it, we oppose the manner in which these fanatics propose to bring about emancipation, as unconstitutional, unjust and impolitic. Voluntary emancipation by their owners and immediate colonization are the only terms upon which we desire a change in the condition of the blacks in this country. These we understand to be the principles of the colonization society, but how different are those of the abolitionists. The 2nd article of their constitution says, 'It shall aim to convince by argument, that slavery is a *heinous crime in the sight of God, and the duty, safety, and best interests of all concerned, is immediate emancipation, without expatriation*' and the third article of the same says, 'It shall be the object of the society to elevate the condition of the colored people to an *equality with the whites*, and according to their intellectual and moral worth, *to share an equality with them in all civil and religious privileges!*'"

Horatio's grandson, Gavin Payne, wrote this description in 1914[4]:

Mr. Byfield was a well-known character in southern Indiana. It was related of him in a sketch by Mr. Woolen that in one famine year, Mr. Byfield's fine farm yielded corn abundantly and he was offered extravagant cash prices for it by buyers from along the river. Instead of selling, he distributed the crop among his neighbors for miles around, taking their two and three year plain notes for the corn. In this wise much distress was averted and the neighborhood had corn for seeding. The late Wm. H. English and Mr. Byfield were friends and when Mr. English came to Indianapolis and made realty investments that enabled him to accumulate several millions before he died, he urged Mr. Byfield to sell his large farm and come to the capital city. Mr. Byfield, however, after a trip to the new capital, could see few possibilities to the place.

Spouse: Jennet Griffith.

Jennet was born 22 May 1808 in Virginia. She died on 30 August 1869 in Lancaster, Jefferson County, Indiana, at the age of more than 60 years, 11 months. She was buried in Byfield Cemetery, Lancaster Township, Jefferson County, Indiana. She married Horatio Byfield on 23 November 1822 in Scott County, Indiana. It has been passed down that Jennet's parents both came to this country from Wales.

Most of Horatio and Jennet's children stayed in Indiana. One daughter, Elva, settled in the Oklahoma Territory. Their daughter, Margaretta, and son, Horatio, ended up together in Colorado. Their son, Daniel, became a doctor. Their son, Cass, became a prominent lawyer.

Children of Jennet Griffith and Horatio Byfield

+ 121 i.   Daniel Byfield. Daniel was born on 11 September 1823 in Indiana. He died on 2 November 1850 in Lancaster Township, Jefferson County, Indiana.

+ 122 ii.   Alford Byfield. Alford was born on 15 March 1825 in Indiana. He died on 7 October 1846 in Indiana.

+ 123 iii.   Henrietta Byfield. Henrietta was born 19 July 1827 in Indiana. She died 1 March 1896 in Shelbyville, Shelby County, Indiana.

+ 124 iv.   Margaretta Byfield. Margaretta was born about 1829 in Indiana. She probably died in Colorado between 1905 and 1910.

125 v.   Corbin Byfield. Corbin was born 10 June 1832 in Indiana. He died on 25 July 1894 in Indianapolis, Marion County, Indiana.

---

4   See Appendix C for a copy of the complete article.

126 vi.   Horatio Byfield. Horatio was born 25 October 1834 in Indiana. He died in Alder, Colorado on 8 September 1890.

+ 127 vii.   Casabianca 'Cass' Byfield. Casabianca was born 17 October 1837 in Indiana. He died on 6 August 1888 in Indianapolis, Marion County, Indiana.

+ 128 viii.   Emily Byfield. Emily was born 7 August 1840 in Indiana. She died 8 June 1906 in Indianapolis, Marion County, Indiana.

+ 129 ix.   Elva Byfield. Elva was born 7 August 1840 in Indiana. She died 29 April 1908 in Oklahoma.

+ 12A x.   Whitcomb Byfield. Whitcomb was born on 11 July 1843 in Indiana. He died on 29 August 1916 in Indianapolis, Marion County, Indiana.

+ 12B xi.   Mary Byfield. Mary was born on 11 February 1846 in Lancaster, Jefferson County, Indiana. She died on 17 December 1919 in Indianapolis, Marion County, Indiana.

+ 12C xii.   Charles A Byfield. Charles A was born about 1850 in Indiana. He died on 5 March 1900 in Franklin County, Indiana.

13.   **Stella Harriet Byfield.** (Abraham H Byfield-1)

Stella was born on 27 August 1798 in Ohio. She died on 13 October 1859 in Goodhue County, Minnesota at the age of 61 years, 1 month. She was the daughter of Abraham H Byfield and Patience Corbin. She married George McGaughey on 14 May 1818 in Hamilton, Ohio.

Stella was the first of Abraham's children to marry. She married George McGaughey in 1818 while the family was still in Hamilton County, Ohio. Many genealogies of the Byfield's show that Abraham had three daughters – Stella, Harriet, and Eliza Ann. I believe that there were only two daughters – Stella and Eliza Ann. On the marriage return for Stella and George, the minister listed her as "Hetty" Byfield. Hetty is usually short for Harriet or Henrietta, so I believe Stella was probably Harriet Stella Byfield or Stella Harriet Byfield. Every record after the marriage lists her as Stella.

Stella and George moved to Indiana along with the rest of the Byfield family. They stayed in Indiana until the mid-1850s when they moved to Goodhue County in southeastern Minnesota. I believe that there were already some McGaugheys in that area or they moved there around the same time since the censuses show many McGaugheys in that area. Stella died just three or four years after the family moved to Minnesota.

Spouse: George McGaughey.

George was born in 1796 in Ohio. He died in 1883 in Arkansas at the age of 87 years. He married Stella Byfield on 14 May 1818 in Hamilton, Ohio.

George is probably the son of David McGaughey that was living in Hamilton County, Ohio around 1820. George stayed in Minnesota until just shortly before his death, when he moved to Arkansas to live with his son, Horatio.

Children of Stella Byfield and George McGaughey

+ 131 i.   Albert Edwin McGaughey. Albert Edwin was born about 1820 in Indiana. He died in 1888 in Ortonville, Big Stone County, Minnesota.

132 ii.   David J McGaughey. David was born between 1 January 1823 and 28 September 1823 in Indiana. He died in August 1875 in Shelby County, Indiana.

+ 133 iii.   Samuel Newton McGaughey. Samuel was born in 1827 in Indiana. He died in _____ in _____.

134 iv.   SonA McGaughey. SonA was born between 1830 and 1835 in _____.

+ 135 v.   Catherine R McGaughey. Catherine was born 29 December 1832 in Indiana. She died 6 January 1906 in Decatur County, Indiana.

+ 136 vi.   George Calvin McGaughey. George Calvin was born about 1831 in Indiana. He died in _____ in _____.

137 vii.   DaughterA McGaughey. DaughterA was born between 1835 and 1840 in _____.

+ 138 viii.   Horatio M McGaughey. Horatio M was born 20 November 1836 in Franklin County, Indiana. He died 25 December 1911 in Rogers, Benton County, Arkansas.

+ 139 ix.   Mary P McGaughey. Mary P was born November 1835 in Indiana. She died 16 May 1927 in _____.

14.   **Holmes Byfield.** (Abraham H Byfield-1)

Holmes was born in 1801 in Pennsylvania during the years when his parents were making their way from Maryland to Ohio. He died on 5 June 1874 in Goliad, Goliad County, Texas at the age of 73 years, 5 months. He was the son of Abraham H Byfield and Patience Corbin. He married Sally Nation on

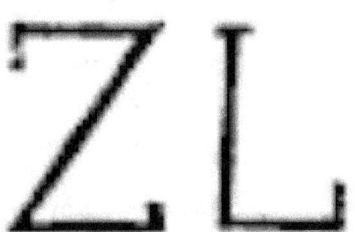

The Holmes Byfield Brand

4 January 1826 in Jennings County, Indiana. He later married Lucinda Ferguson about 1856 in Shelby County, Texas.

Holmes was the first of the Byfields to leave Indiana. Shortly after his marriage to Sally Nation in early 1826, he moved to central Illinois, near Springfield. Holmes and Sally's first two children, Serilla and James were born in Illinois. After about ten years in Illinois, the Byfields pulled up stakes and headed south to take advantage of a new opportunity.

By 1835, Texas was preparing to declare it's independence from Mexico and their new constitution gave a large parcel of land to the head of any family residing in the new republic before March 4th of 1836. In January of 1836 Holmes' family made the 700 mile trek south from Illinois to the new Republic of Texas. They settled around the border of Shelby and Panola Counties, in east Texas, to the west of present day Shreveport, Louisiana. Since Holmes was an immigrant to the republic, he was given a headright grant of a league and a labor of land. The league and labor were old Spanish land measures and would be equal to about 4,700 acres. Usually the league, which was around 4,500 acres would be range land away from a river, and the labor was a much smaller area but located near a river and more suitable for farming. Holmes volunteered for the Army of the Republic of Texas for three months during 1838 and was granted an additional 320 acres for his service.

Holmes also served as Mounted Texas Ranger in Captain Robert Barclay's Company, for which he later received a pension. Holmes and Sally had two more children in Texas, William Anthony, and Elizabeth. Sally died sometime between 1840, when Elizabeth was born, and 1850.

Holmes married Lucinda Ferguson in 1856 and moved the family 300 miles southwest to Goliad County, Texas, north of Corpus Christi. There they had five children, Martha Jane, George Washington, Benjamin Franklin, Sallie, and Nancy Caroline. Holmes died in 1874 and is buried in an unmarked grave near Fannin in Goliad County.

Spouse: Sally Nation.

Sally was born 1810-1815, probably in southeastern Indiana. She died before 1850 in Texas. She married Holmes Byfield on 4 January 1826 in Jennings County, Indiana. Sally is possibly the daughter of John Nation, who lived in Scott County, Indiana in 1820. There are marriage records for Sally and Holmes in both Jennings and Scott Counties, with marriage dates ranging from January 1 to January 4.

Children of Sally Nation and Holmes Byfield

141 i.   Serilla or Zerilda Byfield. Serilla was born about 1830 in Illinois. She probably died before 1856 in Panola County, Texas.

+ 142 ii.   James Byfield. James was born 12 April 1834 in Illinois. He died 17 February 1898 in Oklahoma.

143 iii.   William Anderson Byfield. William Anderson was born about 1837 in Texas. He died in _____ in _____.

+ 144 iv.   Elizabeth Byfield. Elizabeth was born about 1840 in Texas. She died in 1911 in Texas.

Spouse: Lucinda Ferguson.

Lucinda was born on 10 February 1830 in North Carolina. She is listed with her parents in the 1850 census in Randolph County, North Carolina, so she probably moved with her parents to Texas after 1850 then met and married Holmes Byfield there a few years later. She died on 24 January 1904 in Llano County, Texas at the age of 73 years, 11 months. She married Holmes Byfield about 1856 in Shelby County, Texas. At the time of their marriage, Holmes was about 55 years old and Lucinda was about 25. After Holmes' death, Lucinda and several of the children moved to Llano, Texas, just northwest of Austin.

Children of Lucinda Ferguson and Holmes Byfield

+ 145 i.   Martha Jane Byfield. Martha Jane was born about 1858 in Goliad, Goliad County, Texas. She died on 5 Mar 1883 in Llano, Texas.

+ 146 ii.   Benjamin Franklin Byfield. Benjamin Franklin was born in April 1860 in Goliad, Goliad County, Texas. He died in 1940 in Atlanta, Georgia.

+ 147 iii.   George Washington 'Link' Byfield. George Washington was born on 16 March 1861 in Goliad County, Texas. He died on 11 August 1924 in Llano County, Texas.

+ 148 iv.   Sarah 'Sallie' Byfield. Sallie was born about 1864 in Goliad County, Texas. She died on 20 July 1906 in Llano, Texas.

+ 149 v.   Nancy Caroline Byfield. Nancy Caroline was born about 1866 in Goliad County, Texas. She died on 27 April 1930 in Llano, Texas.

15.   **Massia Byfield.** (Abraham H Byfield-1)

Massia Byfield, Abraham and Patience's fourth son, was born about 1805 in Adams County, Ohio. The family had probably only been in Ohio a short time. It's not certain if Massia was the first child born in Ohio since his older sister, Stella, was often recorded as having been born in Ohio, but Holmes, who was supposed to have been born after Stella and before Massia, claims to have been born in Pennsylvania.

Massia's father, Abraham, died when he was about 10 years old and the family moved shortly thereafter to Hamilton County, Ohio. An 1817 probate record in Hamilton County states that guardianship of 16 year old Massia and his estate were assigned to a man named George Bell. The age shown in this record disagrees with later records. He must have been only 12 or 13 years old at the time the guardianship was assigned. This was probably done because Massia was not yet 18 years old and had received an inheritance from his father. Abraham may have left a sizable estate, as his sons were buying large tracts of land in Indiana within just a few years. Abraham probably recorded a will in Adams County, Ohio, but the courthouse burned in 1910 and the old records were lost.

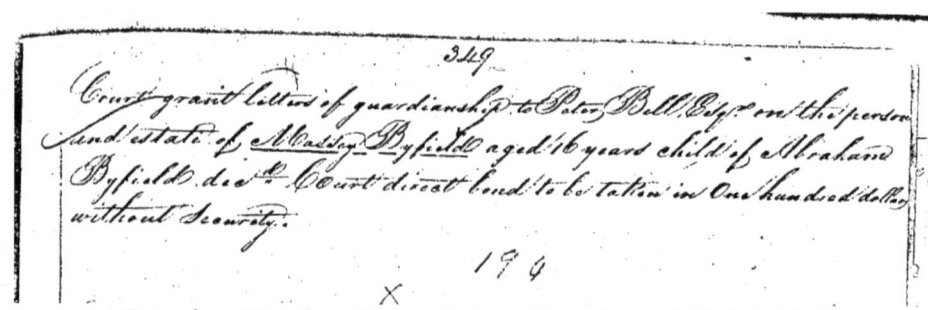

Entry from Hamilton County Probate Court Journal 29 July 1817

Massia was living in Hamilton County with his brother George in 1820. Sometime shortly after, the family moved to Indiana and Massia probably continued to live with his brother for a few years. On the 11th of May, 1826, Massia married Mary 'Polly' Griffith. Massia was 21 years old and Mary was 15 years old. There were a few Griffith families in the area and the Byfields and Griffiths intersect several times in the family tree. Massia's brother, Horatio, also married a Griffith. The Griffiths were prone to having twins and Massia and Mary had two sets of twins in their family.

Massia spent a few years farming in Scott County, Indiana, after his marriage. He was appointed Justice of the Peace from 1828 through 1830. By 1832 he was involved in starting the new town of Paris in neighboring Jennings County. He purchased a lot in the newly formed town in 1832 and then purchased several more lots in 1834, including a lot with a saloon that he purchased along with his brother-in-law, James Griffith.

The town of Paris flourished in the early years and, for a while, was the largest town in southern Indiana. It was known for its many shops and wide variety of goods that couldn't be found elsewhere. Originally, the east-west main street in the town was also the county line between Jennings and Jefferson

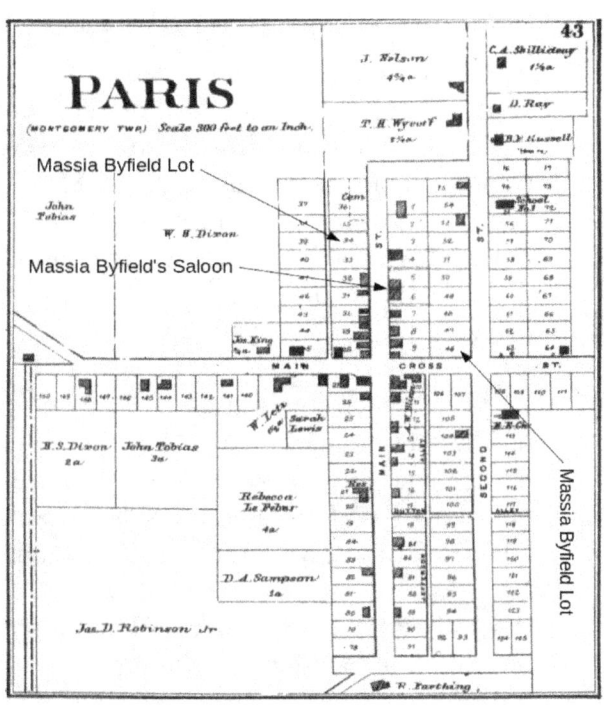

Counties. The Jefferson County Sheriff complained about having to run up to Paris all the time to handle problems so the county line was moved to put all of Paris into Jennings County where the Sheriff was closer. Eventually, a railroad was built that passed well north of Paris and the town dwindled while other towns closer to the railway thrived. However, by the time of Paris' decline, Massia had already moved on.

By 1846 Massia and his family had moved to Union Township, Fulton County, Illinois, west of Peoria. His oldest son, Benjamin, was 20 years old at the time of the move and opted to stay in Indiana and start his own family. Several of Massia's children went to school at a typical one room schoolhouse just across the county line to the west of their land in Illinois. Mary Ann, Julia Ann, Vermilion, and Harvey are listed in a record of the school between 1842 and 1845. The schoolhouse would have been made of logs, very similar to a typical log cabin. There would be a large fireplace at one end, one door, and one or two small windows. The children sat on benches made from logs split in half.

In the early 1850s, people across the country were hearing about gold in California. Thousands went there to seek their fortune in the stream beds. Massia was one of those who participated in the California Gold Rush. So many were coming into the area that California did a census during 1852 to take stock of their sudden population increase. Massia was there in Napa County, so he must have left his sons to manage the farm while he went to California. There is no record of Massia coming back with bags of gold so the trip probably didn't "pan out".

In 1865, a census records Massia in Knox County, the next county north of Fulton. As his home was in Fulton County at the northwest corner, this may have been more a matter of spreading out into the next county rather than an actual move. By 1870, after nearly 25 years in Illinois, Massia moved the family to Kansas.

All of Massia's sons, except Benjamin who had remained in Indiana, moved with Massia to Kansas in the late 1860s. Vermilion was already married at the time, but his brothers were still single. Massia's daughters had all married before the move and went in different directions. The eldest daughter, Mary Ann, ended up in Missouri, while Louisa went to Iowa with her family. The others ended up in eastern Kansas with the rest of the Byfields, sometimes by a round-a-bout route. None of the Byfields stayed in Illinois.

The twin daughters, Mary Ann and Julia Ann, each married an Imel brother and several complicated relationships ensued. Mary Ann's husband, William Imel, had a daughter Elizabeth, from an earlier marriage, who married Vermilion Byfield. So, Vermilion married his own "niece". His children's aunt Mary Ann would also have qualified as their grandmother.

Julia Ann married Peche Imel who, after Julia Ann's death, married her sister, Jeanette Byfield. So, Peche married his sister-in-law and became both step-father and uncle to the children from Jeanette's previous marriage. Likewise, she was both step-mother and aunt to his children.

Massia died in Coffey County, Kansas, in 1880, at the age of 75. His wife, Mary Griffith, died there about 5 years later.

Spouse: Mary Polly Griffith.

Mary Polly was born in 1812 in Ohio. Her parents are believed to be Evan and Eleanor Griffith who had come to America from Wales. She died in 1885 in Leroy, Coffey County, Kansas at the age of 73 years. She married Massia Byfield on 11 May 1826 in Scott County, Indiana.

Children of Mary Polly Griffith and Massia Byfield

+ 151 i.   Benjamin F Byfield. Benjamin F was born on 3 September 1826 in Indiana. He died on 7 April 1890 in Indiana.

+ 152 ii.   Mary Ann Byfield. Mary Ann was born on 11 February 1830 in Scott County, Indiana. She died on 9 August 1891 in Bates County, Missouri.

+ 153 iii.   Julia Ann Byfield. Julia Ann was born about 1830 in Indiana. She died about 1873 in Coffey County, Kansas.

+ 154 iv.   Vermilion Wright Byfield. Vermilion Wright was born on 4 September 1837 in Scott County, Indiana. He died on 8 February 1905 in Leroy, Coffey County, Kansas.

+ 155 v.   Jennette Byfield. Jennette was born in 1842 in Scott County, Indiana. She died 1925 to 1930 in Kansas or Missouri.

+ 156 vi.   Marion Josephus Byfield. Marion Josephus was born on 13 April 1846 in Union, Fulton County, Illinois. He died on 7 August 1907 in Boise, Ada County, Idaho.

+ 157 vii.   Louisa Byfield. Louisa was born on 13 April 1846 in Union, Fulton County, Illinois. She died on 21 February 1908 in Council Bluffs, Pottawatomie County, Iowa.

+ 158 viii.   Milton Cass Byfield. Milton Cass was born in February 1848 in Fulton County, Illinois. He died on 7 August 1909 in Greenfield, Dade County, Missouri.

159 ix.   Harvey N Byfield. Harvey N was born in _____ in Union, Fulton County, Illinois. He died about 1849 in Illinois.

15A x.   Anderson Byfield. Anderson was born about 1862 in Illinois. He died in _____ in _____ .

16.   **Andrew G Byfield.** (Abraham H Byfield-1)

Andrew G Byfield was the son of Abraham H Byfield and Patience Corbin. He was born May 6, 1808 in Adams County, Ohio. He died on 2 March 1882 in Jennings County, Indiana at the age of 73 years, 9 months. He was buried in Jennings County, Indiana. His father died when Andrew was about seven years old. He then moved to Hamilton County, Ohio with his mother and the rest of the family. Around 1820 the family moved again, this time to southeastern Indiana. He probably lived with his brother George or with brother Horatio for a few years. By 1827 he had met his future wife Rhoda, and was ready to start his own family.

Andrew G Byfield married Rhoda Burnett on July 12, 1827 in Scott County, Indiana. Andrew was 19 and Rhoda was 17 years old. They had three children, Catherine, Frederick, and Alexander. Rhoda died in December of 1834, at the age of 24.

On December 18, 1834, Andrew married Mary Bruner in Scott County, Indiana. Andrew and Mary had eleven children together. In 1838, Andrew patented a tract of land in Scott County, from the federal government, but probably didn't live on that land. Shortly after their marriage, Andrew and Mary moved the family a short distance south to a new farm in Graham Township, Jefferson County, Indiana, where they would spend the rest of their lives. Over the years, like his brothers, Andrew purchased several tracts of land in the area, but his home was near Bear Creek, on the border of Jefferson and Jennings counties, not far north of the town of Paris where his brother, Massia, had lived.

Andrew died before Mary, on March 2, 1882, at the age of 73 years, 9 months. Mary died a few years later, on July 15, 1888, at the age of 70. They were both buried near their home, at the Bear Creek Cemetery.

Spouse: Rhoda Burnett.

Rhoda was born in 1810 in Scott County, Indiana. She died in December 1834 in Scott County, Indiana, at the age of 24 years, 11 months. She married Andrew G Byfield on 12 July 1827 in Scott County, Indiana.

Children of Rhoda Burnett and Andrew G Byfield

+ 161 i.   Catherine Byfield. Catherine was born in 1828 in Scott County, Indiana. She died 1871-1880 in Indiana or Illinois.

+ 162 ii.   Frederick W Byfield. Frederick W was born on 13 October 1829 in Scott County, Indiana. He died on 20 March 1906 in Sorento, Bond County, Illinois.

163 iii.   Alexander Hamilton Byfield. Alexander Hamilton was born in 1831 in Scott County, Indiana. He died in _____ in _____.

Spouse: Mary Bruner.

Mary was born on 13 March 1818 in Pennsylvania. She died on 15 July 1888 in Jefferson County, Indiana, at the age of 70 years, 4 months. She was buried in Jennings County, Indiana. She married Andrew G Byfield on 18 December 1834 in Scott County, Indiana.

Children of Mary Bruner and Andrew G Byfield

+ 164 i.   Susan Elizabeth Byfield. Susan Elizabeth was born on 21 January 1836 in Indiana. She died on 9 June 1917 in Laclede County, Missouri.

+ 165 ii.   Martha P Byfield. Martha P was born on 30 October 1837 in Indiana. She died on 20 February 1905 in Jennings County, Indiana.

+ 166 iii.   James M Byfield. James M was born 22 August 1840 in Jefferson County, Indiana. He died 13 September 1906 in Graham Township, Jefferson County, Indiana.

167 iv.   John C Byfield. John C was born on 30 October 1842 in Jefferson County, Indiana. He died on 11 August 1918 in Jennings County, Indiana.

168 v.   Eliza Olivia Byfield. Eliza Olivia was born in November 1844 in Jefferson County, Indiana. She died in _____ in _____.

169 vi.   Andrew Byfield. Andrew was born on 10 August 1847 in Jefferson County, Indiana. He died on 3 January 1890 in Jennings County, Indiana.

16A vii.   Cyrus L D Byfield. Cyrus L D was born on 5 October 1852 in Graham Township, Jefferson County, Indiana. He died on 20 May 1870 in Jennings County, Indiana.

+ 16B viii.   Mary Alvoretta Byfield. Mary Alvoretta was born in October 1854 in Graham Township, Jefferson County, Indiana. She died about 1925 in Indianapolis, Marion County, Indiana.

16C ix.   Corban Byfield. Corban was born on 13 September 1856 in Graham Township, Jefferson County, Indiana. He died on 7 August 1863 in Jennings County, Indiana.

16D x.   Benjamin F Byfield. Benjamin F was born on 10 October 1858 in Indiana. He died on 25 July 1863 in Jennings County, Indiana.

+ 16E xi.   Rose Emma Lucinda Byfield. Rose Emma Lucinda was born in January 1863 in Jefferson County, Indiana. She died in 1937 in Jennings County, Indiana.

17.   **Vincent Byfield.** (Abraham H Byfield-1)

Vincent, the youngest of Abraham Byfield and Patience Corbin's sons, was born about 1810 in Adams County, Ohio. Vincent's father died when he was about 5 years old. After the father's death, the family moved to Hamilton County, Ohio, and stayed there for just a few years. By 1820 Vincent was in Scott County, Indiana, with his mother and his brother, George's, family.

On May 28, 1829, at the age of 19, Vincent married Eliza E Daugherty, who was 17 years old. They were married in Scott County, but moved to Ohio within a few years. Their first child was born in Ohio, probably around Dayton. In fact, all of Vincent and Elizabeth's four children were born in Ohio. There is no record of the reason that they moved from Indiana to Ohio.

Vincent and Eliza's fourth child was born in 1843. In 1850 Elizabeth was a widow and living back in Madison, Jefferson County, Indiana. Vincent must have died between 1843 and 1850, before reaching the age of 40, probably in Ohio. Eliza and the children likely moved back to Indiana to be nearer to Eliza's family, who were in Scott County, Indiana.

Spouse: Eliza E Daugherty.

Eliza was born December 11, 1811 in Kentucky. Her father, Jesse Daugherty, had moved his family to Scott County, Indiana, sometime in the 1820s. After Vincent's death, Eliza moved back from Ohio to Indiana, settling in the town of Madison in Jefferson County. She stayed in Madison for the remainder of her life. She died on June 2, 1887, at the age of 75, and was buried in the Springdale Cemetery in Madison.

Children of Eliza E Daugherty and Vincent Byfield

+ 171 i.   Ann Maria Byfield. Ann Maria was born about 1834 in Ohio. She died on 19 October 1896 in Jefferson County, Indiana.

172 ii.   Addie Valita Byfield. Addie Valita was born about 1836 in Ohio. She died November 1913 in Cairo, Alexander County, Illinois.

+ 173 iii.   Vinson Delas Byfield. Vinson Delas was born on 27 October 1840 in

Akron, Ohio. He died on 6 November 1911 in Madison, Indiana.

+ 174 iv.   Elizabeth Byfield. Elizabeth was born about 1843 in Ohio. She died in _____ in _____.

18.   **Eliza Ann Byfield.** (Abraham H Byfield-1)

Eliza Ann was the last child of Abraham Byfield and Patience Corbin. She was born around 1813 in Adams County, Ohio. After her father's death around 1815, her mother and the rest of the children moved to Hamilton County, Ohio, and then around 1822 to Scott County, Indiana. Eliza probably lived with her mother near her brother George's home until her marriage to James Downs on May 9, 1833, at the age of 20. They were married in Jennings County.

Eliza Ann and James lived in Scott County, Indiana, where they lived near Eliza Ann's niece, Harriet Byfield (daughter of George Washington Byfield) and Harriet's husband, Evan Griffith. Eliza Ann and James had three children, all born in Scott County. By 1850, Eliza Ann's husband had died before the age of 40. In 1850 she was a widow, living in Jennings County near her brother, Andrew Byfield.

In 1851, Eliza Ann departed the Coffee Creek Baptist Church, where she had been a member since the early 1830s. This was probably because she remarried and moved farther from the church. She married William Hoyt on May 5, 1851, in Jennings County, Indiana. Eliza Ann and William had two children, Ann and William. Eliza Ann's second husband, William, died in 1854 leaving her, once again, a widow. In 1860 Eliza Ann was living in Lancaster Township, Jefferson County, Indiana. She had her youngest three children living with her and was near her married daughter, Rebecca.

By 1870, Eliza Ann, her two youngest children, and her daughter Rebecca's family were all living in Marion County, Illinois. At this point, the trail grows cold. There is no record of Eliza Ann or her youngest children, Ann and William, after 1870.

Spouse: James Downs.

James was born about 1810 in Ohio. He died about 1849 in Indiana, at the age of about 39 years. He married Eliza Ann Byfield on 9 May 1833 in Jennings County, Indiana.

Children of Eliza Ann Byfield and James Downs

+ 181 i.   George Washington Downs. George Washington was born on 1 March 1833 in Jefferson County, Indiana. He died on 20 April 1906 in Grant, Mecosta

County, Michigan.

+ 182 ii.   Rebecca A Downs. Rebecca was born in 1837 in Indiana.

+ 183 iii.   James Andrew Downs. James Andrew was born in 1838 in Indiana. He died on 13 June 1863 in Nashville, Tennessee.

Spouse: William Marion Hoyt.

William Marion was born in 1799 in Fairfield, Connecticut. He died on 3 October 1854 in Dupont, Jefferson County, Indiana at the age of 55 years, 9 months. William married Nancy Harding in 1818 and they had nine children before Nancy's death in 1850. William married Eliza Ann Byfield on 5 May 1851 in Jennings County, Indiana.

Children of Eliza Ann Byfield and William Marion Hoyt

184 i.   Ann E Hoyt. Ann E was born about 1852 in Indiana. She died in _____ in _____.

185 ii.   William Hoyt. William was born about 1855 in Indiana. He died in _____ in _____.

GENERATION THREE

CHILDREN OF GEORGE WASHINGTON BYFIELD

111. **George Washington Byfield.** (George Washington Byfield-2; Abraham H Byfield-1)

George Washington Byfield, first child of George Washington Byfield and Magdelena Simonson, was born in Hamilton County, Ohio, on August 11, 1821. After his birth, the family moved to Indiana and settled in Jennings County. George married Eleanor Ann Griffith on September 2, 1841 in Jennings County. George was 20 years old and Eleanor was 18. They farmed in Indiana until 1856 when they traveled to Benton County, Iowa, in a covered wagon, and established a farm on land purchased from the government.

George and Eleanor stayed in Iowa for 25 years before moving west again. In 1880 George went to Smith County, Kansas and established a homestead near the geographic center of the United States. At the same time, Eleanor and the children, Charles, Joseph, Margaret, and Lewis, were listed in the census just north of Smith County, Kansas, in Webster County, Nebraska. They were probably in the process of moving at the time the census was taken. Some of the older children stayed in Iowa, but followed their father to Kansas later. The two eldest children remained in Iowa the rest of their lives.

In 1888, George rented out his farm and moved to Lincoln County, Missouri, for a while, but moved back to western Kansas by 1890. He died on April 2, 1895 in Haddam, Washington County, Kansas at the age of 73 years, 7 months. He was buried at the Pleasant View Cemetery in Washington County.

Spouse: Eleanor Ann Griffith.

Eleanor Ann was born on 18 February 1823 in Baltimore, Maryland.

Eleanor's father had come to Baltimore from Wales. Her mother was also Welsh. She died on 11 September 1898 in Haddam, Washington County, Kansas at the age of 75 years, 6 months. She was buried in Haddam, Washington County, Kansas. She married George Washington Byfield on 2 September 1841 in Vernon, Jennings County, Indiana.

Children of Eleanor Ann Griffith and George Washington Byfield

+ 1111 i. Cornelius Simon Byfield. Cornelius Simon was born in November 1848 in Jennings County, Indiana. He died on 13 May 1902 in Buchanan County, Iowa.

+ 1112 ii. Mary Catherine Byfield. Mary Catherine was born in April 1849 in Scott County, Indiana. She died on 30 November 1937 in Iowa.

+ 1113 iii. George Griffith Byfield. George Griffith was born on 20 June 1849 in Marion Township, Jennings County, Indiana. He died on 28 December 1930 in Butler, Custer County, Oklahoma.

+ 1114 iv. Elinor Jane Byfield. Elinor Jane was born on 29 February 1856 in Independence, Buchanan County, Iowa. She died on 8 May 1937 in Fairbury, Jefferson County, Nebraska.

+ 1115 v. Charles Evans Byfield. Charles Evans was born on 25 December 1858 in Vinton, Benton County, Iowa. He died on 19 April 1924 in Cedar, Smith County, Kansas.

+ 1116 vi. Joseph Abraham Lincoln Byfield. Joseph Abraham Lincoln was born on 1 November 1861 in Red Oak, Montgomery County, Iowa. He died on 20 January 1949 in Stockton, Rooks County, Kansas.

1117 vii. Margaret Olivio Byfield. Margaret Olivio was born in 1863 in Vinton, Benton County, Iowa. She died after 1 June 1900 in Kansas.

1118 viii. Lewis David Byfield. Lewis David was born in 1866 in Vinton, Benton County, Iowa. He died on 10 October 1926 in the Philippines.

112. **Harriet Byfield.** (George Washington Byfield-2; Abraham H Byfield-1)

Harriet Byfield was the first daughter of George Washington Byfield and Magdelena Simonson. She was born in Indiana about 1823. She lived with her parents in Scott County until the age of 16 when she married Evan Griffith, who was 24 years old. They married in Scott County on March 14, 1839. In 1840 they were living near her father and her aunt, Eliza Ann. Harriet and Evan had a daughter, Olivia, in 1843, and Harriet died shortly afterward. By 1846 Evan had remarried.

Spouse: Evan Griffith.

Evan was born about 1815 in Wales. He died on 11 August 1901 in Vernon, Jennings County, Indiana, at the age of about 86 years, 7 months. He married Harriet Byfield on 14 March 1839 in Scott County, Indiana. He married Mary Taulman on 17 May 1846 in Jennings County, Indiana.

Children of Harriet Byfield and Evan Griffith

+ 1121 i.   Olivia Griffith. Olivia was born on 3 August 1843 in Indiana. She died on 5 November 1918 in Heman, Oklahoma.

113.   **Lewis Freeman Byfield.** (George Washington Byfield-2; Abraham H Byfield-1)

Lewis Freeman was born to George Washington Byfield and Magdelena Simonson on 21 January 1825 in Jennings County, Indiana. He lived with his parents in Scott County until his marriage to Ruth Ann Kashow on 3 April 1845. He was 20 years old and Ruth was 19. Lewis and Ruth's first child died as an infant. Lewis died, at the age of 23, on 10 January 1849, less than a month before the birth of his second child. He was buried in the Old Coffee Creek Cemetery in Jennings County, Indiana.

Spouse: Ruth Ann Kashow.

Ruth Ann was born on 5 July 1826 in Ohio. She died on 6 May 1907 in Clatskanie, Columbia County, Oregon, at the age of 80 years, 10 months. She married Lewis Freeman Byfield on 3 April 1845 in Jefferson County, Indiana. She married William J Young on 18 December 1851 in Scott County, Indiana. William Young was the brother of Christian Young, who married Lewis Freeman's sister, Mariah.

Ruth Ann Kashow

Children of Ruth Ann Kashow and

Lewis Freeman Byfield

1131 i.   James Madison Byfield. James Madison was born on 13 October 1846 in Scott County, Indiana. He died on 22 May 1847 in Scott County, Indiana.

+ 1132 ii.   Lewis Freeman Byfield. Lewis Freeman Jr was born on 4 February 1849 in Scott County, Indiana. He died on 5 October 1874 in Scott County, Indiana.

114.   **Mariah Byfield.** (George Washington Byfield-2; Abraham H Byfield-1)

Mariah was born on 17 May 1828 in Scott County, Indiana. She was the daughter of George Washington Byfield and Magdelena Simonson. She married Christian Waldsmith Young on 1 October 1846 in Scott County, Indiana. Mariah and Christian had eleven children before Christian's death in 1871. She then married David T Tobias on 27 April 1879. David died in 1881. Finally, she married James W Bovard on 6 June 1889. James died about three months after their marriage and she collected a Civil War widow's pension from his service. She had no children with David Tobias or James Bovard. Mariah died in Scott County, Indiana, in May of 1899.

Spouse: Christian Waldsmith Young.

Christian Waldsmith was born on 18 October 1824 in Hamilton, Ohio. He died on 15 March 1871 in Jefferson County, Indiana, at the age of 46 years, 4 months. He married Mariah Byfield on 1 October 1846 in Scott County, Indiana.

Children of Mariah Byfield and Christian Waldsmith Young

1141 i.   Harriet Young. Harriet was born on 2 August 1847 in Scott, Lagrange County, Indiana. She died on 2 August 1847 in Scott, Lagrange County, Indiana.

+ 1142 ii.   Lewis Cassius Young. Lewis Cassius was born on 21 September 1848 in Alpha, Scott County, Indiana. He died on 12 October 1886 in Scott County, Indiana.

1143 iii.   William Crawford Young. William Crawford was born on 11 December 1850 in Scott, Lagrange County, Indiana. He died on 11 March 1853 in Scott, Lagrange County, Indiana.

1144 iv.   Olive Clara Young. Olive Clara was born on 30 May 1857 in Jennings County, Indiana. She died on 20 September 1857 in Jennings County, Indiana.

1145 v.   Minerva Jane Young. Minerva Jane was born on 2 November 1856 in Jennings County, Indiana. She died on 29 September 1857 in Jennings County, Indiana.

+ 1146 vi.   Deborah C Young. Deborah C was born on 17 August 1858 in Scott County, Indiana. She died about 1880 in Indiana.

1147 vii.   Infant Girl Young. Infant was born on 28 December 1860 in Jennings County, Indiana. She died on 28 December 1860 in Jennings County, Indiana.

1148 viii.   Jefferson Young. Jefferson was born on 21 December 1861 in Scott, Lagrange County, Indiana. He died on 11 May 1863 in Scott, Lagrange County, Indiana.

+ 1149 ix.   Malana Mary Young. Malana Mary was born on 5 June 1865 in Alpha, Scott County, Indiana. She died on 26 August 1927 in Oklahoma City, Oklahoma County, Oklahoma.

+ 114A x.   Clarence Mclure Young. Clarence Mclure was born in August 1867 in Indiana. He died on 13 March 1937 in Jennings County, Indiana..

114B xi.   Leamon C Young. Leamon C was born on 11 June 1870 in Indiana. He died in 1905 in _____.

Spouse: David T Tobias.

David T was born 22 June 1816 in Wales. He died on 14 January 1881 in Johnson, Scott County, Indiana. He married Mariah Byfield on 27 April 1879 in Scott County, Indiana.

Spouse: James W Bovard.

James W was born on 23 March 1823 in Steubenville, Tuscarawas County, Ohio. He died on 19 October 1889 in Alpha, Scott County, Indiana, at the age of 66 years, 6 months. He married Mariah Byfield on 6 June 1889 in Scott County, Indiana.

115.   **Ida Byfield.** (George Washington Byfield-2; Abraham H Byfield-1)

Ida was born in 1831 in Indiana. She was the daughter of George Washington Byfield and Magdalena Simonson. She married Wesley Hoard on 11 June 1848 in Scott County, Indiana. She died on 30 March 1852 in Graham, Jefferson County, Indiana at the age of 21 years, 2 months.

Spouse: Wesley Hoard.

Wesley was born about 1825 in Mercer, Kentucky. He died on 7 February 1889 in Jefferson County, Indiana at the age of about 64 years, 1 month. He married Ida Byfield on 11 June 1848 in Scott County, Indiana. He later married Rebecca Wheat on 4 August 1854 in Jefferson County, Indiana.

Children of Ida Byfield and Wesley Hoard

+ 1151 i.   Sarah F Hoard. Sarah F was born about 1849 in Jefferson County, Indiana. She died in _____ in _____.

116.   **Albert Byfield.** (George Washington Byfield-2; Abraham H Byfield-1)

Albert was born December 20, 1833 in Indiana. He was the son of George Washington Byfield and Magdalena Simonson. He married Delilah Gross on 4 January 1857 in Jennings County, Indiana. He died July 23, 1888 in Codey's Bluff, Nowata County, Oklahoma.

Albert and Delilah lived in Scott County, Indiana, for over 20 years before moving to Oklahoma in 1880. They settled in Nowata County, which is in northeastern Oklahoma just south of the Kansas state line. Most of the children made the move along with their parents. Delilah died soon after the move and Albert died about 7 years later.

Spouse: Delilah Gross.

Delilah was born about 1835 in Indiana. She died in 1880 in Nowata, Nowata County, Oklahoma, at the age of about 45 years. She married Albert Byfield on 4 January 1857 in Jennings County, Indiana.

Children of Delilah Gross and Albert Byfield

1161 i.   Dorcas Byfield. Dorcas was born about 1858 in Indiana. She died in _____ in _____.

+ 1162 ii.   Harriet Matilda Byfield. Harriet Matilda was born on 5 April 1863 in Scott County, Indiana. She died on 23 February 1936 in Nowata, Nowata County, Oklahoma.

+ 1163 iii.   Maria Byfield. Maria was born in 1866 in Indiana. She died in

_____ in _____ .

1164 iv.   William A Byfield. William A was born in 1866 in Indiana. He died on 1 January 1937 in Nowata, Nowata County, Oklahoma.

+ 1165 v.   Charles C Byfield. Charles C was born in 1870 in Indiana. He died on 26 November 1928 in Nowata, Nowata County, Oklahoma.

+ 1166 vi.   Emma Retta Byfield. Emma Retta was born on 8 February 1872 in Indiana. She died on 9 December 1955 in Alameda, Alameda County, California.

1167 vii.   George Byfield. George was born in 1875 in Indiana. He died on _____ in _____ .

1168 viii.   Loret 'Nellie' Byfield. Loret 'Nellie' was born on 1 March 1878 in Jennings, Jennings County, Indiana. She died on 20 August 1888 in Nowata, Nowata County, Oklahoma.

117.   **Francis Marion Byfield.** (George Washington Byfield-2; Abraham H Byfield-1)

Francis Marion was born on 8 November 1836 in Scott County, Indiana. He was the son of George Washington Byfield and Magdalena Simonson. The name "Francis Marion" is after a hero of the Revolutionary war who was known for his guerrilla tactics and had the nickname "Swamp Fox". Francis married Harriet M Smith on 14 December 1855 in Scott County, Indiana, at 19 years old.

When the Civil War started, Francis Marion already had a young family, so he didn't enlist as did many of his cousins. Still, he was drafted into service on 21 September 1864. He participated in the Campaign of the Carolinas, part of Sherman's March. He died in the war, less than six months after being drafted, on 2 March 1865 in Taxahaw, South Carolina. He was 28 years, 3 months old. His widow, Harriet, applied to the government for a widow's pension for herself and minor's pensions for the three children.

Harriet's second husband, Moses Morrison, became guardian of the three children until the marriage of daughter, Nancy Josephine. Nancy's husband, Oliver Whitsett, then became guardian of her young brothers, George and Francis.

Spouse: Harriett M Smith.

Harriett M was born 26 October 1834 in Indiana. She died on 27 August 1884 in Scott County, Indiana. She married Francis Marion Byfield on 14 December 1855 in Scott County, Indiana. She later married Moses Morrison on 17 January 1868 in Scott County, Indiana.

Children of Harriett M Smith and Francis Marion Byfield

+ 1171 i.   Nancy Josephine Byfield. Nancy Josephine was born on 7 September 1856 in Scott County, Indiana. She died 10 February 1937 in Wainwright, Muskogee County, Oklahoma.

+ 1172 ii.   George W Byfield. George W was born on 28 December 1858 in Scott County, Indiana. He died on 16 March 1917 in Jefferson County, Indiana.

+ 1173 iii.   Francis Alaska Byfield. Francis Alaska was born on 17 June 1862 in Indiana. He died on 28 December 1903 in _____.

118.   **Charles Carel Byfield.** (George Washington Byfield-2; Abraham H Byfield-1)

Charles Carel was born on 17 March 1840 in Scott County, Indiana. He was the son of George Washington Byfield and Magdalena Simonson. He married Mary A Tobias on 11 April 1861 in Scott County, Indiana. Charles was 21 years old and Mary was 24.

In the late 1860s, Charles and Mary moved their young family to Kansas. They had one son, Charley, in Missouri while headed to their homestead in Linn County, Kansas, about 40 miles southwest of Kansas City. Around 1885 the family moved to Montgomery County in southern Kansas, not far from his brother, Albert, who was in northern Oklahoma.

Charles died on 10 March 1899 in Costello, Kansas, at the age of 58 years, 11 months. He was buried in Montgomery County, Kansas.

Spouse: Mary A Tobias.

Mary A was born 25 July 1836 in Indiana. She died on 27 December 1899 in Montgomery County, Kansas, at the age of about 58 years, 11 months. She married Charles Carel Byfield on 11 April 1861 in Scott County, Indiana.

Children of Mary A Tobias and Charles Carel Byfield

1181 i.   Elmira M Byfield. Elmira M was born on 5 March 1862 in
                    _____. She died on 6 May 1865 in Indiana.

+ 1182 ii.   Martha Byfield. Martha was born about 1864 in Indiana. She died
                between 1886 and 1900 in Kansas.

1183 iii.   Charley W Byfield. Charley was born about 1868 in Missouri. He
                    died in _____ in _____.

+ 1184 iv.   Sarah Elmina Byfield. Sarah Elmina was born about 1870 in Kansas.
                She died in 1939 in Idaho.

+ 1185 v.   Bernard S Byfield. Bernard S was born on 25 October 1872 in
                Kansas. He died in 1962 in Oklahoma.

+ 1186 vi.   George Washington Byfield. George Washington was born on 7
                August 1875 in Lawrence, Douglas County, Kansas. He died on 19 April 1915
                in Fairview, Major County, Oklahoma.

+ 1187 vii.   John Boman Byfield. John Boman was born on 4 November 1879 in
                Kansas. He died on 17 December 1953 in Oklahoma.

CHILDREN OF HORATIO BYFIELD

121.   **Daniel Byfield.** (Horatio Byfield-2; Abraham H Byfield-1)

Daniel was born on 11 September 1823 in Indiana. He was the first child of Horatio Byfield and Jennet Griffith. Daniel was trained as a physician. He married Martha M Baldwin on 19 September 1847 in Jennings County, Indiana. He died on 2 November 1850 in Lancaster Township, Jefferson County, Indiana at the age of 27 years, 1 month.

Spouse: Martha M Baldwin.

Martha M was born on 2 August 1829 in Indiana. Martha was the daughter of Ebienezer Baldwin and Elizabeth Hess. She married Daniel Byfield on 19 September 1847 in Jennings County, Indiana. She also married Leland Payne on 20 May 1854 in Johnson County, Indiana. She died on 1 April 1915, at the age of 85, in Johnson County, Indiana.

Children of Martha M Baldwin and Daniel Byfield

1211 i.   Willis Byfield. Willis was born on 4 December 1848 in Indiana. He died on 5 July 1850 in Indiana.

122.   **Alford Byfield.** (Horatio Byfield-2; Abraham H Byfield-1)

Alford was born on 15 March 1825 in Jefferson County, Indiana. He was the son of Horatio Byfield and Jennet Griffith. He married Nancy Graham on 12 October 1843 in Jefferson County, Indiana. Alford was 18 years old and Nancy was 15 at the time of their marriage. Alford died on 7 October 1846 in Indiana at the age of 21 years, 6 months. He was buried in Jefferson County, Indiana, at the Byfield Family Cemetery on his father's farm.

Spouse: Nancy Graham.

Nancy was born about 1828 in Pennsylvania. She married Alford Byfield on 12 October 1843 in Jefferson County, Indiana. By the age of 20 Nancy was a widow. In October 1850 she was living with her parents and her 4 year old daughter, listed as "Hannah J Byfield", was living adjacent to her parents with a family of Guthries. Between 1850 and 1860 she went to the town of Madison and became a dressmaker. The census in 1860 lists her and her daughter along with eight young seamstresses. She died after 1880 in Indianapolis, Indiana.

Children of Nancy Graham and Alford Byfield

1221 i.   James Byfield. James was born 21 August 1844 in Indiana. He died 11 February 1847 in Indiana.

+ 1222 ii.   Hannah Janet 'Catherine' 'Kate' Byfield. Hannah Janet was born 30 June 1846 in Indiana. She died 22 April 1926 in Indiana.

123.   **Henrietta Byfield.** (Horatio Byfield-2; Abraham H Byfield-1)

Henrietta was born 19 July 1827 in Indiana. She was the first daughter of Horatio Byfield and Jennet Griffith. She married William Simeon Reynolds on 21 December 1848 in Jefferson County, Indiana. She was 21 years old when she married. She died, at age 68, on 1 March 1896 in Shelbyville, Shelby County, Indiana.

Spouse: William Simeon Reynolds.

William Simeon was born 24 November 1824 in Indiana. He married Henrietta Byfield on 21 December 1848 in Jefferson County, Indiana. He died 6 April 1912 in Dupont, Indiana.

Children of Henrietta Byfield and William Simeon Reynolds

1231 i.   Levi B Reynolds. Levi B was born on 12 September 1849 in Jefferson County, Indiana. He died on 31 January 1851 in Jefferson County, Indiana.

1232 ii.   Jeanett Reynolds. Jeanett was born on 3 August 1852 in Jefferson County, Indiana. She died on 12 September 1853 in Jefferson County, Indiana.

1233 iii.   Anna C Reynolds. Anna C was born in December 1856 in Indiana. She died after 1930 in Hamilton County, Indiana.

+ 1234 iv.   Maggie Reynolds. Maggie was born December 1861 in Indiana. She died in January 1906 in Clinton County, Indiana.

+ 1235 v.   Ivy Lester Reynolds. Ivy Lester was born 8 September 1876 in Franklin, Johnson County, Indiana. He died 22 April 1952 in Jackson, Jackson

County, Michigan.

124.   **Margaretta Byfield.** (Horatio Byfield-2; Abraham H Byfield-1)

Margaretta was born about 1829 in Jefferson County, Indiana. She was the daughter of Horatio Byfield and Jennet Griffith. She married Green Malcom on 30 December 1856 in Johnson County, Indiana. Green died before 1860. In the 1860 census, Margaretta and her young son, Horatio, were living back with Margaretta's mother.

In 1870 Margaretta and her son were living with two of her unmarried brothers, Horatio and Corbin. The next place we find Margaretta and her son is in Schell City, Missouri, where her son was working as a telegrapher. By 1885 Margaretta, her son, Horatio, and her brother, Horatio, were in the mining town of Alder in Saguache County, Colorado. They ran a store in that town and all three served as Postmasters there at different times.

By 1905 Margaretta was living by herself in the town of Salida, not far from Alder, in Colorado. She died in March 1906, probably in Colorado, but there is no record of her place of burial.

Spouse: Green Malcom.

Green was born in Kentucky. He died about 1859 in Indiana. He married Margaretta Byfield on 30 December 1856 in Johnson County, Indiana.

Children of Margaretta Byfield and Green Malcom

1241 i.   Horatio W Malcom. Horatio W was born 15 September 1858 in Indiana. He died in _____ in _____.

125.   **Corbin⁵ Byfield.** (Horatio Byfield-2; Abraham H Byfield-1)

Corbin was born 10 June 1832 in Indiana. His name comes from his grandmother, Patience Corbin's, family name. He was the son of Horatio Byfield and Jennet Griffith. He was listed with his brother,

---

5   Corbin is listed in the 1850 Census as "Cornelius".

Horatio, in the 1862, Jefferson County, Lancaster Township, militia enrollment. In 1863, at the age of 30, Corbin registered for the draft, but he never served in the Civil War. Corbin never married. He died on 25 July 1894[6] in Indianapolis, Marion County, Indiana at the age of about 62 years, 6 months. He was buried in Indianapolis, Marion County, Indiana.

126.   **Horatio Byfield.** (Horatio Byfield-2; Abraham H Byfield-1)

Horatio was born 25 October 1834 in Indiana. He was the son of Horatio Byfield and Jennet Griffith. Horatio never married.

In 1862 Horatio is listed as a member of the Indiana militia, but he didn't serve in the Civil War. In 1869 he inherited all his mother's land. It's likely that this is the farm where Jennet remained after her husbands death. Horatio lived with his mother until her death. He stayed and took care of the farm in Jefferson County, Indiana for several years, but in the late 1870s he moved to Colorado and became a merchant in the mining area around Leadville. In 1883 he was the Postmaster in Alder, Colorado, a smaller town to the south of Leadville. By 1885 he was joined by his sister, Margaretta, and her son, Horatio.

He died on 8 September 1890 in Alder, Saguache County, Colorado at the age of about 56 years, 8 months. The *Shelby Democrat* newspaper in Indiana reported " Mrs. W. S. Reynolds [Henrietta Byfield] received a telegram last Monday announcing the death of her brother, Horace Byfield in Alder, Colorado. Mr. Byfield was well known in this City". After Horatio's death, his sister, Margaretta took over as the Postmaster of Alder.

127.   **Casabianca 'Cass' Byfield.** (Horatio Byfield-2; Abraham H Byfield-1)

Casabianca was born 17 October 1837 in Indiana, the son of Horatio Byfield and Jennet Griffith. The name Casabianca likely comes from the popular poem of the same name by British poet Felicia Dorothea

---

6   Horatio Byfield's family Bible gives Corbin's death date as 30 July 1893.

Hemans. The poem was well known by the time of Cass' birth and became a standard memorized by school children.

Cass was educated in the practice of law and graduated in the class of 1860 from Franklin College in Franklin County, Indiana. He was a founding member of the Phi Delta Theta fraternity at Franklin College. By age 25 he was partner in the Woolen and Byfield law firm in the town of Franklin in Johnson County, Indiana. He married Jessie Mary Ann Heineken on 22 December 1863 in Johnson County, Indiana. Cass was active in the community and in politics throughout his life. He was a staunch Democrat.

In 1866 Cass was City Attorney for the city of Franklin, Indiana. His future law partner, Thomas W Woolen, was on the city council. In 1871 the Indiana House of Representatives elected Casabianca Byfield as Trustee of the Blind Asylum and he served in that capacity through 1874. In 1872 Casabianca and Daniel Howe, left the Woolen and Byfield law firm in Franklin to start a new law practice in Indianapolis. In 1875 and 1876 Cass was City Attorney for Indianapolis. In 1878 he ran for the office of Superior Court Judge.

In 1880 he ran for the House of Representatives for his district but lost to the Republican candidate. At the time there was a Greenbacker Party that was similar to the Democratic Party, but had stronger anti-monopoly leanings and supported reinstatement of the gold standard. Since they were also running a candidate in 1880, the Democratic leaning voters were split and the Republicans assured of a victory.

Casabianca died of heart disease on 6 August 1888 in Indianapolis, at the age of about 51 years, 7 months. He was buried at the Crown Hill Cemetery in Indianapolis.

Spouse: Jessie Mary Ann Heineken.

Jessie Mary Ann was born in July 1841 in England. She was the daughter of Samuel Heineken, a saloon keeper, and his wife, Caroline, who was a milliner. The family came to the United States from Llanelly, Camarthenshire, Wales, when Jessie was 11 years old. She married Casabianca Byfield on 22 December 1863 in Johnson County, Indiana. She died in 1919 in Indianapolis, Marion County, Indiana, at the age of 77 years, 6 months. She was buried on 14

January 1919 in Indianapolis, Marion County, Indiana.

Children of Jessie Mary Ann Heineken and Casabianca Byfield

1271 i.　　Charles W Byfield. Charles W was born about 1864 in Indiana. He died in October 1923 in Indianapolis, Marion County, Indiana.

1272 ii.　　Arthur H Byfield. Arthur H was born about 1866 in Indiana. He died in 1918 in Indianapolis, Marion County, Indiana.

1273 iii.　　Harry N Byfield. Harry M was born about 1868 in Indiana. He died in _____ in _____.

1274 iv.　　Emma C Byfield. Emma C was born about 1871 in Indiana. She died in October 1949 in Indianapolis, Marion County, Indiana.

1275 v.　　Bessie Byfield. Bessie was born about 1873 in Indiana. She died on 2 May 1915 in New York, New York.

128.　　**Emily Byfield.** (Horatio Byfield-2; Abraham H Byfield-1)

Emily was born 7 August 1840 in Indiana, daughter of Horatio Byfield and Jennet Griffith. She was the twin sister of Elva Byfield. She married William Conway 21 February 1859 in Jefferson County, Indiana. After her husband's death she lived in Indianapolis with her daughters. She died 8 June 1906 in Indianapolis, Marion County, Indiana. She was buried in Indianapolis, Indiana, at the Crown Hill Cemetery, near her daughters, Mary and Elva.

Emily and her husband, William, took a boy off of the Orphan Train on 19 March 1861 whose name was Levi Cornell. He was never formally adopted.

Spouse: William Conway.

William was born 24 November 1831 in Jefferson County, Indiana. He died 16 June 1889 in Johnson County, Indiana. He married Emily Byfield 21 February 1859 in Jefferson County, Indiana.

William Conway's family were founding members of Lancaster Baptist Church, an abolitionist church in *Paris Crossing*.

Children of Emily Byfield and William Conway

1281 i.　　Whitcomb Conway. Whitcomb was born 10 January 1860 in

Lancaster, Jefferson County, Indiana. He died on 12 March 1863 in Lancaster, Jefferson County, Indiana.

1282 ii.   Cora Tripp Conway. Cora Tripp was born 8 August 1862 in Lancaster, Jefferson County, Indiana. She died in 1920 in Marion County, Indiana.

+ 1283 iii.   Elizabeth Janette 'Nettie' Conway. Elizabeth Janette 'Nettie' was born on 18 May 1864 in Lancaster, Jefferson County, Indiana. She died 12 July 1915 in Indianapolis, Marion County, Indiana.

+ 1284 iv.   Mary Mildred Conway. Mary Mildred was born 30 November 1866 in Dupont, Jefferson County, Indiana. She died in 1937 in Indianapolis, Indiana.

1285 v.   Jessie Adelade Conway. Jessie A was born 27 March 1870 in Lancaster, Jefferson County, Indiana. She died on 31 May 1938.

1286 vi.   Elva Walker Conway. Elva Walker was born on 6 July 1872 in Indiana. She died December 1948 in Detroit, Wayne County, Michigan.

+ 1287 vii.   Emily 'Emma' Byfield Conway. Emily 'Emma' Byfield was born 19 April 1875 in Franklin County, Indiana. She died 24 September 1932 in Denver, Colorado.

129.   **Elva Byfield.** (Horatio Byfield-2; Abraham H Byfield-1)

Elva was born 7 August 1840 in Indiana, the daughter of Horatio Byfield and Jennet Griffith. She was the twin sister of Emily Byfield. She married Thomas T Walker 3 September 1861 in Lancaster, Jefferson County, Indiana. Elva and Thomas had six sons, all born in Indiana. Sometime after 1880 the family moved to Custer County, west of Oklahoma City, in Oklahoma. She died 29 April 1908 in Oklahoma. She was buried in Weatherford, Custer County, Oklahoma.

Spouse: Thomas T Walker.

Thomas T was born on 17 September 1837 in Indiana. He died on 15 December 1902 in Oklahoma at the age of 65 years, 2 months. He married Elva Byfield 3 September 1861 in Lancaster, Jefferson County, Indiana.

Children of Elva Byfield and Thomas T Walker

1291 i.   Tanner Walker. Tanner was born 2 January 1864 in Jefferson County, Indiana. He died 13 September 1864 in Lancaster, Jefferson County, Indiana.

1292 ii.   Byfield Walker. Byfield was born about 1865 in Indiana. He died in

_____ in _____.

+ 1293 iii.   William Baxter Walker. William Baxter was born about 1870 in Indiana. He died on 1 March 1933 in Guthrie, Oklahoma.

1294 iv.   John Harris Walker. John Harris was born 24 February 1872 in Indiana. He died on 31 May 1904 in Custer County, Oklahoma.

1295 v.   James Walker. James was born about 1874 in Indiana. He died in _____ in _____.

12A.   **Whitcomb Byfield.** (Horatio Byfield-2; Abraham H Byfield-1)

Whitcomb was born on 11 July 1843 in Indiana. He was the son of Horatio Byfield and Jennet Griffith. In 1864 he enlisted in Indiana Regiment 132, Company D, and fought in the Civil War. He married Margaret Anna Payne on 8 August 1869 in Jefferson County, Indiana. By his mid thirties, Whitcomb moved his family from Madison to Indianapolis. He worked as a custodian. He died on 29 August 1916 in Indianapolis, Marion County, Indiana at the age of 73 years, 1 month. He was buried on 1 September 1916 in Indianapolis, Indiana.

Spouse: Margaret Anna Payne.

Margaret Anna was born on 17 December 1851 in Indiana. She was the daughter of Lydia Godman and Elihu Rudd Payne. Margaret was the sister of John Godman Payne, who married Whitcomb's sister, Mary. She died in 1924 in Indiana at the age of 72 years, 15 days. She was buried on 19 June 1924 in Indianapolis, Marion County, Indiana. She married Whitcomb Byfield on 8 August 1869 in Jefferson County, Indiana.

Children of Margaret Anna Payne and Whitcomb Byfield

12A1 i.   Ralph Godman Byfield. Ralph Godman was born in 1870 or 1871 in Madison, Jefferson County, Indiana. He died on 7 August 1871 in Lancaster, Jefferson County, Indiana.

12A2 ii.   Louise G Byfield. Louise G was born on 30 July 1872 in Indiana. She died on 1 December 1906 in Indianapolis, Indiana.

+ 12A3 iii.   Harry Whitcomb Byfield. Harry Whitcomb was born on 18 January 1876 in Indiana. He died on 16 June 1930 in Buffalo, Erie County, New York.

12B.   **Mary Byfield.** (Horatio Byfield-2; Abraham H Byfield-1)

Mary was born on 11 February 1846 in Lancaster, Jefferson County, Indiana. She was the daughter of Horatio Byfield and Jennet Griffith. During the Civil War she attended Glendale College.   She married John Godman Payne on 25 October 1868 in Jefferson County, Indiana.   Mary and John lived in Indianapolis, Indiana their entire lives.   She died on 17 December 1919 in Indianapolis, Marion County, Indiana at the age of 73 years, 10 months. She was buried on 18 December 1919 in Indianapolis, Marion County, Indiana.

Spouse: John Godman Payne.

John Godman was born on 14 May 1847 in Madison, Jefferson County, Indiana. He was the son of Lydia Godman and Elihu Rudd Payne.   John was a drummer boy in the Civil War.   He worked as an auctioneer.   He died on 19 June 1889 in Indianapolis, Indiana.   He married Mary Byfield on 25 October 1868 in Jefferson County, Indiana.

Children of Mary Byfield and John Godman Payne

+ 12B1 i.   Gavin Lodge Payne. Gavin Lodge was born 3 September 1869 in
          Wirt, Jefferson County, Indiana. He died on 12 September 1939 in
          Indianapolis, Marion County, Indiana.

+ 12B2 ii.   Janet P Payne. Janet P was born about 1872 in Indianapolis, Marion
          County, Indiana. She died on 20 August 1948 in Indianapolis, Indiana.

12C.   **Charles A Byfield.** (Horatio Byfield-2; Abraham H Byfield-1)

Charles A was born about 1850 in Jefferson County, Indiana. He was the youngest child of Horatio Byfield and Jennet Griffith.   In 1870 Charles was living with his sister, Henrietta's family in the town of Franklin, Indiana. At that time he was working as a clerk in a store in Franklin.   In 1870, 1871, and 1872, Charles was listed as treasurer of the new project to build and staff a colored school in Franklin County, Indiana.   Charles was a member of the Independent Order of Odd Fellows, Johnson Lodge No. 76, and filled the office of noble grand at one time.

He married Mattie Milhous on 15 February 1873 in Boone County,

Indiana. In 1874 Charles was listed as a "stave dealer" in Boone County. Charles was a druggist in Franklin, Johnson County, Indiana, in the 1880 census. He was town clerk for the city of Franklin from 1878 to 1880. Charles was a Franklin Township Trustee from 1881 to 1883. Charles served as Clerk of the Johnson County Circuit Court from 1891 to 1899. He was admitted to the county bar but never practiced law. In 1895 Charles was a stockholder in the Franklin Building and Loan Association. He died on 5 March 1900 in Franklin at the age of about 50 years, 2 months.

Spouse: Martha 'Mattie' Milhous.

Mattie was born on 10 October 1853 in Ohio, daughter of Thomas Milhous and Sarah A Hamer. Martha lived in Franklin County, Indiana all her married life. After her husband's death she lived with her daughter, Bonnie, in Texas, and with her son, Charles, in Indianapolis. She died on 28 June 1942 in Indiana at the age of 88 years, 8 months. She was buried in Franklin, Johnson County, Indiana. She married Charles A Byfield on 15 February 1873 in Indiana.

Children of Mattie Milhous and Charles A Byfield

+ 12C1 i. Harold Ragsdale Byfield. Harold R was born on 21 November 1874 in Franklin, Johnson County, Indiana. He died in February 1921 in Indiana.

+ 12C2 ii. Ralph Clermont Byfield. Ralph Clermont was born on 18 July 1876 in Franklin, Johnson County, Indiana. He died in 1933 in Greenberg, Decatur County, Indiana.

+ 12C3 iii. Charles Augustus Byfield. Charles Augustus was born in October 1884 in Franklin, Johnson County, Indiana. He died on 24 November 1942 in Indianapolis, Indiana.

+ 12C4 iv. Raymond Frank Byfield. Raymond Frank was born on 28 March 1889 in Franklin, Johnson County, Indiana. He died 20 January 1937 in Kerrville, Kerr County, Texas.

12C5 v. Bonnie Vivian Byfield. Bonnie Vivian was born on 7 August 1895 in Franklin, Johnson County, Indiana. She died on 27 December 1978 in San Antonio, Bexar County, Texas.

CHILDREN OF STELLA HARRIET BYFIELD

131.   **Albert Edwin McGaughey.** (Stella Harriet Byfield-2; Abraham H Byfield-1)

Albert Edwin was born on 17 February 1820 in Indiana. He was the son of George McGaughey and Stella Harriet Byfield. He married Charlotte B Raymond on Tuesday, 15 April 1845 in Franklin County, Indiana. Albert and his new family moved from Indiana to Minnesota along with his parents. By 1857 they were in Goodhue County near Red Wing in southern Minnesota. In 1859, Albert and his brother, Samuel, were co-inventors of an improvement to steam plows and were awarded U.S. Patent 26,279 for that invention.

Albert farmed in that area until around 1866, when he moved north to the Minneapolis area where he co-founded the North Star Iron Works. Around

The North Star Iron Works in 1874

1870 he sold his interest in the Iron Works. About age 60 he moved west to Big Stone County, Minnesota, where he and his wife lived the rest of their lives. He died 8 June 1888 in Ortonville, Big Stone County, Minnesota, at the age of 68. He was buried in Ortonville, Big Stone County, Minnesota.

Spouse: Charlotte B Raymond.

Charlotte B was born on 30 May 1825 in Indiana. She died 20 June 1897 in Ortonville, Big Stone County, Minnesota. She was buried in Ortonville, Big Stone County, Minnesota. She married Albert Edwin

McGaughey on 15 April 1845 in Franklin County, Indiana.

Children of Charlotte B Raymond and Albert Edwin McGaughey

1311 i. Stella Ann McGaughey. Stella Ann was born on 31 March 1846 in Franklin County, Indiana. She died on 2 January 1917 in Minneapolis, Minnesota.

+ 1312 ii. Martha Elizabeth McGaughey. Martha Elizabeth was born on 15 September 1849 in Indiana. She died on 25 November 1928 in Jefferson County, Montana.

1313 iii. John Henry McGaughey. John Henry was born on 15 January 1853 in Indiana. He died on 10 October 1908 in Ortonville, Big Stone County, Minnesota.

+ 1314 iv. George E McGaughey. George E was born on 11 June 1859 in St Anthony, Hennepin County, Minnesota. He died on 20 February 1934 in Burbank, Los Angeles County, California.

1315 v. Wiley Allen McGaughey. Wiley Allen was born on 15 August 1861 in Minnesota. He died on 4 November 1871 in Minneapolis, Hennepin County, Minnesota.

132. **David J McGaughey.** (Stella Harriet Byfield-2; Abraham H Byfield-1)

David J was born in 1823 in Indiana. He was the son of George McGaughey and Stella Harriet Byfield. He moved to Minnesota with his parents. David is with his younger brother, Horatio, in 1860 in Goodhue County, Minnesota. He died in _____ in _____.

133. **Samuel Newton McGaughey.** (Stella Harriet Byfield-2; Abraham H Byfield-1)

Samuel Newton was born in 1827 in Mount Carmel, Franklin County, Indiana. He was the son of George McGaughey and Stella Harriet Byfield. He married Isabella Wynn on 28 December 1848 in Franklin County, Indiana. Samuel and Isabella move to Decatur County, Indiana, where Samuel worked in the saw mill business. Samuel's family came to Minnesota along with his parents around 1855. In 1859, Samuel and his brother, Albert, were awarded U.S. Patent

26,279 for "Improvement in Steam-Plows". In 1860 Samuel was elected chairman of the Supervisor's Committee for the Leon Township in Goodhue County. In 1858 to 1860 he was also a Justice of the Peace.

By 1863 Samuel had moved the family to the Minneapolis area where he worked for a few years manufacturing pumps and then went to work with his brother at the North Star Iron Works. In 1875 he went to work at the Union Planing Mill. In 1883 he was awarded U.S. Patent 280,843 for a combination cane and folding camp chair. He died about 1900 in Minnesota at the age of about 73 years.

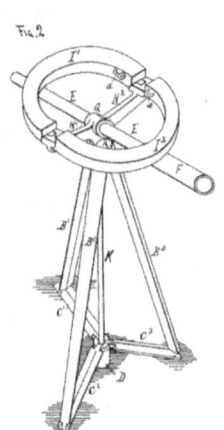

Spouse: Isabella Wynn.

Isabella was born 8 January 1823 in Indiana. She was the daughter of Joseph Wynn and Margaret Armstrong. She married Samuel N McGaughey on 28 December 1848 in Franklin County, Indiana. It appears that after her husband's death she moved back to be with her family in Indiana. She died on 24 June 1903 in Decatur County, Indiana. She was buried in Decatur County, Indiana.

Drawing from one of Samuel Newton McGaughey's patents.

Children of Isabella Wynn and Samuel N McGaughey

+ 1331 i. Viola Wynn McGaughey. Viola Wynn was born in August 1856 in Leon Township, Goodhue County, Minnesota. She died on 10 September 1920 in Minneapolis, Hennepin County, Minnesota.

+ 1332 ii. Margaret McGaughey. Margaret was born on 16 May 1859 in Leon Township, Goodhue County, Minnesota. She died on 18 April 1916 in Florida.

+ 1333 iii. Cora Ellen McGaughey. Cora Ellen was born about 1862 in Minnesota. She died on 8 May 1943 in Hennepin County, Minnesota.

134.   **SonA McGaughey.** (Stella Harriet Byfield-2; Abraham H Byfield-1)

SonA was born between 1830 and 1835 in _____. He was the son of George McGaughey and Stella Harriet Byfield. This is a person that appeared in the early censuses that just tallied numbers of people and ages. It could be that this is a McGaughey that stayed in Indiana when the rest of the family moved to Minnesota.

135.   **Catherine R McGaughey.** (Stella Harriet Byfield-2; Abraham H Byfield-1)

Daughter of George McGaughey and Stella Harriet Byfield. Born 29 December 1832 in Indiana. Died 6 January 1906 in *Decatur County, Indiana* (73 years, 8 days). Buried in Mount Olivet Cemetery, Decatur County, Indiana. Married David Shafer 8 October 1849 in Decatur County, Indiana.

Spouse: David Shafer.

Born 8 March 1822 in Indiana. Died 15 June 1881 in *Decatur County, Indiana* (59 years, 3 months). Buried in Mount Olivet Cemetery, Decatur County, Indiana. Married Catherine R McGaughey 8 October 1849 in Decatur County, Indiana.

Children of Catherine R McGaughey and David Shafer

+ 1351 i.   Stella A Shafer. Born 19 August 1851 in Indiana. Died 17 July 1882 in _____.

+ 1352 ii.   Mary C Shafer. Born about 1854 in Indiana. Died _____ in _____.

+ 1353 iii.   Horatio W Shafer. Born 2 April 1856 in Jackson, Decatur County, Indiana. Died 19 July 1946 in Alert, Decatur County, Indiana.

+ 1354 iv.   Addie E Shafer. Born about 1858 in Indiana. Died _____ in _____.

1355 v.   Harriet E Shafer. Born about 1861 in Indiana. Died _____ in _____.

1356 vi.   Sarah E Shafer. Born 1862 in Alert, Decatur County, Indiana. Died 1944 in _____.

1357 vii.   Nelson David Shafer. Born 1868 in Indiana. Died 1955 in _____.

136.   **George Calvin McGaughey.** (Stella Harriet Byfield-2; Abraham H Byfield-1)

George Calvin was born about 1831 in Indiana. He was the son of George McGaughey and Stella Harriet Byfield. He married Elizabeth Henderson on 9 May 1850 in Decatur County, Indiana.[7] George and Elizabeth moved their family to Minnesota along with the rest of George's family. George's wife, Elizabeth, died in 1873. He married Julia Ann Allen on 15 August 1874 in Big Bend, Cottonwood County, Minnesota. The family moved around some in Minnesota, but ended up in Big Stone County along with several other McGaughey families.

George and several family members moved to Little Rock, Arkansas sometime around 1885. George worked there as a carpenter and his sons, James and Horatio, worked as painters. The last record I can find for George is a 1906 city directory for Little Rock that shows him there and also lists his youngest son, William, who is working as a boilermaker. He died in _____ in _____.

Spouse: Elizabeth Henderson.

Elizabeth was born about 1832 in Ohio. She died in 1873 in Minnesota at the age of about 41 years. She married George C McGaughey on 9 May 1850 in Decatur County, Indiana.

Children of Elizabeth Henderson and George C McGaughey

1361 i.   Clarissa E McGaughey. Clarissa was born about 1852 in Indiana. She died in _____ in _____.

1362 ii.   Mary S L McGaughey. Mary S was born about 1854 in Indiana. She died in _____ in _____.

1363 iii.   Hariett McGaughey. Hariett was born in 1857 in Goodhue County, Minnesota. She died in _____ in _____.

1364 iv.   James T McGaughey. James T was born about 1857 in Minnesota. He died in _____ in _____.

1365 v.   Edward Horatio McGaughey. Edward Horatio was born about 1864 in Minnesota. He died in _____ in _____.

1366 vi.   Lucinda McGaughey. Lucinda was born about 1868 in Minnesota. She died in _____ in _____.

Spouse: Julia Ann Allen.

---

7   In the 1850 census, George and Elizabeth have 18 year old Hamilton Byfield living in their household. I have not identified Hamilton Byfield or how he fits into the family.

Julia Ann was born about 1850 in Canada. She died in _____ in _____. She married George C McGaughey on 15 August 1874 in Big Bend, Cottonwood County, Minnesota. She had previously been married to an Allen.

Children of Julia Ann Allen and George McGaughey

1367 vii.   William A McGaughey. William A was born about 1885 in Arkansas.

137.   **DaughterA McGaughey.** (Stella Harriet Byfield-2; Abraham H Byfield-1)

DaughterA was born between 1835 and 1840 in _____. She was the daughter of George McGaughey and Stella Harriet Byfield. She died before 1850 in Indiana at the age of less than 15 years. This is based on the fact that the 1840 census for George McGaughey shows a female family member less than 5 years old, but there is no child listed in the 1850 census to match that person.

138.   **Mary P McGaughey.** (Stella Harriet Byfield-2; Abraham H Byfield-1)

Mary P was born in November 1835 in Indiana. She was the daughter of George McGaughey and Stella Harriet Byfield. She came to Minnesota with her parents around 1855 and remained in Goodhue County all her life. She married Benjamin F Davis on 12 July 1860 in Leon Township, Goodhue County, Minnesota. She married Robert Smithson in 1880. Mary and Robert had no children together, but raised all the children from their first marriages. She died on 16 May 1927 in Dakota, Minnesota at the age of 91 years, 6 months.

Spouse: Benjamin F Davis.

Benjamin F was born in October 1828 in Lile, Broome, New York. He died on 19 August 1873 in Goodhue County, Minnesota at the age of 44 years, 10 months. He married Mary P McGaughey on 12 July 1860 in Leon Township, Goodhue County, Minnesota.

Children of Mary P McGaughey and Benjamin F Davis

+ 1381 i.   Franklin E Davis. Franklin E was born about 1864 in Goodhue
              County, Minnesota. He died in _____ in _____.

+ 1382 ii.   Harriet E Davis. Harriet E was born 27 November 1865 in Goodhue
              County, Minnesota. She died 8 June 1924 in Goodhue County, Minnesota.

+ 1383 iii.   Bertram E Davis. Bertram E was born about 1867 in Goodhue
              County, Minnesota. He died in _____ in _____.

  1384 iv.   William E Davis. William E was born about 1872 in Goodhue
              County, Minnesota. He died in _____ in _____.

Spouse: Robert Smithson.

Robert was born on 1 April 1829 in England. He died on 12 January
1906 in Goodhue County, Minnesota at the age of 76 years, 9 months.
He was buried in Belle Creek, Goodhue County, Minnesota. He first
married Sarah P Muff. He married Mary P McGaughey in 1880.
Robert had served in the civil war and Mary received a widow's
pension after his death.

139.   **Horatio M McGaughey.** (Stella Harriet Byfield-2; Abraham H
       Byfield-1)

Horatio M was born on 20 November 1836 in Franklin County,
Indiana. He was the son of George McGaughey and Stella Harriet
Byfield. At the age of 20, Horatio moved with his parents to Goodhue
County, Minnesota.

When the Civil War started, Horatio enlisted and served for the entire
war. He was with the 3rd Minnesota Infantry during Sibley's
campaign against the Indians in Minnesota. Later he was with the
regiment during the siege of Vicksburg, was wounded at Helen,
Arkansas and spent several months in the hospital. He later rejoined
his regiment at Little Rock. He was promoted to the rank of 1st
Lieutenant and later commissioned as an officer in the U.S. Colored
Troops 112th Infantry. After the war, he returned to his home in
Goodhue County.

 He married Eliza Ann Shafer on 3 March 1874 in Minnesota. Horatio
and his wife purchased a homestead in Cottonwood County,
Minnesota, and settled there after their marriage. Horatio was active
in the Cottonwood County government, serving as the second

Superintendent of Public Instruction, the first legal clerk of the county court, justice of the peace and chairman of the county commission. After two years of having his crops eaten by grasshoppers and then a few years of uncooperative weather, Horatio decided to move the family south.

In 1881 he moved his family to Benton County, Arkansas, near the town of Rogers. Over the years the town of Rogers grew out to meet his property. This is the origin of the McGaughey Orchard Addition on the south side of Rogers. He finally gave up his farm and moved into town. He opened an office specializing in notary work and made a specialty of helping his G.A.R. brethren with pension papers and legal work. He died on 25 December 1911 in Rogers, Benton County, Arkansas at the age of 75 years, 1 month.

Spouse: Eliza Ann Shafer.

Eliza Ann was born about 1848 in Indiana. She died in 1931 in Rogers, Benton County, Arkansas. She married Horatio M McGaughey on 3 March 1874 in Minnesota.

Children of Eliza A Shafer and Horatio M McGaughey

+ 1391 i.   Frank McGaughey. Frank was born 14 January 1877 in Goodhue County, Minnesota. He died 19 October 1929 in Carthage, Jasper County, Missouri.

+ 1392 ii.   Cora I McGaughey. Cora was born 25 July 1878 in Cottonwood County, Minnesota. She died 19 August 1967 in Contra Costa County, California.

CHILDREN OF HOLMES BYFIELD

141.   **Serilla Byfield.** (Holmes Byfield-2; Abraham H Byfield-1)

Serilla Zeralda was born about 1830 in Illinois. She was the first child of Holmes Byfield and Sally Nation. Her family moved to Texas when she was just five years old. Serilla married Reubin Fisher Sessums on 10 November 1850 in Panola, Texas. She died about 1856 in Panola County, Texas, at the age of about 26 years. Serilla and Reubin had no children together.

Spouse: Reubin Fisher Sessums.

Reubin Fisher was born on 28 December 1824 in Hinds, Mississippi. He married Serilla Byfield on 10 November 1850 in Panola, Texas. After Serilla's death, he married Nancy Flemmings. He died on 12 March 1873 in Fannin, Texas, at the age of 48 years, 2 months.

142.   **James Byfield.** (Holmes Byfield-2; Abraham H Byfield-1)

James was born on 12 April 1834 in Illinois. He was the son of Holmes Byfield and Sally Nation. His family moved from Illinois to Texas when he was barely a year old. James fought for the South during the Civil War, serving in the Texas Second Mounted Rifles.

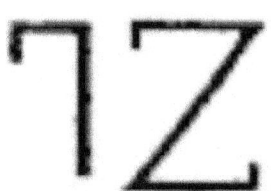

James Byfield's Brand

He married Elizabeth Hines around 1868 in Texas. Sometime after 1880 he moved his family to Oklahoma, which was still Indian Territory. They lived in what is now Carter County, along the southern border of Oklahoma, directly south of Oklahoma City. He died on 17 February 1898 in Reck, Carter County, Oklahoma Indian Territory, at the age of 63 years, 10 months. He was buried in Wilson, Carter County, Oklahoma, at the Reck Cemetery.

Spouse: Elizabeth Hines.

Elizabeth was born 27 November 1839 in Indiana. She was the daughter of Jacob Hines and Sarah Noble. She married James Byfield about 1868 in Texas. She died on 10 March 1910 in Nogal, Lincoln, New Mexico. She was buried in Nogal, Lincoln County, New Mexico.

Children of Elizabeth Hines and James Byfield

1421 i.   James Byfield. James was born in 1869 in Goliad, Goliad County, Texas. He died before 1880 in _____.

+ 1422 ii.   Columbus H. 'Lum' Byfield. Columbus H. 'Lum' was born in September 1872 in Texas. He died on 6 February 1931 in Gila, Arizona.

+ 1423 iii.   Sarah Alice Byfield. Sarah Alice was born on 18 August 1876 in Texas. She died on 28 February 1941 in Gila, Arizona.

143.   **William Anderson Byfield.** (Holmes Byfield-2; Abraham H Byfield-1)

William Anderson was born about 1837 in Texas. He was the son of Holmes Byfield and Sally Nation. William fought for the South in the Civil War, serving in the Texas Eighth (Hobby's) Infantry. He may have married Elizabeth F Brown on 15 December 1869 in Kerrville, Texas.[8] He died in _____ in _____.

Spouse: Elizabeth F Brown.

Elizabeth F was born in _____ in _____. She died in _____ in _____. She had a possible relationship with William Anderson Byfield on 15 December 1869 in Kerrville, Texas.

144.   **Elizabeth Byfield.** (Holmes Byfield-2; Abraham H Byfield-1)

Elizabeth was born about 1840 in Texas. She was the daughter of Holmes Byfield and Sally Nation. She married Lea Ferguson around 1858 in Texas. Her husband must have died young as Elizabeth and her son are living back with her parents in 1870. She died in June 1911, probably in Edwards, Texas at the age of about 71 years, 5 months.

Elizabeth Furgeson Brand

---

8   The marriage record lists the groom as "Oscar William Byfield" so this my be wrong. Don't seem to have more on either William or Oscar beyond the Civil War.

Spouse: Lea Ferguson.

Lea was born about 1837 in Tennessee, the son of William Warren Ferguson and Mary Crouch. He would have been the right age to have fought in the Civil War, but I've found no record of a Lea Ferguson that enlisted. He married Elizabeth Byfield about 1858 in Texas. He probably died between 1860 and 1870 in Texas.

Children of Elizabeth Byfield and Lea Ferguson

+ 1441 i.   Holmes Ferguson. Holmes was born on 5 January 1859 in Shelby County, Texas. He died on 28 January 1923 in Edwards County, Texas.

145.   **Martha Jane 'Jenny' Byfield.** (Holmes Byfield-2; Abraham H Byfield-1)

Martha Jane 'Jenny' was born on 16 March 1858 in Texas. She was the daughter of Holmes Byfield and Lucinda Ferguson. She married Benjamin Franklin Loe on 30 October 1877 in Goliad County, Texas. She died on 5 March 1883 in Llano County, Texas at the age of 24 years, 11 months. She was buried in Comanche Creek West Cemetery, Blanco County, Texas.

Spouse: Benjamin Franklin Loe.

Benjamin Franklin was born on 5 September 1857 in Lavaca County, Texas. He married Martha Jane 'Jenny' Byfield on 30 October 1877 in Goliad County, Texas. He died on 23 September 1882 in Llano County, Texas, at the age of 25 years, 18 days.

Children of Martha Jane 'Jenny' Byfield and Benjamin Franklin Loe

+ 1451 i.   Cicero Loe. Cicero was born on 19 December 1878 in Goliad County, Texas. He died in 1939 in Tempe, Maricopa County, Arizona.

+ 1452 ii.   Alice Loe. Alice was born on 13 August 1880 in Llano County, Texas. She died on 1 March 1962 in Llano County, Texas.

1453 iii.   Elizabeth 'Bettie' Loe. Elizabeth 'Bettie' was born on 12 March 1882 in Llano County, Texas. She died on 3 May 1959 in San Antonio, Bexar County, Texas.

146.   **Benjamin Franklin Byfield.** (Holmes Byfield-2; Abraham H Byfield-1)

Benjamin Franklin was born in April 1860 in Goliad, Goliad County, Texas. He was the son of Holmes Byfield and Lucinda Ferguson. Sometime after 1880 he moved to the Atlanta area in Georgia. He married Kentucky C Toland on 10 March 1889 in Clayton County, Georgia. Their child, Ovid Vance, was born in Texas so they may have gone back to Texas for a while, but returned to the Atlanta area. His wife, Kentucky, died soon after the marriage. He later married Lula E Donahoe on 18 October 1896 in Fulton County, Georgia. By 1900 Benjamin was established as a grocer in Atlanta and continued in that business for the rest of his life. He died in 1940 in Atlanta, Fulton, Georgia at the age of 79 years, 9 months.

SAFE WAS BLOWN OPEN, BUT NO MONEY FOUND

Third Time Cracksmen Have Operated in City Within a Month.

A safe was blown open at the store of B F Byfield 452 West Hunter street, early Saturday morning but the burglar and cracksman failed to secure any money

The safe-blowing is supposed to have occurred about 3 o'clock Saturday morning Entrance to the store was gained by breaking the lock of the front door with nitro-glycerine The outside door of the safe was unlocked, and the burglar blew open the inside door with dynamite There was not a penny in the safe, as Mr Byfield had placed all his money in a bank on Friday Mr Byfield, who lives two blocks from his store says he heard the noise of the explosion, but did not think that his store was being burglarized

This is the third safe that has been blown open in the city within a month The first was at the store of Thomas Bradley, on Kennedy street, when $50 was secured the second was at 489 Whitehall street, when $2 was taken from a safe at a soda fount

From the Atlanta Constitution newspaper, 14 February 1909

Spouse: Kentucky C Toland.

Kentucky C was born on 31 January 1869 in Georgia. She died on 9 December 1891 in Riverdale, Clayton, Georgia at the age of 22 years, 10 months. She was the daughter of Thyus Jackson Toland and Nancy Ann McDaniel. She married Benjamin Franklin Byfield on 10 March 1889 in Clayton County, Georgia.

Children of Kentucky C Toland and Benjamin Franklin Byfield

+ 1461 i.   Ovid Vance Byfield. Ovid Vance was born on 14 March 1890 in Texas. He died on 2 January 1970 in Dallas, Dallas County, Texas.

Spouse: Lula E Donahoe.

Lula E was born in August 1871 in Georgia. Lula was the daughter of Jennie E Baker and James Donahou. She died in _____ in

_____. She married Benjamin Franklin Byfield on 18 October 1896 in Fulton County, Georgia.

Children of Lula E Donahoe and Benjamin Franklin Byfield

+ 1462 i.　　Ibera 'Bera' Byfield. Ibera 'Bera' was born in August 1892 in Texas. She died 3 March 1945 in _____.

1463 ii.　　Clyde King Byfield. Clyde King was born on 15 October 1894 in Georgia. He died on 12 May 1952 in Dallas, Texas.

147.　　**George Washington 'Link' Byfield.** (Holmes Byfield-2; Abraham H Byfield-1)

George Washington 'Link' was born on 16 March 1861 in Goliad County, Texas. He died on 11 August 1924 in Llano County, Texas, at the age of 63 years, 4 months. He was buried in Llano, Llano County, Texas. He was the son of Holmes Byfield and Lucinda Ferguson. He married Mary Siambra Barnett on 27 June 1883 in Llano, Texas.

George Washington Byfield came to Llano County, Texas, in the mid-1870s after the death of his father in Goliad County, Texas. The family lived south of the town of Llano near the town of Click where George served as Postmaster for about 20 years. He had taken the Postmaster job after the death of his brother-in-

Click, Llano County, Texas, Post Office

law, Benjamin Franklin Loe, who was the first postmaster in Click. Click is now a Texas ghost town with only the old general store and post office still standing.

The censuses over the years list George as a merchant, farmer, and bookkeeper for a gentleman's furnishings business.

Spouse: Mary Siambra Barnett.

Mary Siambra was born on 18 March 1866 in Llano County, Texas. Mary was the daughter of James F Barnett and Nancy Ann Smith.

She died on 6 July 1923 in Llano County, Texas, at the age of 57 years, 3 months. She married George Washington 'Link' Byfield on 27 June 1883 in Llano, Texas.

Children of Mary Siambra Barnett and George Washington 'Link' Byfield

+ 1471 i.   Raymond Anderson Byfield. Raymond Anderson was born on 6 November 1885 in Texas. He died on 20 May 1947 in Llano County, Texas.

1472 ii.   Zora Ann Byfield. Zora Ann was born 12 March 1886 in Texas. She died 10 April 1965 in Harris, Texas.

+ 1473 iii.   Augusta Lucinda 'Gussie' Byfield. Augusta Lucinda 'Gussie' was born 27 October 1888 in Texas. She died on 17 May 1981 in Travis County, Texas.

+ 1474 iv.   Callie Byfield. Callie was born on 10 December 1892 in Texas. She died 20 January 1981 in Houston, Harris County, Texas.

+ 1475 v.   Frankie Byfield. Frankie was born on 22 July 1895 in Llano, Texas. She died on 19 December 1970 in Houston, Harris County, Texas.

+ 1476 vi.   Dixie Fay Byfield. Dixie Fay was born 10 April 1897 in Texas. She died 5 April 1997 in Oklahoma.

+ 1477 vii.   George W Byfield. George W was born on 21 September 1899 in Llano County, Texas. He died on 12 July 1939 in Llano County, Texas.

+ 1478 viii.   James Finley Byfield. James Finley was born on 14 August 1901 in Texas. He died on 7 May 1967 in Austin, Travis County, Texas.

148.   **Sarah 'Sallie' Byfield.** (Holmes Byfield-2; Abraham H Byfield-1)

Sarah 'Sallie' was born on 5 May 1864 in Goliad County, Texas. She died on 20 July 1906 in Llano, Llano County, Texas, at the age of 42 years, 2 months. She was buried in Llano County, Texas. She was the daughter of Holmes Byfield and Lucinda Ferguson. She married Charles Tate Moss on 2 August 1882 in Llano, Llano County, Texas.

Spouse: Charles Tate Moss.

Charles Tate was born on 28 December 1845 in Fayette, Texas. He died on 27 October 1916 in Tulare, Tulare County, California at the age of 70 years, 9 months. He married Nellie Button in 1872 and she died a few years later. He married Sarah 'Sallie' Byfield on 2 August

1882 in Llano, Llano County, Texas.[9]

Charles Tate Moss raised cattle in central Texas, at one time owning 30,000 acres of land around the Enchanted Rock area of Llano County.

Children of Sarah 'Sallie' Byfield and Charles Tate Moss

1481 i.   Mary Ann Moss. Mary Ann was born on 15 May 1883 in Llano, Llano County, Texas. She died on 21 April 1891 in Llano, Llano County, Texas.

1482 ii.   Holmes Moss. Holmes was born on 11 February 1885 in Llano, Llano County, Texas. He died on 20 August 1956 in Gillespie, Texas.

1483 iii.   Carlos Smith Moss. Carlos Smith was born on 28 September 1887 in Llano, Llano County, Texas. He died on 16 September 1952 in Llano, Llano County, Texas.

1484 iv.   Dale Moss. Dale was born on 8 July 1890 in Llano, Llano County, Texas. He died on 26 March 1892 in Llano, Llano County, Texas.

1485 v.   Maud Moss. Maud was born on 2 April 1892 in Llano, Llano County, Texas. She died on 2 May 1981 in San Antonio, Bexar County, Texas.

+ 1486 vi.   Cash Moss. Cash was born on 4 May 1894 in Llano, Llano County, Texas. He died on 17 October 1971 in San Angelo, Tom Green, Texas.

+ 1487 vii.   Charles Tate Moss. Charles Tate was born on 14 September 1898 in Llano, Llano County, Texas. He died on 18 December 1955 in Llano, Llano County, Texas.

149.   **Nancy Caroline Byfield.** (Holmes Byfield-2; Abraham H Byfield-1)

Nancy Caroline was born August 23, 1866 in Goliad County, Texas. She died April 27, 1930 in Texas. She was buried in Llano, Llano County, Texas. She was the daughter of Holmes Byfield and Lucinda Ferguson. She married Robert E Lee Wilson on 4 July 1888 in Texas.

Spouse: Robert E Lee Wilson.

Robert E Lee was born December 21, 1862 in Texas. He was the son of James Wilson and Quinna May Wimberly. He died on 25 May 1915 in Bell County, Texas. He married Nancy Caroline Byfield on 4

---

9   Some trees show Charles Tate Moss dying in Tulare, California, but I can't find any evidence of this.

July 1888 in Texas. He was a cattle rancher in Llano County.

Children of Nancy Caroline Byfield and Robert E Lee Wilson

+ 1491 i.   Charles Vernon Wilson. Charles Vernon was born on 29 May 1889 in Click, Llano County, Texas. He died on 7 April 1932 in Temple, Bell County, Texas.

1492 ii.   Ora Wilson. Ora was born in July 1891 in Texas. She died in 1945 in Llano County, Texas.

1493 iii.   Hester 'Hettie' Wilson. Hester 'Hettie' was born on 31 July 1893 in Oxford, Llano County, Texas. She died on 5 October 1974 in Hillsboro, Hill County, Texas.

+ 1494 iv.   Ruth Wilson. Ruth was born November 27, 1900 in Llano, Llano County, Texas. She died October 24, 1976 in Atlanta, Fulton, Georgia.

CHILDREN OF MASSIA BYFIELD

151. **Benjamin F Byfield.** (Massia Byfield-2; Abraham H Byfield-1)

Benjamin F was born on 3 September 1826 in Indiana. He died on 7 April 1890 in Indiana at the age of 63 years, 7 months. He was buried in Jennings County, Indiana. He was the son of Massia Byfield and Mary Polly Griffith. He married Elizabeth M Rector on 2 December 1847 in Jennings County, Indiana. He later married Martha J Redman on 26 February 1884 in Jennings County, Indiana.

Benjamin was the only child of Massia Byfield to stay in Indiana when the rest of the family moved to Illinois. He had already met Elizabeth Rector and stayed around Paris, Indiana, where he had been raised. Although he had a wife and four children he joined in the Civil War in 1861 and participated in most of the war, serving in Indiana's 9th Regiment, 3rd Brigade. He was promoted to 1st Lieutenant and later promoted again to the rank of Captain.

Spouse: Elizabeth Mary Rector[10].

Elizabeth Mary was born on 23 November 1824 in Indiana. Elizabeth was the daughter of Hezekiah Rector and Mary Hughes. She died 10 February 1881 in Montgomery, Jennings County, Indiana. She was buried in Commiskey, Jennings County, Indiana. She married Benjamin F Byfield on 2 December 1847 in Jennings County, Indiana.

Children of Elizabeth Mary Rector and Benjamin F Byfield

1511 i.   Thomas Delmar Byfield. Thomas Delmar was born 25 October 1849 in Jennings County, Indiana. He died 6 October 1864 in Montgomery, Jennings County, Indiana.

+ 1512 ii.   Lester Rector Byfield. Lester Rector was born 9 March 1853 in Jennings County, Indiana. He died on 19 December 1929 in Greene County, Missouri.

---

10 Elizabeth's maiden name may have been Lard. Her Missouri death certificate lists her maiden name as "Elizabeth Lard". In the 1870 census, Elizabeth's widowed mother is living with the family and is listed as "Mary Lard" since she married Samuel Lard after her marriage to Hezakiah Rector, however marriage records show Elizabeth's last name as Rector and Hezakiah Rector died in 1827, after Elizabeth's birth.

+ 1513 iii.   Sardius Henry Byfield. Sardius Henry was born about 1855 in Jennings County, Indiana. He died in 1924 in Indiana.

+ 1514 iv.   Marietta Byfield. Marietta was born 17 March 1858 in Jennings County, Indiana. She died 2 March 1935 in Pacific, Franklin, Missouri.

Spouse: Martha J Redman.

Martha J was born in May 1845 in Jennings County, Indiana. She was the daughter of Reason Redman and Francis Eliza Payne. She died in _____ in _____ . She married Benjamin F Byfield on 26 February 1884 in Jennings County, Indiana. She later married Abel Dunham on 28 November 1891 in Jennings County, Indiana.

152.   **Mary Ann Byfield.** (Massia Byfield-2; Abraham H Byfield-1)

Mary Ann was born on 11 February 1830 in Scott County, Indiana, twin sister of Julia Ann Byfield. She died on 9 August 1891 in Bates County, Missouri at the age of 61 years, 5 months. She was buried in Bates County, Missouri. She was the daughter of Massia Byfield and Mary Polly Griffith. She married William Henry Imel on 21 December 1856 in Knox County, Illinois. She later married Jesse Mullies on 27 March 1864 in Knox County, Illinois.

Mary Ann came to Illinois with her parents in the mid-1840s. She is listed, along with several other Byfield children as a student of John Wingate at the school in Greenbush, Illinois. She married William Henry Imel after the death of his first wife and so started her married life with a family of seven children, the oldest of which was only ten years younger than Mary Ann and who would later marry her brother Vermilion.

William died just two years after his marriage to Mary Ann, leaving her to raise his seven children from a previous marriage and the two children he had with Mary Ann. Mary Ann married Jesse Mullies a few years later. She added the two children from her marriage with William Imel to the five children, from Jesse's previous marriage, still living with him. Mary Ann's step-children from her marriage to William Imel either struck out on their own or went to live with their uncle Peche Imel, who had married Mary Ann's twin sister, Julia Ann.

By 1870, Jesse and Mary Ann had moved the family to Walnut Township in Bates County, Missouri. They stayed in Bates County for the rest of their lives.

Spouse: William Henry Imel.

William Henry was born in January 1811 in Frederick, Frederick County, Maryland. He was the son of Henry Imel and Margaret Kiser. He died on 29 April 1859 in Indian Point, Knox County, Illinois at the age of 48 years, 3 months. He married Temperance Moore on 26 May 1839 in Union County, Indiana. William and Temperance had seven children before Temperance's death in 1856. William and Temperance's oldest daughter would later marry Massia Byfield's son, Vermilion. William married Mary Ann Byfield on 21 December 1856 in Knox County, Illinois.

Children of Mary Ann Byfield and William Henry Imel

+ 1521 i.   Charles Harrison Imel. Charles Harrison was born on 21 September 1857 in Indian Point, Knox County, Illinois. He died on 29 January 1944 in Foster, Bates County, Missouri.

1522 ii.   M Westfall Imel. M Westfall was born in May 1859 in Illinois. He died in _____ in _____.

Spouse: Jesse Mullies.

Jesse was born on 2 November 1814 in Iredell, North Carolina. He died on 5 August 1905 in Bates County, Missouri, at the age of 90 years, 9 months. He married Ruth Cralle in 1840 in _____. He married Mary Ann Byfield on 27 March 1864 in Knox County, Illinois.

Passed down in the family is the story of Jesse Mullies and the Confederate Ruffians:

Jesse Mullies

Jess Mullis was pro-union during the Civil War. One day a group of ex-Confederate soldiers came to his home, called him out and told him they were going to hang him because he was pro-union. He said to them "let me go in me house and get me old pipe so I can smoke one last time." They let him go back in the house and when he came back out he had a gun pointed at them and his grown children had gone out the back door and came around the house with guns pointed at the soldiers. Needless to say the soldiers left rather quickly and did not bother the family the rest of that day.

This story was told to Dora Maxine Adams by her mother Florence May (Jennings)

Adams.

Children of Mary Ann Byfield and Jesse Mullies

1523 i.   Henry Mason Mullies. Henry Mason was born on 4 February 1865 in Knox County, Illinois. He died on 21 December 1944 in Polk County, Arkansas.

+ 1524 ii.   Elfreda Florence Mullies. Elfreda Florence was born on 11 November 1866 in Illinois. She died on 21 April 1956 in Nevada, Vernon County, Missouri.

153.   **Julia Ann Byfield.** (Massia Byfield-2; Abraham H Byfield-1)

Julia Ann was born about 1830 in Indiana. She died about 1873 in Coffey County, Kansas at the age of about 43 years. She was the daughter of Massia Byfield and Mary Polly Griffith. She married Peche Harrison Imel on 14 January 1855 in Knox County, Illinois.

Julia Ann came to Illinois with her parents in the mid-1840s. She attended the Greenbush country school along with several of her brothers and sisters. Julia Ann was the twin sister of Mary Ann Byfield. The twins married Imel brothers, William and Peche. She married Peche Harrison Imel who was a farmer that lived in the same area as the Byfields. She was 25 years old at the time of her marriage and Peche was about 10 years older.

After the Civil War, the Byfields and the Imels moved from Illinois to Coffey County, Kansas. Julia had three daughters with Peche before her death around 1873. Julia Ann is believed to be buried in the Veteto Cemetery[11] near LeRoy in Coffey County, Kansas.

Spouse: Peche Harrison Imel.

Peche Harrison was born on 22 July 1821 in Wayne, Wayne County, Indiana. He died *after 1883* in *Leroy, Coffey County, Kansas*. He is buried in the Veteto Cemetery, Coffey County, Kansas.

---

11   The Veteto Cemetery is sometimes referred to as the Imel Cemetery. The Veteto Cemetery is located one mile east and 1/2 mile north of LeRoy, in a field. On October 29, 1866, Pechey Harrison Imel purchased from John and Martha Veteto the northeast quarter of Section 35, excluding one square acre already in use as a graveyard. Many of the graves in this cemetery have no markers.

His first marriage was to Mary Moler in Indiana. His second marriage was to Sarah A Moore on 19 January 1845 in Wayne County, Indiana. His third marriage was to Julia Ann Byfield on 14 January 1855 in Knox County, Illinois. His fourth marriage was to Julia Ann's sister, Jennette Byfield, about 1877 in Coffey County, Kansas.

Peche Harrison Imel was probably named for Dr. Peachy Harrison who was prominent in Rockingham, Virginia where most of the Imel children were born. Peche and his brother William married Moore women in Indiana who were either sisters or cousins. After moving to Illinois, their wives died and the Imel brothers each married one of the Byfield twins.

Peche and his father, Henry, moved to Kansas around 1866, along with the Byfields. Peche had registered for the draft, but didn't serve in the Civil War. When Peche's third wife, Julia Ann Byfield died, he married again, this time to Jennette Byfield, another daughter of Massia Byfield and Mary Polly Griffith.

Children of Julia Ann Byfield and Peche Harrison Imel[12]

+ 1531 i.   Harriett B 'Hattie' Imel. Born January 1856 in Illinois. Died about 1929 in Linn County, Kansas.

1532 ii.   Clara May Imel. Born about 1858 in Illinois. Died _____ in _____.

1533 iii.   Mary Lincoln Imel. Born 30 May 1863 in Kansas. Died 17 February 1869 in Kansas.

+ 1534 iv.   Louisa Imel. Born 6 May 1867 in Kansas. Died 1935 in Baldwin City, Douglas County, Kansas.

1535 v.   Lewis Imel. Born 6 May 1867 in Kansas. Died 8 April 1869 in Kansas.

154.   **Vermilion Wright Byfield.** (Massia Byfield-2; Abraham H Byfield-1)

Vermilion Wright was born on 4 September 1837 in Scott County, Indiana. He died on 8 February 1905 in Leroy, Coffey County, Kansas at the age of 67 years, 5 months. He was buried on 10 February 1905 in Logue Cemetery, Leroy, Coffey County, Kansas. He was the son of

---

12 The book *Immel and Imel Families in America* lists additional children Henry, Charles, and Harry. I can't find sources for these children.

Massia Byfield and Mary Polly Griffith. He married Mary Elizebeth Imel on 11 November 1859 in Knox County, Illinois.

Vermilion came to Knox County, Illinois with his parents at the age of five. He was a student of John Wingate at the country school in Greenbush Township[13] in neighboring Warren County, Illinois. At the age of 22, he married 17 year old Mary Elizabeth Imel, oldest daughter of William Henry Imel and Temperance Moore. Mary Elizabeth's father had died earlier in the year and Vermilion's older sister, Mary Ann, William Imel's second wife, was raising the family.

In July of 1863, Vermilion was registered for the Civil War draft, but he didn't serve in the war. In the mid-1860s most of the Massia Byfield clan in Illinois moved to the Spring Creek Township in Coffey County, Kansas. Vermilion moved his wife and two young children to Kansas at that time. Vermilion purchased land in Coffey County, farming and raising stock. His land was adjacent to parcels owned by his brothers, Melton Cass, and Marion Josephus. He is mentioned in the Coffey County section of Cutler's *History of the State of Kansas*, published in 1883.

Spouse: Mary Elizebeth Imel.

Mary Elizebeth was born on 26 February 1842 in Scott County, Indiana. She died on 29 October 1927 in Leroy, Coffey County, Kansas at the age of 85 years, 8 months. She was buried in Logue Cemetery, Leroy, Coffey County, Kansas. She was the daughter of William Henry Imel and Temperance Moore. She married Vermilion Wright Byfield on 11 November 1859 in Knox County, Illinois.

Children of Mary Elizebeth Imel and Vermilion Wright Byfield

+ 1541 i.　　William Albert Byfield. William Albert was born on 24 November 1860 in Illinois. He died on 17 January 1929 in Rural Colony, Anderson County, Kansas.

+ 1542 ii.　　Emma Frances Byfield. Emma Frances was born on 28 September 1863 in Illinois. She died on 24 December 1916 in Neosho Falls, Woodson County, Kansas.

1543 iii.　　Olive May Byfield. Olive May was born on 14 June 1869 in Kansas. She died in 1962 in Neosho Falls, Woodson County, Kansas.

13　A good portrait of this area is in the book *Early days in Greenbush* by William L. Snapp published in 1905.

+ 1544 iv.   Charles Alfred Byfield. Charles Alfred was born on 8 September 1872 in Kansas. He died on 1 March 1940 in Neosho Falls, Woodson County, Kansas.

1545 v.   Sara Florance Byfield. Sara Florance was born on 2 October 1875 in Kansas. She died on 22 April 1903 in Neosho Falls, Woodson County, Kansas.

+ 1546 vi.   Leonard Lee Byfield. Leonard Lee was born on 4 August 1877 in Kansas. He died in September 1960 in Neosho Falls, Woodson County, Kansas.

+ 1547 vii.   Thomas Westfall Byfield. Thomas Westfall was born on 29 May 1881 in Kansas. He died on 19 April 1946 in Los Angeles, California.

155.   **Jennette Byfield.** (Massia Byfield-2; Abraham H Byfield-1)

Jennette was born in 1842 in Scott County, Indiana. She died between 1925 and 1930 in Kansas or Missouri. She was buried in Linn County, Kansas. She was the daughter of Massia Byfield and Mary Polly Griffith. She married Martin Varner Baldwin on 30 August 1866 in Marion County, Missouri. She later married Peche Harrison Imel about 1877 in Coffey County, Kansas.

Jennette came to Illinois with her parents when she was very young. She grew up in Knox County, Illinois and moved west to Kansas in the mid-1860s. Her marriage to Martin Baldwin in Marion County, Missouri, might mean that she married Martin while the Byfields and Baldwins were en-route to Kansas. Martin Baldwin had been married previously and had several young children coming to Kansas with him. Martin was 48 years old and Jennette was 24 at the time of their marriage. They settled in Linn County, Kansas, about 60 miles south of Kansas City.

Martin died when he and Jennette had been married for about 10 years, leaving her with several young step-children and four children that she had with Martin. She took the family to Coffey County, Kansas, near where many of her brothers had settled. Jennette's sister, Julia Ann, had died a few years earlier leaving her husband, Peche Imel, with several children to raise on his own. Jennette and Peche married in 1877 in Coffey County. Jennette raised the combined family of her nieces and nephews, her step-children, the children she had with Martin Baldwin, and two more children that she had with Peche Imel.

After Peche died, probably in the mid-1880s, Jennette lived with her daughters until her death in the late 1920s. In 1905 she is found living with her daughter, Rosa Baldwin, and Rosa's family. In 1910 she is with her daughter, Maude, in Saint Joseph, Missouri. The 1920s find her back with her daughter Rosa's family, around the Saint Joseph area. In the censuses after 1900 she is listed with the last name Baldwin.

Spouse: Martin Varner Baldwin.

Martin Varner was born on 3 March 1818 in Ohio. He died on 3 August 1876 in Potosi, Linn County, Kansas at the age of 58 years, 5 months. Martin was the son of Judge Benjamin Franklin Baldwin and Martha Varner. He, first, married Eliza Crosson in Ohio. He, second, married Jennette Byfield on 30 August 1866 in Marion County, Missouri.

Children of Jennette Byfield and Martin Varner Baldwin

+ 1551 i.　　Willard Elmer Baldwin. Willard E was born 29 September 1867 in Missouri. He died on 22 December 1953 in _____.

+ 1552 ii.　　Rosa Emily Baldwin. Rosa Emily was born in March 1870 in Kansas. She died on 11 May 1957 in Kansas City, Wyandotte County, Kansas.

1553 iii.　　Mary E Baldwin. Born 30 May 1872 in Linn County, Kansas. Died 1 August 1873 in Linn County, Kansas.

1554 iv.　　Martin E Baldwin. Martin E was born about 1874 in Kansas. He died in _____ in _____.

1555 v.　　Louisa Baldwin. Louisa was born about 1876 in Kansas. She died in _____ in _____.

Spouse: Peche Harrison Imel.

Peche Harrison was born on 22 July 1821 in Wayne, Wayne County, Indiana. He died between 1882 and 1905 in Kansas. He, first, married Sarah A Moore on 19 January 1845 in Wayne County, Indiana. He later married Julia Ann Byfield on 14 January 1855 in Knox County, Illinois. He later married Jennette Byfield about 1877 in Coffey County, Kansas.

Children of Jennette Byfield and Peche Harrison Imel

1556 i.　　Minnie Imel. Minnie was born about 1878 in Kansas. She died in _____ in _____.

1557 ii.   Maude M Imel. Maude M was born about 1882 in Kansas. She died in _____ in _____ .

156.   **Marion Josephus Byfield.** (Massia Byfield-2; Abraham H Byfield-1)

Marion Josephus was born on 13 April 1846 in Union, Fulton County, Illinois. He was a twin to Louisa Byfield. He died on 7 August 1907 in Boise, Ada County, Idaho at the age of 61 years, 3 months. He was buried in Boise, Ada County, Idaho. He was the son of Massia Byfield and Mary Polly Griffith. He married Susan Angeline Biers on 3 July 1870 in Leroy, Coffey, Kansas.

Marion Josephus was the first child of Massia Byfield and Mary Polly Griffith to be born in Illinois. He grew up in Knox County, Illinois and then, at the age of 20, moved to Coffey County, Kansas, along with his parents and several of his siblings. Marion met and married his wife, Susan Angeline Biers, within 2 or 3 years of arriving in Kansas. Marion and Susan farmed in Kansas for about ten years.

Around 1880, Marion moved his family to Bates County, Missouri, where he worked as a teamster and also served as a postmaster for several years. Bates County is about 50 miles south of Kansas City, along the western border of Missouri. Marion's sister, Mary Ann, was already living in Bates County with her second husband, Jesse Mullies. Several other Byfields would also come to Bates County, including Melton Cass and Anderson, both brothers of Marion.

Around 1900 Marion moved the family to Owyhee County, Idaho, south of Boise. His two sons went there with their parents. His daughters also moved to Idaho, one marrying in Missouri just prior to the move and one marrying in Idaho shortly after the move.

Spouse: Susan Angeline Biers.

Susan Angeline was born on 11 January 1850 in Ohio. Susan Angeline was the daughter of Johnathan Biers and Elizabeth. She died on 3 December 1931 in Grandview, Owyhee County, Idaho at the age of 81 years, 10 months. She married Marion Josephus Byfield on 3 July 1870 in Leroy, Coffey, Kansas.

After her husband's death in 1907, Susan lived with her son Fay Ora Byfield until her death in 1931.

Children of Susan Angeline Biers and Marion Josephus Byfield

+ 1561 i.   Hattie Etora Byfield. Hattie Etora was born on 30 April 1871 in Leroy, Coffey, Kansas. She died on 28 January 1957 in Boise, Ada County, Idaho.

+ 1562 ii.   Mary Etta Byfield. Mary Etta was born on 19 September 1872 in Leroy, Coffey, Kansas. She died on 8 September 1950 in Nampa, Canyon, Idaho.

1563 iii.   Bernice Blanche Byfield. Bernice Blanche was born on 14 February 1875 in Leroy, Coffey, Kansas. She died on 31 May 1892 in Walnut, Bates County, Missouri.

1564 iv.   Arley Oliver Byfield. Arley Oliver was born on 2 February 1877 in Leroy, Coffey, Kansas. He died on 3 December 1946 in Union, Union, Oregon.

+ 1565 v.   Fay Ora Byfield. Fay Ora was born on 15 September 1879 in Leroy, Coffey, Kansas. He died on 29 March 1953 in Great Falls, Cascade County, Montana.

157.   **Louisa Byfield.** (Massia Byfield-2; Abraham H Byfield-1)

Louisa was born on 13 April 1846 in Union, Fulton County, Illinois. She was a twin to Marion Josephus Byfield. She died on 21 February 1908 in Council Bluffs, Pottawattamie County, Iowa at the age of 61 years, 10 months. She was buried in Council Bluffs, Pottawattamie County, Iowa. She was the daughter of Massia Byfield and Mary Polly Griffith. She married Calvin L Allen on 1 March 1865 in Knox County, Illinois.

Louisa Byfield

Louisa was born and raised in Illinois. When she was 19 years old, she married Calvin Allen. Louisa and Calvin stayed in Illinois when most of the Byfields moved to Kansas in the mid-1860s. They may have been in Kansas for a short time as their first child was born there in late 1865, but by 1870 they were back in Illinois. She and her husband farmed in Fulton County, Illinois until about 1885. They moved their family to Iowa in the mid-1880s, settling in the southeastern part of the state around the town of

Shenandoah.

Louisa was a twin and she had two sets of twins with Calvin Allen; Eddie and Freddie, born in 1877, and Cora and Lora, born in 1882. Most of the children came to Iowa with their parents and settled in the southeastern part of the state.

Spouse: Calvin L Allen.

Calvin L was born on 24 December 1839 in Fulton, Illinois. He was the son of Edwin Allen and Catherine Jenkins. He died on 27 December 1906 in Council Bluffs, Pottawattamie County, Iowa, at the age of 67 years, 3 days. He was buried in Council Bluffs, Pottawattamie County, Iowa. He married Louisa Byfield on 1 March 1865 in Knox County, Illinois.

Calvin Allen

Children of Louisa Byfield and Calvin L Allen

+ 1571 i.   William Melvin Allen. William Melvin was born on 10 October 1865 in Kansas. He died in _____ in _____.

+ 1572 ii.   James M Allen. James M was born on 24 October 1867 in Illinois. He died on 26 November 1954 in _____.

+ 1573 iii.   Clara M Allen. Clara M was born about 1869 in Illinois. She died in _____ in _____.

1574 iv.   John Franklin Allen. John Franklin was born on 15 November 1874 in Illinois. He died in Illinois.

+ 1575 v.   Edwin T Allen. Edwin T was born on 25 July 1877 in Illinois. He died in _____ in _____.

+ 1576 vi.   Freddie Allen. Freddie was born 25 July 1877 in Fulton County, Illinois. He died before 1920 in _____.

1577 vii.   Henry Allen. Henry was born about 1880 in Illinois. He died 15 October 1966 in _____.

+ 1578 viii. Cora F Allen. Cora was born on 21 January 1882 in Illinois. She died in _____ in _____.

+ 1579 ix.   Lora Allen. Lora was born on 21 January 1882 in Illinois. He died on 7 February 1965 in Missouri.

+ 157A x.   Earl Alva Allen. Earl Alva was born on 3 April 1884 in Illinois. He died in _____ in _____.

+ 157B xi.   Mabel Grace Allen. Mabel G was born on 3 March 1888 in Cass, Iowa. She died on 26 March 1942 in _____.

158.   **Melton Cass Byfield.** (Massia Byfield-2; Abraham H Byfield-1)

Melton Cass was born in February 1848 in Fulton County, Illinois. He died on 7 August 1909 in Greenfield, Dade County, Missouri at the age of 61 years, 6 months. He was buried on 9 August 1909 in Greenfield, Dade County, Missouri. He was the son of Massia Byfield and Mary Polly Griffith. He married Hannah Elizabeth Randall on 5 November 1871 in Coffey County, Kansas.

Melton was born and raised in Union and Knox Counties in Illinois. As a young man, he migrated to Coffey County, Kansas, along with his parents and several of his siblings. He established a farm on land adjacent to that of his brothers, Vermilion and Marion. He married Hannah Elizabeth Randall in 1871 and within a year or two had moved his young family east to Bates County, Missouri. He and his brother, Marion, both came to Bates County at about the same time.

During the late 1880s Melton and his family were a little ways southwest in Montgomery County, Kansas. This is the same area that Melton's cousin Charles Carel Byfield had come to in the mid-1880s. By 1890 it appears that Melton had returned the family to Dade County, Missouri.

Spouse: Hannah Elizabeth Randall.

Hannah Elizabeth was born on 5 April 1854 in Illinois. Hannah was the daughter of Benjamin S Randall and Sophronia Sutherland. She died in 1939 probably in Joplin, Missouri at the age of 84 years. She married Melton Cass Byfield on 5 November 1871 in Coffey County, Kansas.

Children of Hannah Elizabeth Randall and Melton Cass Byfield

+ 1581 i.   Eva J Byfield. Eva J was born about 1872 in Kansas. She died in 1906 in Dade County, Missouri.

+ 1582 ii.   James Byfield. James L was born 9 January 1873 in Missouri. He died on 7 Jan 1908 in Dade County, Missouri.

1583 iii.   Mary Louise Byfield. Mary Louise was born about 1876 in Missouri.

She died on 14 December 1887 in Montgomery County, Kansas.

+ 1584 iv.   Flora Ann Byfield. Flora Ann was born on 28 February 1879 in Greenfield, Dade County, Missouri. She died on 29 June 1949 in Joplin, Newton County, Missouri.

+ 1585 v.   Melton Otis Albert Byfield. Melton Otis Albert was born on 22 February 1891 in Greenfield, Dade County, Missouri. He died on 17 January 1954 in Fort Gibson, Muskogee County, Oklahoma.

159.   **Harvey N Byfield.** (Massia Byfield-2; Abraham H Byfield-1)

Harvey N was born in Union, Fulton County, Illinois. He died about 1849 in Illinois. He was the son of Massia Byfield and Mary Polly Griffith.

Harvey must have died as a young child. He is listed as a student at the Greenbush country school about 1845, along with several of his siblings. He is not recorded in the 1850 census, or any later censuses, with his family.

15A.   **Anderson Byfield.** (Massia Byfield-2; Abraham H Byfield-1)

Anderson was born about 1862 in Illinois. Anderson Byfield is a puzzle. He is first recorded with Massia Byfield and Mary Polly Griffith in the 1870 census in Coffey County, Kansas. If he is their son then he was born about 10 years after the last of the other children. In 1875 he is living with Jennett Byfield's family. She would be Anderson's older sister. In 1880 he is with Jordina Imel in Bates County, Missouri. Jordina lists him as her cousin. They are listed adjacent to Melton Cass Byfield. I've found no record of Anderson Byfield after 1880.

CHILDREN OF ANDREW G BYFIELD

161. **Catherine Byfield.** (Andrew G Byfield-2; Abraham H Byfield-1)

Catherine was born in 1828 in Scott County, Indiana. She died between 1871 and 1880 in Indiana or Illinois as her husband was listed as a widower in the 1880 census. She was the daughter of Andrew G Byfield and Rhoda Burnett. She married William A Wells on 26 September 1850 in Jefferson County, Indiana.

Catherine was the oldest child of Andrew Byfield and his first wife, Rhoda Burnett. She and her husband lived near her father in Jennings County, Indiana. The last record of Catherine is her listing in the 1870 census. Ten years later, her husband is found in the census in Illinois along with his youngest daughter.

Spouse: William A Wells.

William A was born about 1829 in Indiana. He died in _____ in _____. He married Catherine Byfield on 26 September 1850 in Jefferson County, Indiana.

Children of Catherine Byfield and William A Wells

1611 i.   Arthur E Wells. Arthur E was born about 1852 in Indiana. He died in _____ in _____.

1612 ii.   John Wells. John was born about 1854 in Indiana. He died in _____ in _____.

1613 iii.   Cyrus A Wells. Cyrus A was born about 1856 in Indiana. He died in _____ in _____.

1614 iv.   Mary Wells. Mary was born about 1860 in Indiana. She died in _____ in _____.

1615 v.   James M Wells. James M was born about 1862 in Indiana. He died in _____ in _____.

1616 vi.   Rebecca Jennie Wells. Rebecca Jennie was born about 1869 in Indiana. She died in _____ in _____.

162. **Frederick W Byfield.** (Andrew G Byfield-2; Abraham H Byfield-1)

Frederick W was born on 13 October 1829 in Scott County, Indiana. He died on 20 March 1906 in Sorento, Bond County, Illinois at the age of 76 years, 5 months. He was buried in Sorento, Bond County, Illinois. He was the son of Andrew G Byfield and Rhoda Burnett. He married Nancy Jane Thorp on 13 March 1851 in Indiana. He later married Elizabeth Elmore Hubbard on 27 April 1876 in Fayette, Illinois. He later married Tabitha Jane 'Bessie' Thacker on 6 August 1890 in Bond County, Illinois.

Frederick was raised in southeastern Indiana and was trained as a physician. As a young man of 20 years, he married his first wife, Nancy Thorp. When the Civil War began, he was 30 years old with a wife and four young children. Still, he enlisted to fight for the Union in the Civil war and had served for about nine months when he was shot in the leg and discharged. After recovering from his injury he re-enlisted and served for the remainder of the war.

By the mid-1870s Frederick had moved his family to Bond County, Illinois about 50 miles east of Saint Louis. There he married his second wife, Elizabeth Hubbard. Frederick and Elizabeth had one child together in 1879. They must have divorced as Frederick remarried in 1890 to his third wife, Tabitha Thacker.

Tabitha was 28 years old when she married 60 year old Frederick. They were together for about 15 years before Frederick died in 1906. Tabitha collected a widow's pension for Frederick's Civil War service after his death.

Spouse: Nancy Jane Thorp.

Nancy Jane was born 15 April 1832 in Decatur County, Indiana. She died between 1870 and 1876 in Indiana or Illinois. She married Frederick W Byfield on 13 March 1851 in Indiana.

Children of Nancy Jane Thorp and Frederick W Byfield

1621 i.   Lucinda Byfield. Lucinda was born on 8 December 1851 in Decatur County, Indiana. She died on 1 January 1852 in Decatur County, Indiana.

+ 1622 ii.   James H Byfield. James H was born on 27 May 1853 in Decatur County, Indiana. He died on 5 June 1928 in Pocahontas, Bond County, Illinois.

1623 iii.   William A Byfield. William A was born on 7 January 1857 in Decatur County, Indiana. He died on 7 October 1859 in Decatur County, Indiana.

+ 1624 iv.   Flora B Byfield. Flora B was born on 10 October 1861 in Decatur County, Indiana. She died on 28 December 1911 in Winfield, Cowley County, Kansas.

+ 1625 v.   Ida Mae Byfield. Ida Mae was born on 15 July 1863 in Indiana. She died on 14 April 1916 in Bond County, Illinois.

+ 1626 vi.   John W Byfield. John W was born on 22 July 1867 in Decatur County, Indiana. He died on 10 April 1912 in Shamrock, Wheeler County, Texas.

1627 vii.   Minnie Byfield. Minnie was born about 1870 in Indiana. She died in _____ in _____ .

Spouse: Elizabeth Elmore Hubbard.

Elizabeth was born on 26 March 1839 in Illinois. She died on 4 April 1915 in Bond County, Illinois at the age of 76 years, 9 days. She was the daughter of Hiram Elmore and Sarah Walker. She married Frederick W Byfield on 27 April 1876 in Fayette, Illinois. She also had a previous marriage to Wiley B Hubbard.

Children of Elizabeth Elmore Hubbard and Frederick W Byfield

1629 i.   Frederick Byfield. Frederick was born about 1879 in Cottonwood Grove, Bond County, Illinois. He died in _____ in _____ .

Spouse: Tabitha Jane 'Bessie' Thacker.

Tabitha Jane 'Bessie' was born on 27 November 1861 in Bond County, Illinois. She died 14 November 1935 in Saint Louis, Missouri at the Deaconess Hospital. She was the daughter of J W Thacker and Elizabeth Tisdale. She married Frederick W Byfield on 6 August 1890 in Bond County, Illinois. Bessie is buried next to Frederick in the Sunnyside Cemetery in Sorento, Illinois.

Children of Tabitha Jane 'Bessie' Thacker and Frederick W Byfield

+ 1628 i.   Rhoda I Byfield. Rhoda I was born 12 November 1892 in Sorento, Bond County, Illinois. She died in _____ in _____ .

163.   **Alexander Hamilton Byfield.** (Andrew G Byfield-2; Abraham H Byfield-1)

Alexander Hamilton was born in 1831 in Scott County, Indiana. He died in _____ in _____ . He was the son of

Andrew G Byfield and Rhoda Burnett.   The last record of Alexander is in the 1850 census where he is listed twice -- once with his parents and also with his young McGaughey cousin, 19 year old George M McGaughey and George's wife, 18 year old Elizabeth.

164.   **Susan Elizabeth Byfield.** (Andrew G Byfield-2; Abraham H Byfield-1)

Susan Elizabeth was born on 21 January 1836 in Indiana. She died on 9 June 1917 in Laclede County, Missouri at the age of 81 years, 4 months. She was buried in Phillipsburg, Laclede County, Missouri. She was the daughter of Andrew G Byfield and Mary Bruner. She married Samuel S Weatherington on 25 January 1860 in Jefferson County, Indiana. She later married William Ferguson on 11 November 1877 in Jennings County, Indiana.

Susan and her first husband, Samuel Weatherington, lived in Jefferson County, Indiana near Susan's parents. Samuel died sometime around 1870 and Susan remarried. By 1885 her second husband was gone and she was living with her children in Laclede County, in central Missouri. In 1880 Susan's youngest daughter, Addie, was living with Susan's sister, Mary Alvoretta, but a few years later was in Missouri with the rest of the family.

Spouse: Samuel S Wetherington.

Samuel S was born in _____ in _____ . He died in _____ in _____ . He married Susan Elizabeth Byfield on 25 January 1860 in Jefferson County, Indiana.

Children of Susan Elizabeth Byfield and Samuel S Wetherington

1641 i.   Martha Weatherington. Martha was born in 1861 in Indiana. She died in _____ in _____ .

+ 1642 ii.   Mary Ellen Weatherington. Mary Ellen was born on 28 November 1863 in Graham, Jefferson County, Indiana. She died on 24 September 1943 in Phillipsburg, Laclede County, Missouri.

1643 iii.   John Weatherington. John was born in 1867 in Graham, Jefferson County, Indiana. He died in _____ in _____ .

+ 1644 iv.   Sarah Adaline Weatherington. Sarah Adaline was born 26 Sept 1870 in Indiana. She died on 18 June 1934 in Todd, Kentucky.

Spouse: William Ferguson.

William was born about 1816 in Ohio. He died in _____ in _____. He married Elizabeth in _____ in _____. He later married Susan Elizabeth Byfield on 11 November 1877 in Jennings County, Indiana.

---

165.   Martha P Byfield. (Andrew G Byfield-2; Abraham H Byfield-1)

Martha P was born on 30 October 1837 in Indiana. She died on 20 February 1905 in Jennings County, Indiana at the age of 67 years, 3 months. She was buried in Jennings County, Indiana. She was the daughter of Andrew G Byfield and Mary Bruner. She married Joshua Miller on 11 June 1867 in Indiana.

Martha married Joshua Miller after he returned from fighting in the Civil War. They farmed land that was part of Joshua's father's original farm. Joshua's brother, Robert, remembered that Joshua and Martha had four children but only John survived early childhood.

Spouse: Joshua Miller.

Joshua was born 27 May 1835 in Indiana. He died 25 September 1915 in Jennings County, Indiana and was buried at the Bear Creek Cemetery. He was the son of Robert Miller and Hannah Chapman. He married Martha P Byfield on 11 June 1867 in Indiana. After Martha died, Joshua married Asenith Coryea.

Children of Martha P Byfield and Joshua Miller

+ 1651 i.   John Andrew Miller. John Andrew was born on 16 April 1868 in Indiana. He died on 11 May 1936 in Jefferson, Kentucky.

---

166.   James M Byfield. (Andrew G Byfield-2; Abraham H Byfield-1)

James M was born on 22 August 1840 in Jefferson County, Indiana. He died on 13 September 1906 in Bond County, Illinois at the age of

66 years, 22 days. He was the son of Andrew G Byfield and Mary Bruner. He married Mahala Robinson on 14 October 1868 in Jefferson County, Indiana.

James grew up in Jefferson County, Indiana and stayed there for many years after his marriage. At the age of 28, he married 17 year old Mahala Robinson, who had come to the area from England with her parents. Around 1900 all their children had been born and they moved the family to Bond County in Illinois near where James' brother Frederick had settled. James died a few years after the move and was buried in the Montrose Cemetery in Greenville, Illinois.

Spouse: Mahala Robinson.

Mahala was born on 3 July 1851 in England. She died on 23 June 1921 in East Saint Louis, Saint Clair County, Illinois at the age of 69 years, 11 months. She was buried on 25 June 1921 in Greenville, Illinois. She was the daughter of Mathew Robinson and Rachel Vickerman. She married James M Byfield on 14 October 1868 in Jefferson County, Indiana.

After her husband's death, Mahala remained in Greenville, Illinois, for a few years and then went to Montana to live with her daughter, Jeannette's family in Lincoln County. Her daughter, Mary, went there, too. By the time of her death in 1921 she was living in East Saint Louis where her daughter, Anna, lived with her family. She was buried with her husband in the Montrose Cemetery in Greenville, Illinois.

Children of Mahala Robinson and James M Byfield

+ 1661 i.   Anna Byfield. Anna was born on 11 December 1869 in Jefferson County, Indiana. She died on 4 May 1936 in East Saint Louis, Saint Clair County, Illinois.

1662 ii.   James Edward Byfield. James Edward was born about 1870 in Indiana. He died on 12 July 1941 in Wood River, Madison County, Illinois.

1663 iii.   Mary Byfield. Mary was born in September 1872 in Indiana. She probably died in Idaho after 1940.

+ 1664 iv.   Elizabeth L Byfield. Elizabeth L was born in August 1874 in Madison, Jefferson County, Indiana. She died on 23 May 1937 in Chicago, Cook County, Illinois.

+ 1665 v.   Jeannette Paulina Byfield. Jeannette Paulina was born on 23

November 1876 in Indiana. She died on 22 November 1967 in Spokane, Spokane County, Washington.

+ 1666 vi.   Rose Emma Byfield. Rose Emma was born on 11 May 1878 in Jennings County, Indiana. She died in March 1965 in Idaho.

1667 vii.   John Mathew Byfield. John Mathew was born on 24 October 1880 in Indiana. He died on 28 July 1929 in Spokane, Spokane County, Washington.

1668 viii.   Albert Cleveland Byfield. Albert Cleveland was born on 9 March 1884 in Illinois. He died in 1954 in Idaho.

1669 ix.   Lillian Francis Byfield. Lillian Francis was born in 1887 in Indiana. She died in _____ in _____ .

167.   **John C Byfield.** (Andrew G Byfield-2; Abraham H Byfield-1)

John C was born on 30 October 1842 in Jefferson County, Indiana. He died on 11 August 1918 in Jennings County, Indiana at the age of 75 years, 9 months. He was buried in Jennings County, Indiana, at the Bear Creek Cemetery. He was the son of Andrew G Byfield and Mary Bruner. He married Lizzie E Morcy on 25 November 1891 in Paris, Jennings County, Indiana.

John married Lizzie when he was 49 and she was 31 years old. They had no children.

Spouse: Lizzie E Morcy.

Lizzie E was born in July 1860 in Indiana. She died after 1930 in _____ . She was the daughter of Robert G Morcy and Sarah M Barger. She married John C Byfield on 25 November 1891 in Paris, Jennings County, Indiana.

168.   **Eliza Olivia Byfield.** (Andrew G Byfield-2; Abraham H Byfield-1)

Eliza Olivia was born in November 1844 in Jefferson County, Indiana. She died in _____ in _____ . She was the daughter of Andrew G Byfield and Mary Bruner. She married Henry Tapp on 17 March 1878 in Jefferson County, Indiana.

Spouse: Henry Tapp.

Henry was born in February 1841 in Indiana. He died in _____ in _____. He was the son of Burkett Tapp and Sarah Corya. He married Eliza Olivia Byfield on 17 March 1878 in Jefferson County, Indiana. He had a previous marriage to Hannah E Barnett.

169.   **Andrew G Byfield.** (Andrew G Byfield-2; Abraham H Byfield-1)

Andrew was born on 10 August 1847 in Jefferson County, Indiana. He died on 3 January 1890 in Jennings County, Indiana at the age of 42 years, 4 months and was buried in the Bear Creek Cemetery in Jennings County. He was the son of Andrew G Byfield and Mary Bruner.

16A.   **Cyrus L D Byfield.** (Andrew G Byfield-2; Abraham H Byfield-1)

Cyrus L D was born on 5 October 1852 in Graham Township, Jefferson County, Indiana. He died on 20 May 1870 in Jennings County, Indiana at the age of 17 years, 7 months. He was buried in the Bear Creek Cemetery in Jennings County, Indiana. He was the son of Andrew G Byfield and Mary Bruner.

16B.   **Mary Alvoretta Byfield.** (Andrew G Byfield-2; Abraham H Byfield-1)

Mary Alvoretta was born in October 1854 in Graham Township, Jefferson County, Indiana. She died January 1925 in Indianapolis, Marion County, Indiana at the age of about 70 years, 3 months. She was buried on 26 January 1925 in Indianapolis, Marion County, Indiana at the Crown Hill Cemetery. She was the daughter of Andrew G Byfield and Mary Bruner. She married James H Spencer on 28 May 1876 in Jefferson County, Indiana.

Mary grew up in Jefferson County, Indiana and married James Spencer at the age of 21 years. She and James lived in Jefferson and Decatur counties and then, by 1900, were in Indianapolis. In the 1900 census Mary says that she had 8 children, 3 of which are living in 1900. There are two boys with her and James in 1900, so there is a third child that must have been born after 1880 but isn't at home in 1900.

Mary's husband died sometime between 1900 and 1910. Her sons lived with her in Indianapolis until her death in January of 1925.

Spouse: James H Spencer.

James H was born in November 1854 in West Virginia. He died 1901-1910 in Indianapolis, Marion County, Indiana. He married Mary Alvoretta Byfield on 28 May 1876 in Jefferson County, Indiana.

Children of Mary Alvoretta Byfield and James H Spencer

16B1 i.   Willford Dallas Spencer. Willford Dallas was born on 20 October 1877 in Jennings County, Indiana. He died on 6 July 1961 in Indianapolis, Marion County, Indiana.

16B2 ii.   Edgar John Spencer. Edgar John was born on 15 January 1880 in Jennings County, Indiana. He died in November 1954 in Indianapolis, Marion County, Indiana.

16C.   **Corban Byfield.** (Andrew G Byfield-2; Abraham H Byfield-1)

Corban was born on 13 September 1856 in Graham Township, Jefferson County, Indiana. He died on 7 August 1863 in Jennings County, Indiana at the age of 6 years, 10 months. He was the son of Andrew G Byfield and Mary Bruner.

16D.   **Benjamin F Byfield.** (Andrew G Byfield-2; Abraham H Byfield-1)

Benjamin F was born on 10 October 1858 in Indiana. He died on 25 July 1863 in Jennings County, Indiana at the age of 4 years, 9 months and was buried in the Bear Creek Cemetery. He was the son of Andrew G Byfield and Mary Bruner.

16E.　　**Rose Emma Lucinda Byfield.** (Andrew G Byfield-2; Abraham H Byfield-1)

Rose Emma Lucinda was born in January 1863 in Jefferson County, Indiana. She died in 1937 in Jennings County, Indiana at the age of 74 years. She was buried in Vernon, Jennings County, Indiana. She was the daughter of Andrew G Byfield and Mary Bruner. She married John Elmer McGuire on 4 April 1888 in Jefferson County, Indiana.

Rose's name causes some confusion in tracing her over the years[14]. She first appears as a young girl with her parents in the 1870 census as Rose. The next census with her parents she is listed as Lucinda. A land map from 1884, two years after her father's death, shows Lucinda Byfield owning land around her brothers, probably inherited from her father. She marries John Elmer McGuire in 1888 and used the name Rose E. on the marriage records. All later records list her as Rose.

She and her husband remained in Jennings County their entire lives and are buried together in the Vernon Cemetery in Jennings County.

Spouse: John Elmer McGuire.

John Elmer was born in March 1867 in Jennings County, Indiana. He died in 1952 in Jennings County, Indiana at the age of 84 years, 10 months. He was buried in Vernon, Jennings County, Indiana. He was the son of William Edward McGuire and Nancy Violetta Deputy. He married Rose Emma Lucinda Byfield on 4 April 1888 in Jefferson County, Indiana.

John and his brother, James, got their marriage licenses on the same day. His brother married Flora Abrams.

Children of Rose Emma Lucinda Byfield and John Elmer McGuire

16E1 i.　　　Alford E McGuire. Alford E was born on 2 July 1889 in Jennings County, Indiana. He died on 23 October 1889 in Jennings County, Indiana.

16E2 ii.　　　Walter McGuire. Walter was born on 29 March 1890 in Paris Crossing, Jennings County, Indiana. He died on 19 August 1963 in Philadelphia, Philadelphia County, Pennsylvania.

14　Rose Emma Lucinda Byfield (Henry number 16E) has a niece, daughter of James Byfield, that is also named Rose Emma (Henry number 1666.)

16E3 iii.   Hazel McGuire. Hazel was born on 12 October 1895 in Jefferson County, Indiana. She died 16 April 1972 in Jennings County, Indiana.

CHILDREN OF VINCENT BYFIELD

171.   **Ann Maria Byfield.** (Vincent Byfield-2; Abraham H Byfield-1)

Ann Maria was born about 1834 in Ohio. She died on 19 October 1896 in Jefferson County Indiana at the age of about 62 years, 9 months. She was buried in Madison, Jefferson County, Indiana. She was the daughter of Vincent Byfield and Eliza E Daugherty. She married Henry Stephens on 9 October 1855 in Jefferson County, Indiana.

Ann and her husband, Henry Stephens, spent their married lives in the river town of Madison, Indiana. They had seven children together. Many of the children died young of "consumption" as did her husband. Consumption was the term used in those days for tuberculosis. None of the children married. Ann is buried in the Springdale Cemetery in Madison as is her mother.

Spouse: Henry Stephens.

Henry was born in 1832 in Elizabeth, Allegheny County, Pennsylvania. He died on 23 April 1892 in Jefferson County Indiana at the age of 60 years, 3 months. He was buried in Madison, Jefferson County, Indiana. He married Ann Maria Byfield on 9 October 1855 in Jefferson County, Indiana.

Henry was a ship carpenter, building boats to travel the Ohio and Mississippi rivers. Henry is buried with his wife and several of the children in the Springdale Cemetery.

Children of Ann Maria Byfield and Henry Stephens

1711 i.   Melvina 'Mellie' R Stephens. Melvina 'Mellie' R was born on 6 December 1856 in Madison, Jefferson County, Indiana. She died on 30 May 1932 in Cincinnati, Hamilton County, Ohio.

1712 ii.   John W Stephens. John W was born about 1859 in Indiana. He died in _____ in _____ .

1713 iii.   Joseph G Stephens. Joseph G was born about 1862 in Indiana. He died on 14 January 1888 in Jefferson County, Indiana.

1714 iv.   Adelaide Stephens. Adelaide was born about 1865 in Indiana. She died on 19 November 1886 in Jefferson County, Indiana.

1715 v.   Frank Stephens. Frank was born about 1867 in Indiana. He died 28 January 1894 in Jefferson County, Indiana.

1716 vi.   Delos Stephens. Delos was born about 1871 in Indiana. He died on 10 May 1895 in Jefferson County, Indiana.

1717 vii.   Fannie Stephens. Fannie was born on 28 March 1872 in Indiana. She died on 29 June 1912 in Cincinnati, Hamilton County, Ohio.

172.   **Addie Valita Byfield.** (Vincent Byfield-2; Abraham H Byfield-1)

Addie Valita was born about 1836 in Ohio. She died November 1913 in _____. She was buried in Madison, Jefferson County, Indiana. She was the daughter of Vincent Byfield and Eliza E Daugherty. She married Henry B Davidson Jr on 24 March 1869 in Jefferson County, Indiana.

Addie was hard to track down as her mother was flexible with the names she called the children in the early censuses. Addie and Henry moved to Cairo, Illinois, soon after their marriage and remained there for the rest of their lives. Henry was listed in the censuses as a collector. They had no children. Addie is buried in the Springdale Cemetery in Madison, Indiana.

Spouse: Henry B Davidson Jr.

Henry B was born in October 1844 in Indiana. He died in _____ in _____. He was the son of Henry B Davidson Sr and Catharine Peters. He married Addie Valita Byfield on 24 March 1869 in Jefferson County, Indiana.

173.   **Vinson Delas Byfield.** (Vincent Byfield-2; Abraham H Byfield-1)

Vinson Delas was born on 27 October 1840 in Akron, Ohio. He died on 6 November 1911 in Madison, Indiana at the age of 71 years, 10 days. He was buried in Indianapolis, Marion County, Indiana. He was the son of Vincent Byfield and Eliza E Daugherty. He married Rebecca Turner Johnson on 15 October 1871 in Hamilton, Ohio.

Vinson Delas was born in Ohio, but the location in Ohio is uncertain. His obituary claims he was born in Akron, but his record from the veteran's home lists his birthplace as Greene County which would be closer to Xenia or Dayton. He served in the Civil War in Company C of the 67th Indiana Volunteers.

He lived with his mother in Madison, Indiana until his marriage at age 30 to Rebecca Turner Johnson. Although they were both from Indiana, Vinson and Rebecca were married in Hamilton County, Ohio and their first child was born in Kentucky. The couple moved to Indianapolis where Vinson continued in his profession as a machine moulder. They lived in Indianapolis for the rest of their lives and are buried together at the Crown Hill Cemetery.

Photo from Vinson D Byfield funeral notice in Indianapolis Star newspaper 8 November 1911

Spouse: Rebecca Turner Johnson.

Rebecca Turner was born on 18 November 1841 in Indiana. She died on 13 June 1893 in Indianapolis at the age of 51 years, 6 months. She was buried in Indianapolis, Marion County, Indiana. She was the daughter of Nicholas Johnson and Malinda Cloud. She married Vinson Delas Byfield on 15 October 1871 in Hamilton, Ohio.

Children of Rebecca Turner Johnson and Vinson Delas Byfield

+ 1731 i.   Charles Howard Byfield. Charles Howard was born on 23 May 1873 in Kentucky. He died in May 1935 in Marion County, Indiana.

+ 1732 ii.   Delila Elizabeth Byfield. Delila Elizabeth was born on 2 January 1875 in Indiana. She died on 6 May 1950 in Bethel, Clermont County, Ohio.

+ 1733 iii. Helen Malinda Byfield. Helen Malinda was born on 11 August 1879 in Indiana. She died on 8 October 1949 in Los Angeles County, California.

1734 iv.   Harriet B 'Hattie' Byfield. Harriet B 'Hattie' was born on 27 August 1882 in Marion County, Indiana. She died on 12 August 1930 in Indianapolis, Marion County, Indiana.

1735 v.   Florence J Byfield. Florence J was born on 22 July 1884 in Indianapolis, Marion County, Indiana. She died on 2 June 1964 in Los

Angeles, Los Angeles County, California.

174.   **Elizabeth D 'Lizzie' Byfield.** (Vincent Byfield-2; Abraham H Byfield-1)

Elizabeth D 'Lizzie' was born about 1843 in Ohio. She died in _____ in _____. She was the daughter of Vincent Byfield and Eliza E Daugherty. She married William B Davis on 8 October 1863 in Jefferson County, Indiana.

Elizabeth's story is very uncertain. She appears in the 1860 census at age 17, but is not listed in the 1850 census when she would most certainly be with her mother. A Lizzie Byfield marries William B Davis in 1863, but there is no later census showing the two together. In 1870 an Emma Davis with young son Charles is living with the Byfield family in Madison, Indiana.

This leaves a lot of unanswered questions. Where is Elizabeth in 1850? Is the Emma in 1870 actually Elizabeth and if so, where is her husband? What happens to Elizabeth (Emma) and her son after 1870?

Spouse: William B Davis.

William B was born about 1844 in Kentucky. He died in _____ in _____. He was the son of Davis and Elizabeth. He married Elizabeth D 'Lizzie' Byfield on 8 October 1863 in Jefferson County, Indiana.

Children of Elizabeth D 'Lizzie' Byfield and William B Davis

1741 i.   Charles Davis. Charles was born in 1866 in Indiana. He died in _____ in _____.

CHILDREN OF ELIZA ANN BYFIELD

181.   **George Washington Downs.** (Eliza Ann Byfield-2; Abraham H Byfield-1)

George Washington was born on 1 March 1833 in Jefferson County, Indiana. He died on 20 April 1906 in Grant, Mecosta County, Michigan at the age of 73 years, 1 month. He was buried in Hersey, Osceola County, Michigan. He was the son of James Downs and Eliza Ann Byfield. He married Lenora Marie Byram on 3 November 1853 in Jennings County, Indiana.

George grew up in Jefferson County, Indiana and there married Lenora Byram. Some years after their marriage the Civil War commenced and George enlisted and fought through most of the war. After the war, George moved the family to southern Michigan where he farmed for the rest of his life.

Spouse: Lenora Marie Byram.

George Washington Downs

Lenora Marie was born on 25 November 1834 in Indiana. She died on 20 June 1926 in Grant, Mecosta County, Michigan at the age of 91 years, 6 months. She married George Washington Downs on 3 November 1853 in Jennings County, Indiana.

Children of Lenora Marie Byram and George Washington Downs

1811 i.   James Samuel Downs. James Samuel was born on 30 November 1854 in Indiana. He died on 27 January 1937 in Yuma, Yuma County, Arizona.

1812 ii.   Sarah Jane Downs. Sarah Jane was born on 26 August 1856 in Indiana. She died on 18 August 1938 in _____.

1813 iii.   William Riley Downs. William Riley was born on 23 April 1858 in Indiana. He died in 1939 in _____.

1814 iv.   John Wesley Downs. John Wesley was born on 11 August 1859 in Indiana. He died on 29 November 1860 in Indiana.

1815 v.   Hannah Belle Downs. Hannah Belle was born on 30 November 1860 in Vernon, Hancock County, Indiana. She died on 13 August 1943 in Pontiac, Oakland County, Michigan.

1816 vi.   Elizabeth Alice Downs. Elizabeth Alice was born on 16 February 1866 in Indiana. She died on 30 July 1889 in _____ .

1817 vii.   George Elmer Downs. George Elmer was born on 17 June 1872 in Michigan. He died on 18 February 1935 in Reed City, Osceola County, Michigan.

1818 viii.   Henry Ansel Downs. Henry Ansel was born on 25 December 1875 in Michigan. He died on 11 October 1876 in Michigan.

1819 ix.   Vincent A Downs. Vincent A was born on 14 April 1877 in Michigan. He died on 26 December 1916 in Port Huron, Saint Clair County, Michigan.

181A x.   Anna Belle Downs. Anna Belle was born on 22 May 1878 in Michigan. She died on 26 February 1937 in _____ .

182.   Rebecca A Downs. (Eliza Ann Byfield-2; Abraham H Byfield-1)

Rebecca A was born in 1837 in Indiana. She died in _____ in _____ . She was the daughter of James Downs and Eliza Ann Byfield. She married Nelson Smith on 9 October 1852 in Decatur County, Indiana.

Rebecca and Nelson moved to Illinois in the midst of the Civil War. His parents are there as are some of his brothers. Rebecca's mother and her half-brother and half-sister are also there in Marion County, Illinois. After 1870 they disappear from the area.

Spouse: Nelson Smith.

Nelson was born about 1828 in Indiana. He died in _____ in _____ . He was the son of James Peter Smith and Eliza Ann Beachum. He married Rebecca A Downs on 9 October 1852 in Decatur County, Indiana.

Children of Rebecca A Downs and Nelson Smith

1821 i.   Ann Eliza Smith. Ann Eliza was born about 1854 in Indiana. She died in _____ in _____ .

1822 ii.   Thomas C Smith. Thomas C was born about 1856 in Indiana. He died in _____ in _____ .

1823 iii.   James C Smith. James C was born about 1859 in Indiana. He died in _____ in _____ .

1824 iv.   Lydia J Smith. Lydia J was born about 1862 in Indiana. She died in _____ in _____ .

1825 v.   Jennie S Smith. Jennie S was born about 1865 in Illinois. She died in _____ in _____ .

1826 vi.   Samuel S Smith. Samuel S was born about 1869 in Illinois. He died in _____ in _____ .

183.   **James Andrew Downs.** (Eliza Ann Byfield-2; Abraham H Byfield-1)

James Andrew was born in 1838 in Indiana. He died on 13 June 1863 in Nashville, Davidson County, Tennessee at the age of 25 years, 5 months. He was the son of James Downs and Eliza Ann Byfield. He married Sarah Jane Perry on 5 February 1861 in Jefferson County, Indiana.

James' father died when he was very young. James lived with his mother until his marriage to Sarah Jane Perry in 1861. The Civil War started around the time of his marriage and in 1862 James went off to fight. He died from pneumonia in a Civil War hospital in Nashville, Tennessee. He left his young wife and a baby daughter.

Spouse: Sarah Jane Perry.

Sarah Jane was born in _____ in _____ . She died in _____ in _____ . She was the daughter of Eliza. She married James Andrew Downs on 5 February 1861 in Jefferson County, Indiana.

Children of Sarah Jane Perry and James Andrew Downs

1831 i.   Rebecca Ann Downs. Rebecca Ann was born in 1862 in Jefferson County, Indiana. She died in _____ in _____ .

184.   **Ann E Hoyt.** (Eliza Ann Byfield-2; Abraham H Byfield-1)

Ann E was born about 1852 in Indiana. She died in _____ in _____ . She was the daughter of William Marion Hoyt and

Eliza Ann Byfield. Ann's father died when she was very young. She is last recorded in 1870 in Marion County, Illinois, living with her mother and brother and near her half-sister, Rebecca Downs.

185.   **William Hoyt.** (Eliza Ann Byfield-2; Abraham H Byfield-1)

William was born about 1855 in Indiana. He died in _____ in _____. He was the son of William Marion Hoyt and Eliza Ann Byfield. As with his sister, Ann, William is last found in the 1870 census living with his mother in Marion County, Illinois.

GENERATION FOUR

GRANDCHILDREN OF GEORGE WASHINGTON BYFIELD

1111.   **Cornelius Simon Byfield.** (George Washington Byfield-3; George Washington Byfield-2; Abraham H Byfield-1)

Cornelius Simon was born in November 1848 in Jennings County, Indiana. He died on 13 May 1902 in Buchanan County, Iowa at the age of 53 years, 6 months. He was buried in Estherville, Emmet County, Iowa in the Oak Hill Cemetery. He was the son of George Washington Byfield and Eleanor Ann Griffith. He married Nancy Emily Gilliam in 1868.

Cornelius came to Benton County, Iowa with his parents when he was nine or ten years old. Benton County is between Cedar Rapids and Waterloo in eastern Iowa. By 1860 the family had moved to Buchanan County, just north of Cedar Rapids. It was there that he met and married Nancy Gilliam. The couple made several moves within Iowa, ending up in Emmet County near Estherville in northwest Iowa.

C S. Byfield,

Successors to Neville & Horswell.

Livery and Feed STABLE.

Single and Double Rigs.
Fine City Turnouts,
Saddle Horses.

Prices Reasonable.

East Lincoln Street. **C.S.BYFIELD**

From the Emmet County Republican, 2 June 1892

Cornelius ran a livery stable in Estherville for many years. In spring of 1902 Cornelius was seriously injured while scraping out a ditch with a team of horses. He suffered internal injuries when the scraper struck a rock and he was thrown over the scraper and down an embankment. He died of his injuries within a few days.

Spouse: Nancy Emily Gilliam.

Nancy Emily was born on 16 April 1853 in Wisconsin. She died on 11 July 1931 in Winona, Winona County, Minnesota at the age of 78 years, 2 months. She was the daughter of Martin Gilliam and Sarah Darling. She married Cornelius Simon Byfield in 1868. She later married R F Gleason.

Children of Nancy Emily Gilliam and Cornelius Simon Byfield

+ 11111 i.   William A Byfield. William A was born on 20 June 1869 in Brandon, Buchanan County, Iowa. He died on 24 September 1914 in Estherville, Emmet County, Iowa.

1112.   **Mary Catherine Byfield.** (George Washington Byfield-3; George Washington Byfield-2; Abraham H Byfield-1)

Mary Catherine was born on 4 April 1849 in Scott County, Indiana. She died on 30 November 1937 in Aurora, Buchanan County, Iowa at the age of 88 years, 7 months. She was buried in Urbana, Iowa at the Urbana Cemetery. She was the daughter of George Washington Byfield and Eleanor Ann Griffith. She married John Adams McFarlan on 25 August 1872 in Spencer's Grove, Benton County, Iowa.

Mary's parents made the trip from Indiana to Iowa around 1855 in a covered wagon when Mary was about six years old. They settled in eastern Iowa in the rural area between the towns of Waterloo and Cedar Rapids. They were near a place known as Spencer's Grove which was a stagecoach stop. There Mary married John McFarlan.

The McFarlans lived in Garrison, Iowa where they had their first three children who all died of diphtheria in early childhood. The McFarlans later moved to Nebraska where they had four children. In 1888 they moved back to Iowa near their original home and stayed there for the rest of their lives.

Spouse: John Adams McFarlan.

John Adams was born on 18 July 1848 in Pennsylvania. He died on 26 June 1923 in Iowa City, Wright County, Iowa at the age of 74 years, 11 months. He was buried in Urbana, Iowa in the Urbana Cemetery. He married Mary Catherine Byfield on 25 August 1872 in Spencer's Grove, Benton County, Iowa.

Children of Mary Catherine Byfield and John Adams McFarlan

11121 i.   Josephine May McFarlan. Josephine May was born in 1874. She died on 3 August 1879.

11122 ii.   George William McFarlan. George William was born in 1876. He died on 22 August 1879.

11123 iii.   Rosie Ann McFarlan. Rosie Ann was born in 1878. She died on 17 August 1879.

+ 11124 iv.   William Henry McFarlan. William Henry was born on 12 December 1880 in Nebraska. He died on 9 December 1943 in Cass, North Dakota.

11125 v.   Mary Elizabeth McFarlan. Mary Elizabeth was born on 30 July 1884 in Nebraska. She died in 1906.

+ 11126 vi.   John Emmert McFarlan. John Emmert was born on 3 August 1886 in Hubble, Nebraska. He died on 4 October 1965 in Hennepin County, Minnesota.

+ 11127 vii.   Sadie Elmira McFarlan. Sadie Elmira was born 2 October 1888 in Hubbell, Thayer County, Nebraska. She died 9 December 1961 in Independence, Buchanan County, Iowa.

11128 viii.   Simon Peter McFarlan. Simon Peter was born on 4 July 1892 in Iowa. He died on 19 May 1964 in Cedar Rapids, Linn County, Iowa.

11129 ix.   Arthur James McFarlan. Arthur James was born on 22 December 1895 in Vinton, Benton County, Iowa. He died on 24 September 1963.

1113.   **George Griffith Byfield.** (George Washington Byfield-3; George Washington Byfield-2; Abraham H Byfield-1)

George Griffith was born on 20 June 1849 in Marion Township, Jennings County, Indiana. He died on 28 December 1930 in Butler, Custer County, Oklahoma at the age of 81 years, 6 months. He was buried in Butler, Custer County, Oklahoma at the Antioch Cemetery. He was the son of George Washington Byfield and Eleanor Ann Griffith. He married Sarah Ann Sherman on 5 April 1874 in Benton County, Iowa.

George came to Iowa with his parents around 1855. He married Sarah Ann Sherman in Iowa and then the young couple moved to Kansas following George's parents to the northeastern part of the state. George ended up in Washington County just a county or two east of where his parents settled. In the early 1900s the family moved south to Custer County, Oklahoma which is west of Oklahoma City. There is a biography of George in the *Portrait and Biographical Album of Washington, Clay and Riley Counties Kansas*, published in 1890.

George Griffith Byfield and Sarah Ann Sherman

Spouse: Sarah Ann Sherman.

Sarah Ann was born on 9 April 1858 in Cayuga County, New York. She was the daughter of Joseph Sherman and Kate Stalls. She died on 16 February 1937 in Custer County, Oklahoma at the age of 78 years, 10 months. She was buried in Butler, Custer County, Oklahoma in the Antioch Cemetery. She married George Griffith Byfield on 5 April 1874 in Benton County, Iowa.

Children of Sarah Ann Sherman and George Griffith Byfield

+ 11131 i.   Frank Ellsworth Byfield. Frank Ellsworth was born on 16 September 1875 in Buchanan County, Iowa. He died on 3 September 1950 in Ceres, Stanislaus County, California.

+ 11132 ii.   Fred Albert Byfield. Fred Albert was born on 26 January 1877 in Benton County, Iowa. He died on 25 November 1956 in Placer, California.

11133 iii.   William Oscar Byfield. William Oscar was born on 21 October 1878 in Benton County, Iowa. He died 1930-1935 in Kansas.

+ 11134 iv.   Rosetta Byfield. Rosetta was born on 1 January 1880 in Kansas. She died on 31 December 1956 in Wichita, Sedgwick County, Kansas.

+ 11135 v.   Charley Lewis Byfield. Charley Lewis was born on 10 December 1881 in Kansas. He died 21 July 1973 in Oklahoma City, Oklahoma County, Oklahoma.

11136 vi.   Martha Jane Byfield. Martha Jane was born on 7 December 1883 in Washington, Iowa.

+ 11137 vii. Lillie Belle Byfield. Lillie Belle was born on 21 November 1885 in

Kansas. She died in 1961 in Clinton, Oklahoma.

+ 11138 viii.   Gertrude Mae Byfield. Gertrude Mae was born on 12 January 1888 in Kansas. She died on 26 March 1949 in Phoenix, Maricopa County, Arizona.

+ 11139 ix.   Clarence Delmer Byfield. Clarence Delmer was born on 28 November 1891 in Kansas. He died in 1957 in Custer County, Oklahoma.

+ 1113A x.   Sylvia Agnes Byfield. Sylvia Agnes was born on 13 June 1893 in Kansas. She died on 20 March 1955 in Custer County, Oklahoma.

+ 1113B xi.   Earl Milton Byfield. Earl Milton was born on 3 May 1896 in Kansas. He died on 14 August 1954 in Saline County, Nebraska.

1114.   **Elinor Jane Byfield.** (George Washington Byfield-3; George Washington Byfield-2; Abraham H Byfield-1)

Elinor Jane was born on 29 February 1856 in Independence, Buchanan County, Iowa. She died on 8 May 1937 in Fairbury, Jefferson County, Nebraska at the age of 81 years, 2 months. She was the daughter of George Washington Byfield and Eleanor Ann Griffith. She married Noah Troxel on 29 November 1873 in Independence, Buchanan County, Iowa.

Elinor Jane was the first Byfield born in Iowa. She was born after her parents came to Iowa from Indiana in 1855. She and her husband moved their family to Smith County, Kansas, following her parents to that area around 1880. By 1910 the family had moved a little way north to Jefferson County, Nebraska where they remained for the rest of their lives.

Spouse: Noah Troxel.

Noah was born on 12 February 1853 in Indianapolis, Marion County, Indiana. He died on 28 February 1932 in Endicott, Jefferson County, Nebraska at the age of 79 years, 16 days. He was the son of Elias Troxel and Catherine Summers. He married Elinor Jane Byfield on 29 November 1873 in Independence, Buchanan County, Iowa.

Children of Elinor Jane Byfield and Noah Troxel

11141 i.   Cora Agnes Troxel. Cora Agnes was born on 19 September 1874 in Iowa City, Wright County, Iowa. She died on 15 September 1968 in Topeka, Shawnee County, Kansas.

11142 ii.   Nora Elizabeth Troxel. Nora Elizabeth was born on 18 January 1876 in Iowa. She died on 4 October 1898 in Saint John, Putnam County, Missouri.

11143 iii.   Enoch Aaron Troxel. Enoch Aaron was born on 29 August 1879 in Iowa. He died on 6 June 1955 in Los Angeles, California.

11144 iv.   Tish Irene Troxel. Tish Irene was born on 19 November 1881 in Kirwin, Phillips County, Kansas. She died on 3 August 1964 in Contra Costa County, California.

11145 v.   Russel Erastus Troxel. Russel Erastus was born on 19 November 1885 in Kirwin, Kansas. He died 10 July 1976 in Spokane, Washington.

11146 vi.   Sylvia Ann Troxel. Sylvia Ann was born on 13 April 1888 in Kirwin, Phillips County, Kansas. She died on 1 February 1955 in Butte, California.

11147 vii.   Charles Noah Troxel. Charles Noah was born on 13 February 1892 in Unionville, Saint Louis County, Missouri. He died on 8 April 1958 in Oakdale, Stanislaus County, California.

11148 viii.   Iva Troxel. Iva was born on 8 October 1895 in Cabool, Texas County, Missouri. She died on 2 January 1988 in Thedford, Thomas County, Nebraska.

11149 ix.   Henry Granville Troxel. Henry Granville was born on 17 September 1899 in Cabool, Texas County, Missouri. He died in December 1918 in Kansas City, Jackson County, Missouri.

1115.   **Charles Evans Byfield.** (George Washington Byfield-3; George Washington Byfield-2; Abraham H Byfield-1)

Charles Evans was born on 25 December 1858 in Vinton, Benton County, Iowa. He died on 19 April 1924 in Cedar, Smith County, Kansas at the age of 65 years, 3 months. He was the son of George Washington Byfield and Eleanor Ann Griffith. He married Mary Elizabeth Crist on 22 October 1883 in Smith Center, Smith County, Kansas.

Charles is listed with his mother and younger siblings in the 1880 census in Webster County, Nebraska. His father had already found a new homestead in Smith County, Kansas, so the family was probably on the way there when the census was taken in early June. Once settled

Back row (left to right): Arthur, Orville, Nellie Jane, George Ernest, Ora, Roy. Front row (left to right): Mary Crist Byfield (mother), Mary Violet, Charles E Byfield (father). Photo courtesy of Debbie Loechner.

in Smith County, Kansas, Charles married Mary Elizabeth Crist and they stayed in the area for the rest of their lives.

Spouse: Mary Elizabeth Crist.

Mary Elizabeth was born 19 June 1867 in Cincinnati, Hamilton County, Ohio. She died 24 June 1951 in Osborne, Osborne County, Kansas. She was buried in Cedar, Smith County, Kansas. She was the daughter of Benjamin R Crist and Lorenda. She married Charles Evans Byfield on 22 October 1883 in Smith Center, Smith County, Kansas.

Children of Mary Elizabeth Crist and Charles Evans Byfield

+ 11151 i.　George Ernest Byfield. George Ernest was born on 1 December 1884 in Dor, Smith County, Kansas. He died on 10 September 1951 in San Bernardino, San Bernardino County, California.

+ 11152 ii.　Charles Leroy Byfield. Charles Leroy was born on 1 June 1889 in Dor, Smith County, Kansas. He died on 24 August 1938 in Smith County, Kansas.

+ 11153 iii.　Nellie Jane Byfield. Nellie Jane was born on 10 February 1891 in Dor, Smith County, Kansas. She died on 14 July 1967 in Alton, Osborne County, Kansas.

+ 11154 iv.　Ora Byfield. Ora was born on 25 June 1893 in Dor, Smith County, Kansas. He died 5 January 1934 in Smith County, Kansas.

+ 11155 v.   Arthur Byfield. Arthur was born on 14 August 1895 in Dor, Smith County, Kansas. He died on 19 May 1960 in Colby, Thomas County, Kansas.

+ 11156 vi.   Orville E Byfield. Orville E was born on 26 June 1897 in Kansas. He died 7 February 1962 in Wichita, Sedgwick County, Kansas.

11157 vii.   Mary Viola Byfield. Mary Viola was born on 19 September 1911 in Smith County, Kansas. She died in January 1996 in Grandview, Jackson County, Missouri.

1116.   Joseph Abraham Lincoln Byfield. (George Washington Byfield-3; George Washington Byfield-2; Abraham H Byfield-1)

Joseph Abraham Lincoln was born on 1 November 1861 in Iowa. He died on 20 January 1949 in Stockton, Rooks County, Kansas at the age of 87 years, 2 months. He was the son of George Washington Byfield and Eleanor Ann Griffith. He married Alice Idell Francisco on 18 March 1899 in Smith County, Kansas.

Joseph settled in Smith County, Kansas just about 50 miles southwest of where his parents lived.

Spouse: Alice Idell Francisco.

Alice Idell was born on 24 April 1879 in Smith County, Kansas. She died on 20 January 1929 in Jewell County, Kansas at the age of 49 years, 8 months. She was the daughter of John Francisco and Louisa Jane Hart. She married Joseph Abraham Lincoln Byfield on 18 March 1899 in Smith County, Kansas.

Children of Alice Idell Francisco and Joseph Abraham Lincoln Byfield

11161 i.   Carl Elmo Byfield. Carl Elmo was born on 26 January 1900 in Kansas. He died on 5 July 1984 in Uvalde, Uvalde County, Texas.

11162 ii.   Emil Grant Byfield. Emil Grant was born on 16 July 1902 in Kansas. He died in May 1970 in Elk Mountain, Carbon County, Wyoming.

11163 iii.   Freeman G Byfield. Freeman G was born on 11 March 1905 in Kansas. He died 21 June 1983 in Stockton, Rooks County, Kansas.

11164 iv.   Ralph Raymond Byfield. Ralph Raymond was born on 1 April 1909 in Kansas. He died before 22 January 1920 in Rooks County, Kansas.

11165 v.   Eugene Kenneth Byfield. Eugene Kenneth was born on 27 October 1910 in Kansas.

1117.   **Margaret Olivio Byfield.** (George Washington Byfield-3; George Washington Byfield-2; Abraham H Byfield-1)

Margaret Olivio was born in 1863 in Vinton, Benton County, Iowa. She was the daughter of George Washington Byfield and Eleanor Ann Griffith. The last record of Margaret is the 1900 census where she is found living with her brother George's family at the age of 39 years.

1118.   **Lewis David Byfield.** (George Washington Byfield-3; George Washington Byfield-2; Abraham H Byfield-1)

Lewis David was born in 1866 in Vinton, Benton County, Iowa. He died on 10 October 1926 in Manila, Philippines at the age of 60 years, 9 months. He was buried in the Fort McKinley Cemetery near Luzon, Philippines. He was the son of George Washington Byfield and Eleanor Ann Griffith. He possibly married Maria Fernando in The Philippines.

Lewis was a career Army soldier. He spent much of his career in The Philippines which is where he is buried. Family stories pass down that he married Maria Fernando in the Philippines.

1121.   **Olivia Griffith.** (Harriet Byfield-3; George Washington Byfield-2; Abraham H Byfield-1)

Olivia was born on 3 August 1843 in Indiana. She died on 5 November 1918 in Heman, Oklahoma at the age of 75 years, 3 months. She was the daughter of Evan Griffith and Harriet Byfield. She married Jonas Morse Doughty on 14 March 1863 in Jennings County, Indiana.

Oliva and her husband, Jonas, had five children in Jennings County, Indiana. Olivia's husband and the four youngest children died before 1900, leaving her with just her oldest son, Joseph. Joseph left Indiana and lived a while in Illinois, where he met his wife, then moved to Iowa and finally to Oklahoma. Olivia joined her son in Oklahoma which is where she died.

Spouse: Jonas Morse Doughty.

Jonas Morse was born about 1827 in New Jersey. He died on 20 March 1890 in Alpha, Scott County, Indiana at the age of about 63 years, 2 months. He was buried in Paris Crossing, Jennings County, Indiana at the Coffee Creek Christian Church Cemetery. He married Elanor M Hudson who died young. He then married Olivia Griffith on 14 March 1863 in Jennings County, Indiana.

Children of Olivia Griffith and Jonas Morse Doughty

+ 11211 i.   Joseph Evan Doughty. Joseph Evan was born on 15 February 1864 in Indiana. He died on 15 July 1925 in Tonkawa, Kay County, Oklahoma.

11212 ii.   Edward Doughty. Edward was born on 30 August 1866 in Jennings County, Indiana. He died on 31 August 1867 in Jennings County, Indiana.

11213 iii.   Ezra Doughty. Ezra was born on 4 October 1868 in Indiana. He died on 27 February 1896 in Jennings County, Indiana.

11214 iv.   Llewwilyn M Doughty. Llewwilyn M was born on 15 July 1872 in Indiana. He died on 31 August 1874 in Indiana.

11215 v.   Lillian Edna Doughty. Lillian Edna was born on 31 December 1873 in Indiana. She died on 3 March 1899 in Jennings County, Indiana.

1131.   **James Madison Byfield.** (Lewis Freeman Byfield-3; George Washington Byfield-2; Abraham H Byfield-1)

James Madison was born on 13 October 1846 in Scott County, Indiana. He died on 22 May 1847 in Scott County, Indiana at the age of 7 months, 9 days. He was the son of Lewis Freeman Byfield and Ruth Ann Kashow.

1132.   **Lewis Freeman Byfield Jr.** (Lewis Freeman Byfield-3; George Washington Byfield-2; Abraham H Byfield-1)

Lewis Freeman Jr was born on 4 February 1849 in Scott County, Indiana He died on 5 October 1874 in Scott County, Indiana at the age of 25 years, 8 months. He was the son of Lewis Freeman Byfield and

Ruth Ann Kashow. He married Nancy Josephine Whitsitt on 22 September 1870 in Scott County, Indiana.

Spouse: Nancy Josephine Whitsitt.

Nancy Josephine was born on 9 September 1849 in Indiana. She died on 1 November 1935 in , Scott County, Indiana at the age of 86 years, 1 month. She married Lewis Freeman Jr Byfield on 22 September 1870 in Scott County, Indiana. She next married Newton E Philips on 6 April 1882 in Scott County, Indiana.

Children of Nancy Josephine Whitsitt and Lewis Freeman Jr Byfield

11321 i.   Freeman O Byfield. Freeman O was born on 12 December 1871 in , Scott County, Indiana. He died on 17 September 1874 in , Scott County, Indiana.

+ 11322 ii.   Lewis Scott Byfield. Lewis Scott was born on 10 October 1874 in Scott County, Indiana. He died on 26 February 1935 in Scott County, Indiana.

1141.   **Harriet Young.** (Mariah Byfield-3; George Washington Byfield-2; Abraham H Byfield-1)

Harriet was born on 2 August 1847 in Scott, Lagrange County, Indiana She died on 2 August 1847. She was buried in Jennings County, Indiana at the Old Coffee Creek Cemetery. She was the daughter of Christian Waldsmith Young and Mariah Byfield.

1142.   **Lewis Cassius Young.** (Mariah Byfield-3; George Washington Byfield-2; Abraham H Byfield-1)

Lewis Cassius was born on 21 September 1848 in Alpha, Scott County, Indiana He died on 12 October 1886 in Scott County, Indiana at the age of 38 years, 21 days. He was buried in Austin, Scott County, Indiana at the Wesley Chapel Cemetery. He was the son of Christian Waldsmith Young and Mariah Byfield. He married Mary Jane Peacock.

Spouse: Mary Jane Peacock.

Mary Jane was born on 25 November 1849 in Indiana. She died on 16 December 1900 in Scott County, Indiana at the age of 51 years, 21 days. She was buried in Austin, Scott County, Indiana at the Wesley Chapel Cemetery. She married Lewis Cassius Young.

Children of Mary Jane Peacock and Lewis Cassius Young

+ 11421 i.   Lawrence E Young. Lawrence E was born on 20 December 1872 in Indiana. He died on 14 March 1901 in Scott County, Indiana.

11422 ii.   John W Young. John W was born on 28 June 1878 in Scott County, Indiana. He died on 28 December 1946 in Ida County, Iowa.

+ 11423 iii.   Homer Cass Young. Homer Cass was born on 29 November 1880 in Austin, Scott County, Indiana. He died on 18 December 1934 in Ida Grove, Ida County, Iowa.

1143.   **William Crawford Young.** (Mariah Byfield-3; George Washington Byfield-2; Abraham H Byfield-1)

William Crawford was born on 11 December 1850 in Scott, Lagrange County, Indiana He died on 11 March 1853 in Scott, Lagrange County, Indiana at the age of 2 years, 3 months. He was buried in Jennings County, Indiana at the Old Coffee Creek Cemetery. He was the son of Christian Waldsmith Young and Mariah Byfield.

1144.   **Olive Clara Young.** (Mariah Byfield-3; George Washington Byfield-2; Abraham H Byfield-1)

Olive Clara was born on 21 August 1854 in Jennings County, Indiana. She died 20 September 1857 in Jennings County, Indiana. She was buried in Jennings County, Indiana at the Old Coffee Creek Cemetery. She was the daughter of Christian Waldsmith Young and Mariah Byfield.

1145.   **Minerva Jane Young.** (Mariah Byfield-3; George Washington Byfield-2; Abraham H Byfield-1)

Minerva Jane was born on 2 November 1856 in Jennings County,

Indiana. She died on 29 September 1857 in Jennings County, Indiana at the age of 10 months, 27 days. She was the daughter of Christian Waldsmith Young and Mariah Byfield.

1146. **Deborah C Young.** (Mariah Byfield-3; George Washington Byfield-2; Abraham H Byfield-1)

Deborah C was born on 17 August 1858 in Scott County, Indiana She died about 1880 in Jennings County, Indiana at the age of about 21 years, 4 months. She was the daughter of Christian Waldsmith Young and Mariah Byfield. She married her second cousin, Sardius Henry Byfield on 13 May 1875 in Scott County, Indiana.

Spouse: Sardius Henry Byfield.

Ref: 1513. Sardius Henry Byfield

Children of Deborah C Young and Sardius Henry Byfield

15131 i.   Flora Byfield. Flora was born about 1875 in Indiana.

+ 15132 ii.   Maude Marier Byfield. Maude Marier was born in February 1876 in Lebanon, Boone County, Indiana. She died 10 September 1940 in Boone County, Indiana.

+ 15133 iii.   Claude Clement Byfield. Claude Clement was born on 15 January 1878 in Indiana. He died on 20 July 1949.

1147. **Infant Young.** (Mariah Byfield-3; George Washington Byfield-2; Abraham H Byfield-1)

Infant was born and died on 28 December 1860 in Jennings County, Indiana. She was the daughter of Christian Waldsmith Young and Mariah Byfield.

1148. **Jefferson Young.** (Mariah Byfield-3; George Washington Byfield-2; Abraham H Byfield-1)

Jefferson was born on 21 December 1861 in Scott, Lagrange County, Indiana He died on 11 May 1863 in Scott, Lagrange County, Indiana at the age of 1 year, 4 months. He was buried in Jennings County, Indiana. He was the son of Christian Waldsmith Young and Mariah Byfield.

1149.   **Malana Mary Young.** (Mariah Byfield-3; George Washington Byfield-2; Abraham H Byfield-1)

Malana Mary was born on 5 June 1865 in Alpha, Scott County, Indiana She died on 26 August 1927 in Oklahoma City, Oklahoma County, Oklahoma at the age of 62 years, 2 months. She was the daughter of Christian Waldsmith Young and Mariah Byfield. She married William Morrison Skeels on 12 September 1895 in Scott County, Indiana.

Malana and William moved the family to Oklahoma after 1910.

Spouse: William Morrison Skeels.

William Morrison was born on 26 February 1853 in Scott County, Indiana He died on 29 November 1939 in Oklahoma City, Oklahoma County, Oklahoma at the age of 86 years, 9 months. He married Malana Mary Young on 12 September 1895 in Scott County, Indiana

Children of Malana Mary Young and William Morrison Skeels

11491 i.   William Carl Skeel. William Carl was born on 26 August 1896 in Scott, Lagrange County, Indiana He died on 28 May 1956 in Riverside, Riverside County, California

11492 ii.   Flo Jessie Skeel. Flo Jessie was born on 18 April 1901 in Scott County, Indiana She died on 10 December 1992 in Riverside, Riverside County, California

11493 iii.   Morris Young Skeel. Morris Young was born on 6 March 1903 in Scott County, Indiana He died on 10 October 1969 in Oklahoma City, Oklahoma County, Oklahoma.

114A.   **Clarence Mclure Young.** (Mariah Byfield-3; George Washington Byfield-2; Abraham H Byfield-1)

Clarence Mclure was born in August 1867 in Indiana. He died on 13

March 1937 in Jennings County, Indiana at the age of 69 years, 7 months. He was the son of Christian Waldsmith Young and Mariah Byfield. He married Adda M McClellan on 16 February 1898 in Jennings County, Indiana.

Spouse: Adda M McClellan.

Adda M was born in August 1876 in Indiana. She died on 26 December 1955 at the age of 79 years, 4 months. She was the daughter of Frank McClellan and Olivia Eliza Butler. She married Clarence Mclure Young on 16 February 1898 in Jennings County, Indiana.

Children of Adda M McClellan and Clarence Mclure Young

114A1 i.   Agnes M Young. Agnes M was born on 30 November 1898 in Indiana. She died on 10 February 1997 in Union City, Randolph County, Indiana.

114A2 ii.   Frank C Young. Frank C was born in 1901 in Indiana.

+ 114A3 iii. Lillian O Young. Lillian O was born 31 August 1902 in Indiana. She died on 27 July 1993 in Bel Air, Harford, Maryland.

+ 114A4 iv.   Delcie M Young. Delcie M was born in 1906 in Indiana.

+ 114A5 v.   Ruth Young. Ruth was born on 29 March 1909 in Jennings County, Indiana.

114A6 vi.   Marshall Young. Marshall was born about 1912 in Indiana.

114A7 vii.   Ernest G Young. Ernest G was born about 1915 in Indiana.

114B.   Leamon C Young. (Mariah Byfield-3; George Washington Byfield-2; Abraham H Byfield-1)

Leamon C was born on 11 June 1870 in Indiana. He died in 1905 at the age of 34 years, 6 months. He was the son of Christian Waldsmith Young and Mariah Byfield.

1151.   Sarah F Hoard[15]. (Ida Byfield-3; George Washington Byfield-2;

---

15 Sarah Hoard's family has proven very difficult to trace. There are many near matches, but nothing that gives proof of the family after 1870. Many George and Sarah Neff's can be found in later years but none that can be matched with any confidence.

Abraham H Byfield-1)

Sarah F was born about 1849 in Jefferson County, Indiana. She was the daughter of Wesley Hoard and Ida Byfield. She married George W Neff on 21 November 1864 in Jefferson County, Indiana.

Spouse: George W Neff.

George W was born in 1841 in Lexington, Scott County, Indiana He died in 1880 at the age of 39 years. He married Sarah F Hoard on 21 November 1864 in Jefferson County, Indiana

Children of Sarah L Hoard and George W Neff

+ 11511 i.   Addison Neff. Born August 1865 in Jefferson County, Indiana. Died 9 November 1941 in Clark County, Indiana.

11512 ii.   Edwin Neff. Born 25 May 1869 in Jefferson County, Indiana. Died _____ in _____.

+ 11513 iii.   Ida Mae Neff. Born 4 July 1873 in Jefferson County, Indiana. Died 5 November 1931 in Blocher, Scott County, Indiana.

1161.   **Dorcas Byfield.** (Albert Byfield-3; George Washington Byfield-2; Abraham H Byfield-1)

Daughter of Albert Byfield and Delilah Gross. Born about 1858 in Indiana. Died _____ in _____. Married William S McCan 23 August 1883 in Cana, Jennings County, Indiana.

Dorcas was raised in Scott County, Indiana. In their marriage license William listed his residence as Milford, Illinois. He and Dorcas may have settled in that place. Some records say that William may have died around 1889 in Milford and if so, Dorcas likely remarried, but there are no records of what happened after the couple's marriage.

Spouse: William S McCan.

Son of John McCan and Betsy. Born about 1860 in _____. Died _____ in _____. Married Dorcas Byfield 23 August 1883 in Cana, Jennings County, Indiana.

1162. **Harriet Matilda Byfield.** (Albert Byfield-3; George Washington Byfield-2; Abraham H Byfield-1)

Daughter of Albert Byfield and Delilah Gross. Born 5 April 1863 in Scott, Indiana. Died 23 February 1936 in Nowata, Nowata County, Oklahoma (72 years, 10 months). Married Julian Clinton Keith 5 January 1881 in Scott County, Indiana.

Soon after their marriage Harriet and her husband, Julian headed west, living for a while in Bourbon County in eastern Kansas and then, by 1890, settling in Nowata County in northeastern Oklahoma.

Spouse: Julian Clinton Keith.

Born 25 May 1857 in Jennings, Jennings County, Indiana. Died 15 October 1929 in Nowata, Nowata County, Oklahoma (72 years, 4 months). Married Harriet Matilda Byfield 5 January 1881 in Scott County, Indiana.

Children of Harriet Matilda Byfield and Julian Clinton Keith

+ 11621 i. Charles Theopolis Keith. Born 11 February 1884 in Fort Scott, Bourbon County, Kansas. Died 11 December 1964 in Bartlesville, Washington County, Oklahoma.

+ 11622 ii. Julian Frank Keith. Born 3 September 1886 in Kansas. Died 13 August 1965 in Nowata County, Oklahoma.

+ 11623 iii. Clarence A Keith. Born 29 September 1890 in Indian Territory, Oklahoma. Died 21 November 1966 in Nowata, Nowata County, Oklahoma.

11624 iv. Florance D Keith. Born about 1894 in Indian Territory, Oklahoma. Died _____ in _____.

+ 11625 v. Mary Elizabeth Keith. Born 4 November 1897 in Indian Territory, Oklahoma. Died 23 February 1981 in Oklahoma City, Oklahoma.

11626 vi. Lilly Keith. Born about 1900 in Indian Territory, Oklahoma. Died _____ in _____.

+ 11627 vii. James Alonzo Keith. Born about 1903 in Oklahoma. Died 28 December 1944 in Nowata, Nowata County, Oklahoma.

1163. **Maria Byfield.** (Albert Byfield-3; George Washington Byfield-2; Abraham H Byfield-1)

Daughter of Albert Byfield and Delilah Gross. Born 1866 in Indiana. Died _____ in _____. Married Aurelius Lamb about 1883 in _____.

Maria and her husband went to Pueblo, Colorado after their marriage, where they had two children. By 1900 they moved to Oklahoma near where some of Maria's brothers and sisters were living in Nowata County. They are found there through 1910 but then disappear from the records.

Spouse: Aurelius Lamb.

Born about 1856 in Illinois. Died _____ in _____. Married Maria Byfield about 1883 in _____.

Children of Maria Byfield and Aurelius Lamb

+ 11631 i. Vivian Delila Lamb. Born September 1884 in Colorado. Died 5 May 1910 in Oklahoma City, Oklahoma.

11632 ii. Charles A Lamb. Born 23 October 1896 in Pueblo, Colorado. Died September 1970 in Bentonville, Benton County, Arkansas.

1164. **William A Byfield.** (Albert Byfield-3; George Washington Byfield-2; Abraham H Byfield-1)

Son of Albert Byfield and Delilah Gross. Born 1866 in Indiana. Died _____ in _____.

William migrated from Scott County, Indiana to Oklahoma along with several of his siblings, but he didn't stay there. In 1910 he was in Reno, Nevada, in 1920 in Fergus County, Montana, and in 1930 in Albany County, Wyoming. It's not known where he died and there is no record of a marriage.

1165. **Charles C Byfield.** (Albert Byfield-3; George Washington Byfield-2; Abraham H Byfield-1)

Son of Albert Byfield and Delilah Gross. Born 1870 in Scott County, Indiana. Died 26 November 1928 in Nowata, Nowata County,

Oklahoma (58 years, 10 months). Buried in Nowata, Nowata County, Oklahoma. Married Effie Jane Roland 7 October 1890 in Independence, Montgomery County, Kansas.

Charles was yet another of Albert Byfield's children to follow him to Oklahoma. In 1890 he was in southeastern Kansas where he met and married his wife, Effie. By 1895 they had moved just south across the border to Nowata County in Oklahoma.

Spouse: Effie Jane Roland.

Daughter of William T Rolan and Mary E Rolan. Born January 1872 in Missouri. Died 1938 in Nowata, Nowata County, Oklahoma (66 years). Married Charles C Byfield 7 October 1890 in Independence, Montgomery County, Kansas.

Children of Effie Jane Roland and Charles C Byfield

+ 11651 i.   Lucy Belle Byfield. Born 5 April 1895 in Indian Territory, Oklahoma. Died 21 October 1971 in Nowata County, Oklahoma.

+ 11652 ii.   Walter Ora Byfield. Born 15 October 1901 in Oklahoma. Died 28 October 1966 in Nowata, Nowata County, Oklahoma.

1166.   **Emma Retta Byfield.** (Albert Byfield-3; George Washington Byfield-2; Abraham H Byfield-1)

Daughter of Albert Byfield and Delilah Gross. Born 8 February 1872 in Indiana. Died 9 December 1955 in Alameda, Alameda County, California (83 years, 10 months). Married Tecumsah Sherman Ayers 1896 in Pueblo, Pueblo County, Colorado.

Emma must have migrated to Colorado with her sister, Maria as that is where she married her husband, Tecumsah Ayers. In 1900 they were in Grinell, Iowa, but were back in Pueblo by 1910. Since Tecumsah was born in Iowa they may have moved there for a while to be closer to his family. By 1920 they were in Berkeley, California where Tecumsah died.

Spouse: Tecumsah Sherman Ayers.

Born 7 June, 1866 in Iowa. Died 23 February 1920 in Alameda,

Alameda County, California. Married Emma Retta Byfield 1896 in Pueblo, Pueblo County, Colorado.

Tecumsah was a carpet maker.

Children of Emma Retta Byfield and Tecumsah Sherman Ayers

+ 11661 i.   Melber Welden Ayers. Born 10 September 1896 in Pueblo, Colorado. Died 21 February 1986 in Albany, Alameda County, California.

11662 ii.   Alice M Ayers. Born 20 May 1898 in Colorado. Died 2 October 1966 in _____ .

+ 11663 iii.   Myrtle Fay Ayers. Born 8 October 1900 in Grinnell, Poweshiek County, Iowa. Died 26 April 1973 in _____ .

11664 iv.   Donald Marvin Ayers. Born 14 January 1903 in Iowa. Died 3 June 1972 in Berkeley, Alameda County, California.

+ 11665 v.   Esther Emma Ayers. Born 23 April 1906 in Colorado. Died 21 January 1993 in Antioch, Contra Costa County, California.

11666 vi.   Sherman Wesley Ayers. Born 14 July 1908 in Colorado. Died 18 July 1939 in _____ .

1167.   **George Byfield.** (Albert Byfield-3; George Washington Byfield-2; Abraham H Byfield-1)

Son of Albert Byfield and Delilah Gross. Born 1875 in Indiana.

George would have been young enough to have moved to Oklahoma with his father, but there is no record of him there. He may have died young while still in Indiana.

1168.   **Loret 'Nellie' Byfield.** (Albert Byfield-3; George Washington Byfield-2; Abraham H Byfield-1)

Daughter of Albert Byfield and Delilah Gross. Born 1 March 1878 in Jennings, Jennings County, Indiana. Died 20 August 1888 in Nowata, Nowata County, Oklahoma (10 years, 5 months). Buried in Nowata, Nowata County, Oklahoma in the Coker Cemetery.

Nellie went to Oklahoma with her parents. She died young and shares a headstone with her father.

1171.   **Nancy Josephine Byfield.** (Francis Marion Byfield-3; George Washington Byfield-2; Abraham H Byfield-1)

Daughter of Francis Marion Byfield and Harriett M Smith. Born 7 September 1856 in Scott County, Indiana. Died 10 February 1937 in Wainwright, Muskogee County, Oklahoma (80 years, 5 months). Buried in Muskogee, Muskogee County, Oklahoma in the Greenhill Cemetery. Married Oliver Cromwell Whitsitt 13 August 1874 in Scott County, Indiana.

After their marriage, Nancy's husband, Oliver took over guardianship of Nancy's brothers George and Francis who were receiving money from the government because of their father's death in the Civil War. In 1900 Nancy and Oliver had Nancy's 14 year old niece, Jessie Carol Byfield staying with them while her brother, Francis was shown in Illinois. Since Jessie was married in Indiana it's possible that she lived with the Whitsitts until her marriage.

Nancy and her husband, Oliver raised their family in Scott County, Indiana. Their two daughters married, but both died young. Nancy and Oliver, by 1910, had moved to Muskogee, Oklahoma along with their son-in-law, Oscar Baxter and their two grandsons.

Spouse: Oliver Cromwell Whitsitt.

Son of Joseph Wright Whitsett and Elvira Foster. Born 18 July 1854 in Deputy, Jefferson County, Indiana. Died 13 February 1943 in Wainwright, Muskogee County, Oklahoma (88 years, 6 months). Buried in Muskogee, Muskogee County, Oklahoma in the Greenhill Cemetery. Married Nancy Josephine Byfield 13 August 1874 in Scott County, Indiana.

Children of Nancy Josephine Byfield and Oliver Cromwell Whitsitt

+ 11711 i.   Delma P Whitsitt. Born 1 September 1875 in Indiana. Died 16 September 1902 in Scott County, Indiana.

+ 11712 ii.   Cora G Whitsitt. Born 3 October 1878 in Alpha, Scott County, Indiana. Died 21 February 1906 in Jennings County, Indiana.

1172. **George W Byfield.** (Francis Marion Byfield-3; George Washington Byfield-2; Abraham H Byfield-1)

Son of Francis Marion Byfield and Harriett M Smith. Born 28 December 1858 in Scott County, Indiana. Died 16 March 1917 in Jefferson County, Indiana (58 years, 2 months). Buried in Deputy, Jefferson County, Indiana in the Pisgah Cemetery. Married Iva Chloe Stewart 9 September 1880 in Jennings County, Indiana. Later married Mary Nevada Harrod 13 September 1892 in Scott, Indiana.

George was a farmer in southeast Indiana his entire life. His father died in the Civil War when George was a young boy. He was raised in Scott County then established his home in Jefferson County where he farmed the rest of his life.

Spouse: Iva Chloe Stewart.

Daughter of Peter Stewart and Alviras Stewart. Born 15 July 1861 in Indiana. Died 21 March 1887 in Jennings County, Indiana (25 years, 8 months). Buried in Deputy, Jefferson County, Indiana in the Pisgah Cemetery. Married George W Byfield 9 September 1880 in Jennings County, Indiana.

Children of Iva Chloe Stewart and George W Byfield

+ 11721 i.   Bertha Alma Byfield. Born 16 February 1881 in Indiana. Died 19 January 1954 in _____.

Spouse: Mary Nevada Harrod.

Daughter of Favonious Harrod and Mary Jane Mitchell. Born 15 October 1865 in Scott, Indiana. Died 5 February 1915 in Deputy, Jefferson County, Indiana (49 years, 3 months). Married George W Byfield 13 September 1892 in Scott, Indiana.

Children of Mary Nevada Harrod and George W Byfield

11722 i.   Harold Byfield. Born 13 June 1894 in Jefferson County, Indiana. Died 13 June 1894 in Jefferson County, Indiana.

11723 ii.   Berenice E Byfield. Born 26 November 1896 in Indiana. Died 15 November 1976 in Deputy, Jefferson County, Indiana.

11724 iii.   Grace Byfield. Born 23 October 1899 in Jefferson County, Indiana. Died 23 October 1899 in Jefferson County, Indiana.

+ 11725 iv.   Charles Korbly Byfield. Born 17 October 1900 in Deputy, Jefferson County, Indiana. Died 17 April 1953 in Charleston, Charleston County, South Carolina.

11726 v.   Aleeta Byfield. Born 4 October 1904 in Deputy, Jefferson County, Indiana. Died 2 June 1992 in Deputy, Jefferson County, Indiana.

11727 vi.   Wauneeta Byfield. Born 4 October 1904 in Deputy, Jefferson County, Indiana. Died 4 January 1971 in Cleveland, Cuyahoga County, Ohio.

1173.   **Francis Alaska Byfield.** (Francis Marion Byfield-3; George Washington Byfield-2; Abraham H Byfield-1)

Son of Francis Marion Byfield and Harriett M Smith. Born 17 June 1862 in Indiana. Died 28 December 1903 in _____ (41 years, 6 months). Buried in Jennings County, Indiana in the Coffee Creek Christian Church Cemetery. Married Florence May Peregrine 27 November 1884 in Scott County, Indiana.

Francis was raised in Scott County, Indiana. His father died in the Civil War when Francis was very young. His family was in McLean County, Illinois in 1900. When he died in 1903 the rest of his family moved to Ida Grove, Iowa. His daughter, Jennie had stayed in Indiana with her aunt, Nancy but later she and her husband joined the rest of the family in Ida Grove. Francis' headstone was made for him and his wife but his wife, Florence is buried in Iowa.

Spouse: Florence May Peregrine.

Daughter of Reuben Peregrine and Eleanor Tobias. Born 12 June 1866 in Indiana. Died 30 November 1944 in Ida Grove, Ida County, Iowa (78 years, 5 months). Buried in Ida Grove, Ida County, Iowa in the Ida Grove Cemetery. Married Francis Alaska Byfield 27 November 1884 in Scott County, Indiana.

Children of Florence May Peregrine and Francis Alaska Byfield

11731 i.   Horace Bovard Byfield. Born 9 October 1885 in Indiana. Died _____ in _____.

+ 11732 ii.   Jessie Carol Byfield. Born 26 September 1887 in Indiana. Died 1 November 1957 in Ida Grove, Ida County, Iowa.

11733 iii.   Ethel Byfield. Born 4 May 1890 in Indiana. Died 1 August 1891 in Indiana.

11734 iv.   Lillian Myrl Byfield. Born 8 July 1892 in Indiana. Died 1950 in Ida Grove, Ida County, Iowa.

1181.   **Elmira M Byfield.** (Charles Carel Byfield-3; George Washington Byfield-2; Abraham H Byfield-1)

Daughter of Charles Carel Byfield and Mary A Tobias. Born 5 March 1862 in Indiana. Died 6 May 1865 in Indiana (3 years, 2 months). Buried in Indiana in the Coffee Creek Baptist Church Cemetery.

1182.   **Martha Byfield.** (Charles Carel Byfield-3; George Washington Byfield-2; Abraham H Byfield-1)

Daughter of Charles Carel Byfield and Mary A Tobias. Born about 1864 in Indiana. Died 1886-1900 in Kansas. Married John Limuel Bottrell 18 March 1883 in Liberty, Linn County, Kansas.

Martha met and married her husband, John while her family was in eastern Kansas. The rest of the family moved on to Oklahoma, but Martha and her husband remained in Kansas around Linn County. Martha died young and her husband remarried.

Spouse: John Limuel Bottrell.

Son of John Bottrell and Sarina Bovee. Born 3 December 1858 in Walworth County, Wisconsin. Died 1933 in Duck Creek, Wilson County, Kansas (74 years, 29 days). Married Martha Byfield 18 March 1883 in Liberty, Linn County, Kansas. Later married Mary Emma Watkins 2 March 1899 in Fredonia, Wilson County, Kansas.

In 1930 John is found living with his daughter, Mattie's family in Pueblo, Colorado.

Children of Martha Byfield and John Limuel Bottrell

+ 11821 i.   Mattie Avis Bottrell. Born about 27 February 1886 in Buxton, Wilson County, Kansas. Died about 17 February 1939 in Pueblo, Colorado.

1183.   **Charley W Byfield.** (Charles Carel Byfield-3; George Washington Byfield-2; Abraham H Byfield-1)

Son of Charles Carel Byfield and Mary A Tobias. Born about 1868 in Missouri. Died _____ in _____.

Charley was born in Missouri while the family was making it's way westward to Kansas and Oklahoma. He is found with the family in Shawnee, Montgomery, and Linn Counties in Kansas, but doesn't appear again in any records after 1880.

1184.   **Sarah Elmina Byfield.** (Charles Carel Byfield-3; George Washington Byfield-2; Abraham H Byfield-1)

Daughter of Charles Carel Byfield and Mary A Tobias. Born 5 March 1870 in Kansas. Died 31 July 1939 in Oklahoma. Buried in Major County, Oklahoma. Married George Stong 1 July 1888 in Elk City, Montgomery County, Kansas.

Sarah was the first of Charles Carel Byfield's children to be born in Kansas so we know the family came to the state around 1870. She married her husband, George Stong in Kansas and they moved south to Oklahoma, following her parents. They settled around the Enid area in northwestern Oklahoma. Sarah and George had divorced by 1930. Sarah stayed around Enid with the children. In 1930 Sarah is living with her youngest daughter, Dollie.

Spouse: George Stong.

Born 3 November 1861 in Van Buren, Van Buren, Iowa. Died 17 April 1947 in Elk City, Montgomery County, Kansas (85 years, 5 months). Married Sarah Elmina Byfield 1 July 1888 in Elk City, Montgomery County, Kansas.

George was a farmer all his life.

Children of Sarah Elmina Byfield and George Stong

+ 11841 i.   George Ernest Stong. Born 5 January 1889 in Kansas. Died June 1976 in Seiling, Dewey County, Oklahoma.

+ 11842 ii.   Manderville Stong. Born 15 December 1890 in Louisburg, Montgomery County, Kansas. Died 17 July 1979 in Cleo Springs, Major County, Oklahoma.

+ 11843 iii.   Gracie Stong. Born 7 March 1893 in Kansas. Died 2 March 1989 in Merced, Merced County, California.

11844 iv.   Harl Stong. Born March 1895 in Oklahoma. Died _____ in _____.

+ 11845 v.   Ada Vey Stong. Born 25 August 1897 in Oklahoma. Died 13 February 1979 in Merced, Merced County, California.

11846 vi.   Bessie Stong. Born December 1899 in Oklahoma. Died before 1910 in Oklahoma.

11847 vii.   Roy E Stong. Born 23 December 1903 in Oklahoma. Died March 1987 in Enid, Garfield County, Oklahoma.

11848 viii.   Dollie Stong. Born 28 March 1906 in Oklahoma. Died 12 March 1992 in Enid, Garfield County, Oklahoma.

1185.   **Bernard S Byfield.** (Charles Carel Byfield-3; George Washington Byfield-2; Abraham H Byfield-1)

Son of Charles Carel Byfield and Mary A Tobias. Born 25 October 1872 in Kansas. Died 1962 in Oklahoma (89 years, 2 months). Buried in Major County, Oklahoma in the Cheyenne Valley Cemetery. Married Alpha R Thompson 1899 in _____.

Bernard grew up in eastern Kansas. He probably married Alpha Thompson in Oklahoma as they were there in 1900. They farmed in northwestern Oklahoma around Major County.

Spouse: Alpha R Thompson.

Born April 1878 in Kansas. Died 1963 in Oklahoma (84 years, 9 months). Buried in Major County, Oklahoma in the Cheyenne Valley Cemetery. Married Bernard S Byfield 1899 in _____.

Children of Alpha R Thompson and Bernard S Byfield

11851 i.   Ethel Byfield. Born April 1900 in Oklahoma. Died _____ in _____.

11852 ii.   Mabel Byfield. Born about 1902 in Oklahoma. Died _____ in _____.

+ 11853 iii.   Orville B Byfield. Born 28 January 1904 in Oklahoma. Died 6 May 1983 in Omega, Kingfisher County, Oklahoma.

+ 11854 iv.   Mary Viola Byfield. Born 5 August 1910 in Cheyenne Valley, Woods County, Oklahoma. Died 14 October 2007 in Enid, Garfield County, Oklahoma.

11855 v.   Nora O Byfield. Born about 1914 in Oklahoma. Died _____ in _____.

11856 vi.   Bertha I Byfield. Born about 1917 in Oklahoma. Died _____ in _____.

11857 vii.   Olin A Byfield. Born 2 August 1921 in Oklahoma. Died 14 April 1998 in Muskegon, Muskegon County, Michigan.

1186.   **George Washington Byfield.** (Charles Carel Byfield-3; George Washington Byfield-2; Abraham H Byfield-1)

Son of Charles Carel Byfield and Mary A Tobias. Born 7 August 1875 in Lawrence, Douglas County, Kansas. Died 19 April 1915 in Fairview, Major County, Oklahoma (39 years, 8 months). Buried in Fairview, Major County, Oklahoma in the Roscoe Cemetery. Married Bernettie M _____ in _____. Later married Amy Letitia White _____ in _____.

George was raised in northeastern Kansas and moved to northwestern Oklahoma with his parents as a young man. He probably married both of his wifes in Oklahoma but there is no record of the marriages. His first wife died after delivering triplets. George and his second wife, Amy had three children and George died while they were very young. Amy and the children went west to Los Angeles, California in the 1930s.

Spouse: Bernettie M.

Born 20 October 1882 in _____. Died 20 February 1904 in Major County, Oklahoma (21 years, 4 months). Buried in Fairview, Major County, Oklahoma in the Roscoe Cemetery. Married George Washington Byfield _____ in _____.

Children of Bernettie M and George Washington Byfield

11861 i.   Triplet Infants Byfield. Born 31 January 1904 in Major County, Oklahoma. Died 31 January 1904 in Major County, Oklahoma.

Spouse: Amy Letitia White.

Born 20 February 1888 in Maize, Sedgwick County, Kansas. Died 20 August 1942 in Fall River, Greenwood County, Kansas (54 years, 6 months). Married George Washington Byfield _____ in _____ .

Children of Amy Letitia White and George Washington Byfield

11862 i.   Gordon L Byfield. Born 30 November 1906 in Oklahoma. Died 21 March 1982 in Bell, Los Angeles County, California.

+ 11863 ii.   Avis Letitia Byfield. Born 25 May 1908 in Fairview, Major County, Oklahoma. Died 3 December 2005 in Wheeler, Tillamook County, Oregon.

+ 11864 iii.   Lawrence Everett Byfield. Born 4 September 1910 in Oklahoma. Died 24 January 1952 in Portland, Oregon.

1187.   **John Boman Byfield.** (Charles Carel Byfield-3; George Washington Byfield-2; Abraham H Byfield-1)

Son of Charles Carel Byfield and Mary A Tobias. Born 4 November 1879 in Kansas. Died 17 December 1953 in Major County, Oklahoma (74 years, 1 month). Buried in Fairview, Major County, Oklahoma in the Roscoe Cemetery. Married Ida L _____ in _____ .

John grew up in northeastern Kansas and moved to Major County, Oklahoma with his parents in the late 1890s. He probably married his wife, Ida in Oklahoma. He farmed in Major County for the rest of his life.

Spouse: Ida L.

Born 30 June 1883 in Texas. Died 6 August 1961 in Oklahoma (78 years, 1 month). Buried in Fairview, Major County, Oklahoma in the Roscoe Cemetery. Married John Boman Byfield _____ in _____ .

Children of Ida L and John Boman Byfield

11871 i.   Pearl Byfield. Born 1904 in Oklahoma. Died _____ in _____.

11872 ii.   Ray E Byfield. Born 19 July 1907 in Major County, Oklahoma. Died 3 August 1909 in Major County, Oklahoma.

+ 11873 iii.   Paul L Byfield. Born 22 April 1911 in Oklahoma. Died August 1984 in Purcell, McClain County, Oklahoma.

GRANDCHILDREN OF HORATIO BYFIELD

1211.   **Willis Byfield.** (Daniel Byfield-3; Horatio Byfield-2; Abraham H Byfield-1)

Son of Daniel Byfield and Martha M Baldwin. Born 4 December 1848 in Indiana. Died 5 July 1850 in Indiana (1 year, 7 months). Buried in the Byfield family cemetery on Horatio Byfield's farm.

1222.   **Hannah Janet 'Catherine' 'Kate' Byfield.** (Alford Byfield-3; Horatio Byfield-2; Abraham H Byfield-1)

Daughter of Alford Byfield and Nancy Graham. Born 30 June 1846 in Indiana. Died 22 April 1926 in Indiana. Hannah Janet was named after her maternal grandmother who was named Hannah and her paternal grandmother who was Jennet however, it seems that she was most often called Catherine or Kate. She married John Polasky 24 May 1867 in Jefferson County, Indiana. She later married Thomas Wheeler Woolen 4 March 1872 in Indiana.

Catherine was raised in Jefferson County, Indiana.[16] In 1860 she is enumerated in Madison, Indiana where her mother was working as a dress maker. In 1870 she was again listed with her mother in Madison as a widow with a young daughter.

Catherine and her first husband, John Polasky moved to Louisiana. Her husband and Aurthur Hurd had started a business. John Polasky and Arthur Hurd both died the same day. Catherine and John's daughter, Mary (also called Kate), was born in 1868 in Mississippi. Possibly young Kate's middle name Hurd or "Herdie" has something to do with all this.

---

16 Catherine's father died when she was very young and she is found in 1850 living with a Guthrie family, listed as Hannah J Byfield. The Guthries were living adjacent to two Graham families. Later when she is a widow living with her youngest daughter, Kathryn Woolen Dean, she is again listed as Hannah. In her daughter, Kathryn's DAR application, she records her mother as Hannah Janet Byfield.

Catherine's first husband, John Polasky, died just six months after their marriage. Her second husband was the recently widowed lawyer, Thomas W Woolen. The Woolen household was in Franklin County, Indiana. After Thomas' death in 1898 Catherine remained in Franklin County and there is where she probably died. She lived with her youngest daughter, Kathryn, for many years.

Spouse: John Polasky.

Born 1840 in _____. Died 28 September 1867 in Jefferson County, Indiana (27 years, 8 months). Buried in Jefferson County, Indiana in the Byfield family cemetery on Horatio Byfield's farm. Married Hannah Janet 'Catherine' 'Kate' Byfield 24 May 1867 in Jefferson County, Indiana.

Children of Hannah Janet 'Catherine' 'Kate' Byfield and John Polasky

12221 i.   Mary Hurd 'Kate' 'Herdie' Polasky. Born about 1868 in Mississippi. Died 9 March 1900 in Indiana.

Spouse: Thomas Wheeler Woolen.

Son of Edward Woolen and Anna Wheeler. Born 26 April 1830 in Maryland. Died 12 February 1898 in Franklin County, Indiana. Married Hannah Janet 'Catherine' 'Kate' Byfield 4 March 1872 in Indiana. Previously married Harriet J Williams 6 August 1850 in Brownstown, Jackson, Indiana.

Thomas' family included many prominent lawyers, judges, and doctors. Thomas was a lawyer and a judge. He served as Attorney General for the state of Indiana from 1878 to 1880. His first wife died young and he married Catherine who helped raise his children from his first marriage along with the three children they had together and Catherine's daughter from her first marriage. There is a good biography of Thomas W Woolen in the book *A Biographical History of Eminent and Self-made Men of the State of Indiana* published in 1880.

Children of Hannah Janet 'Catherine' 'Kate' Byfield and Thomas Wheeler Woolen

12222 i.   Agnes Pearl Woolen. Born 20 June 1873 in Indiana. Died 19 August 1881 in Indiana.

+ 12223 ii.   Ruby May Woolen. Born August 1876 in Indiana. Died
          _____ in _____.

+ 12224 iii. Kathryn L Woolen. Born October 1884 in Indiana. Died
          _____ in _____.

1231.   **Levi B Reynolds.** (Henrietta Byfield-3; Horatio Byfield-2; Abraham
        H Byfield-1)

        Son of William Simeon Reynolds and Henrietta Byfield. Born 12
        September 1849 in Jefferson County, Indiana. Died 31 January 1851
        in Jefferson County, Indiana (1 year, 4 months). Buried in Jefferson
        County, Indiana in the Byfield family cemetery on Horatio Byfield's
        farm.

1232.   **Jeanett Reynolds.** (Henrietta Byfield-3; Horatio Byfield-2; Abraham
        H Byfield-1)

        Daughter of William Simeon Reynolds and Henrietta Byfield. Born 3
        August 1852 in Jefferson County, Indiana. Died 12 September 1853 in
        Jefferson County, Indiana (1 year, 1 month). Buried in Madison,
        Jefferson County, Indiana in the Byfield family cemetery on Horatio
        Byfield's farm.

1233.   **Anna C Reynolds.** (Henrietta Byfield-3; Horatio Byfield-2; Abraham
        H Byfield-1)

        Daughter of William Simeon Reynolds and Henrietta Byfield. Born
        December 1856 in Indiana. Died 1932 in Hamilton County, Indiana
        (75 years, 1 month). Buried in Cicero, Hamilton County, Indiana in
        the Cicero Cemetery. Married Koscoliuskio Sperry 1892 in
        _____.

        Anna lived with her family in Johnson County, Indiana until her
        marriage at about age 35. Before her marriage she worked as a dress
        maker. The family had recently move to Bartholomew County when
        she met her husband. The couple spent most of their married lives in

Cicero, Hamilton County, Indiana where her husband had a bakery. They had no children.

Spouse: Koscoliuskio Sperry.

Son of George Sperry and Mary. Born October 1859 in Indiana. Died 1930 in Hamilton County, Indiana (70 years, 3 months). Buried in Cicero, Hamilton County, Indiana in the Cicero Cemetery. Married Anna C Reynolds 1892 in _____.

Koscoliuskio was a baker.

1234. **Maggie Reynolds.** (Henrietta Byfield-3; Horatio Byfield-2; Abraham H Byfield-1)

Daughter of William Simeon Reynolds and Henrietta Byfield. Born December 1861 in Indiana. Died January 1906 in Frankfort, Clinton County, Indiana (44 years, 1 month). Buried in Frankfort, Clinton County, Indiana in the Greenlawn Cemetery. Married John N Dorner 1 October 1884 in Shelby County, Indiana.

Spouse: John N Dorner.

Son of Phillip William Dorner and Mary Magdalena Spitznagle. Born 9 January 1858 in Lafayette, Allen, Indiana. Died 18 January 1921 in Frankfort, Clinton County, Indiana (63 years, 9 days). Buried in Frankfort, Clinton County, Indiana. Married Maggie Reynolds 1 October 1884 in Shelby County, Indiana. Later married Mary Lucetta Horlacher 30 September 1908 in Frankfort, Clinton County, Indiana.

John worked as a tanner with his father.

Children of Maggie Reynolds and John N Dorner

+ 12341 i. Elnora Dorner. Born 2 February 1887 in Indiana. Died 14 March 1969 in _____.

+ 12342 ii. Hazel Kirk Dorner. Born 18 September 1890 in Indiana. Died 29 November 1974 in Frankfort, Clinton County, Indiana.

12343 iii. John Harve Dorner. Born 27 June 1899 in Frankfort, Clinton County, Indiana. Died 11 August 1944 in Frankfort, Clinton County, Indiana.

1235.   **Ivy Lester Reynolds.** (Henrietta Byfield-3; Horatio Byfield-2; Abraham H Byfield-1)

Son of William Simeon Reynolds and Henrietta Byfield. Born 8 September 1876 in Franklin, Johnson County, Indiana. Died 22 April 1952 in Jackson, Jackson County, Michigan (75 years, 7 months). Buried in Jackson, Jackson County, Michigan in the Saint John's Catholic Cemetery. Married Elizabeth Norma Huber 25 July 1898 in Shelbyville, Shelby County, Indiana. Later married Dora B Garber 2 March 1914 in Morenci, Lenawee County, Michigan.

As a young man, Ivy first worked for a printing company in the town of Shelbyville. Later he worked with C Steinhauser in Shelbyville learning about watchmaking. He then went to Indianapolis to work for the Dyer & Matsumoto company, continuing in the jewelry and watchmaking business. In 1897 he opened his own shop on the town square in Shelbyville.

By 1897 the American public had been whipped into a fury over the independence of Cuba from Spain. Across the country states were forming militia groups in preparation for the possibility of war with Spain. Ivy joined the militia and participated in their exercises while he was in Indianapolis and when he returned to Shelbyville.

Second Lieutenant Ivy Lester Reynolds

He had the rank of Second Lieutenant in Company C of the One Hundred Sixty-First Indiana Volunteer Infantry. They were sent to Havana, Cuba For most of the war the company served as special guard at the general's headquarters in Havana.

Ivy married Lizzie Huber in 1898 and they had five children before Lizzie's death in 1914. Ivy married his second wife, Dora Garber just 11 days after the death of his first wife. The circumstances around the death of his first wife and his remarriage led Ivy to be accused by the state of murdering Lizzie by poisoning. The case went to trial but the judge ended the proceedings after the prosecution had presented their case as he felt the case wasn't strong enough to continue.[17]

Ivy and his second wife settled in Toledo, Ohio and then moved later to Jackson, Michigan. Ivy's children from his first marriage were all living with his sister, Anna Reynolds Sperry in 1920, but later followed their father to Ohio.

Spouse: Elizabeth Norma Huber.

Daughter of John Shelby Watkins and Louisa Caroline Huber[18]. Born January 1878 in Indiana. Died 16 February 1914 in Connersville, Indiana (36 years, 1 month). Married Ivy Lester Reynolds 25 July 1898 in Shelbyville, Shelby County, Indiana.

Children of Elizabeth Norma Huber and Ivy Lester Reynolds

12351 i.   Raymond Durban Reynolds. Born 17 May 1899 in Shelbyville, Shelby County, Indiana. Died 13 July 1986 in Durham, Durham County, North Carolina.

12352 ii.   Russel Sperry Reynolds. Born 10 January 1902 in Connersville, Fayette County, Indiana. Died 26 March 1941 in Toledo, Lucas County, Ohio.

+ 12353 iii.   Maria Batista Reynolds. Born 17 April 1905 in Indiana. Died 19 April 1980 in Sylvania, Lucas County, Ohio.

12354 iv.   Anna Katherine Reynolds. Born 14 July 1908 in Indiana. Died 31 July 1981 in Artesia, Eddy County, New Mexico.

+ 12355 v.   Helen J Reynolds. Born 28 March 1912 in Connersville, Fayette County, Indiana. Died 9 April 1990 in Grass Lake, Jackson County, Michigan.

Spouse: Dora B Garber.

Daughter of Benjamin Garber and Rebecca C Vootman. Born December 1894 in Nebraska. Died _____ in _____. Married Ivy Lester Reynolds 2 March 1914 in Morenci, Lenawee County, Michigan.

Dora married 37 year old Ivy Reynolds when she was 19 years old.

---

17 See Appendix A, Newspaper Accounts of the Trial of Ivy Reynolds.
18 Elizabeth Norma Huber was born about two years before her mother's marriage to John Watkins. In 1880 when her daughter would be about two years old, Elizabeth's mother is listed by herself as a servant in a Shelbyville household.

She was living in Morenci, Lenawee County, Michigan with her family at the time of the marriage.

Children of Dora B Garber and Ivy Lester Reynolds

12356 i.   Naida Janet Reynolds. Born about 1915 in Michigan. Died _____ in _____.

12357 ii.   William De Haven Reynolds. Born 1916 in _____. Died 1917 in _____.

12358 iii.   Robert Lester Reynolds. Born 22 June 1918 in Michigan. Died 7 March 1945 in _____.

12359 iv.   Theodore K Reynolds. Born 9 July 1924 in Lucas, Ohio. Died 15 June 2002 in Boca Raton, Palm Beach County, Florida.

1241.   **Horatio W Malcom.** (Margaretta Byfield-3; Horatio Byfield-2; Abraham H Byfield-1)

Son of Green Malcom and Margaretta Byfield. Born 15 September 1858 in Indiana. Died _____ in _____.

Horatio's father died before he was a year old. As a young boy Horatio and his mother lived with his grandparents in Jefferson County, Indiana. In the 1870s he and his mother were living with his single uncles, Horatio Byfield and Corbin Byfield. In 1880 Horatio and his mother were in Schell City, Missouri where Horatio was working as a telegrapher.

In 1885 Horatio and his mother were in the mining area of Saguache County, Colorado along with Horatio's uncle, Horatio Byfield. Horatio's mother is found in that area for many years, but there is no record of her son after 1885.

1271.   **Charles W Byfield.** (Casabianca 'Cass' Byfield-3; Horatio Byfield-2; Abraham H Byfield-1)

Son of Casabianca 'Cass' Byfield and Jessie Mary Ann Heineken. Born about 1864 in Indiana. Died October 1923 in Indianapolis, Marion County, Indiana (about 59 years, 9 months). Buried 12

October 1923 in Indianapolis, Marion County, Indiana in the Crown Hill Cemetery.

Charles moved with his parents from Johnson County, Indiana to Indianapolis as a young boy. He spent his working career with the Postal Service in Indianapolis, moving up from a clerk to eventually head the money order division. In 1913 he was named Assistant Postmaster and head of the financial division.

CHARLES W BYFIELD.

During his career, Charles helped to streamline the Postal Money Order system. He was also active in encouraging people to start savings accounts in the Postal Savings Bank.

1272.   **Arthur H Byfield.** (Casabianca 'Cass' Byfield-3; Horatio Byfield-2; Abraham H Byfield-1)

Son of Casabianca 'Cass' Byfield and Jessie Mary Ann Heineken. Born about 1866 in Indiana. Died 1918 in Indianapolis, Marion County, Indiana (about 52 years). Buried 5 October 1918 in Indianapolis, Marion County, Indiana. Married Hazel M Stevens Barnett 20 August 1904 in Chicago, Cook County, Illinois.

Arthur came to Indianapolis with his parents as a boy. He worked as a building superintendent in Indianapolis for many years. Around age 35 he moved to Chicago to work for a brick manufacturer. He probably died in Chicago as his wife was still there in 1920.

Spouse: Hazel M Stevens Barnett.

Daughter of Mate L Stevens. Born about 1881 in Indiana. Died _____ in _____. Married Arthur H Byfield 20 August 1904 in Chicago, Cook County, Illinois.

1273.   **Harry N Byfield.** (Casabianca 'Cass' Byfield-3; Horatio Byfield-2; Abraham H Byfield-1)

Son of Casabianca 'Cass' Byfield and Jessie Mary Ann Heineken. Born about 1868 in Indiana. Died 1916-1920 in San Francisco, California. Married Olive _____ in _____.

Harry grew up in Indianapolis. He worked as a clerk and later salesman in the hardware business in Indianapolis. Around age 40 he moved to San Francisco, California where he continued in hardware sales. He remained in California for the rest of his life.

Spouse: Olive.

Born 10 September 1884 in Ohio. Died 20 March 1975 in Orange County, California (90 years, 6 months). Married Harry N Byfield _____ in _____.

1274.   **Emma C Byfield.** (Casabianca 'Cass' Byfield-3; Horatio Byfield-2; Abraham H Byfield-1)

Daughter of Casabianca 'Cass' Byfield and Jessie Mary Ann Heineken. Born about 1871 in Indiana. Died October 1949 in Indianapolis, Marion County, Indiana (about 78 years, 9 months). Buried 27 October 1949 in Indianapolis, Marion County, Indiana.

Emma was raised in Indianapolis and lived there her entire life. She was a school teacher.

1275.   **Bessie Byfield.** (Casabianca 'Cass' Byfield-3; Horatio Byfield-2; Abraham H Byfield-1)

Daughter of Casabianca 'Cass' Byfield and Jessie Mary Ann Heineken. Born about 1873 in Indiana. Died 2 May 1915 in Park Avenue Hotel, New York, New York (about 42 years, 4 months). Buried in Indianapolis, Marion County, Indiana.

Bessie grew up in Indianapolis. Bessie was a teacher as was her older sister, Emma. As a young woman, she was an avid golfer and participated in many tournaments. At one of these events she was hit in the back of the head by a golf ball and afterward suffered from severe headaches. A week later, she took a train to New York City, booked a room in the Park Avenue Hotel, and ended her life by taking poison.[19]

GOES TO GOTHAM TO END HER LIFE

Miss Bessie Byfield of Indianapolis Leaves Note Saying She Could Not Commit Suicide Among Loved Ones.

ACCIDENT BELIEVED CAUSE

Young Woman, Who Disappeared Friday, Had Suffered Violent Headaches After Being Hit by Golf Ball.

The Indianapolis Star, 3 May 1915

1281.   **Whitcomb Conway.** (Emily Byfield-3; Horatio Byfield-2; Abraham H Byfield-1)

Son of William Conway and Emily Byfield. Born 10 January 1860 in Lancaster, Jefferson County, Indiana. Died 12 March 1863 in Lancaster, Jefferson County, Indiana. Buried in Jefferson County, Indiana in the Byfield family cemetery on Horatio Byfield's farm.

1282.   **Cora Tripp Conway.** (Emily Byfield-3; Horatio Byfield-2; Abraham H Byfield-1)

Daughter of William Conway and Emily Byfield. Born 8 August 1862 in Lancaster, Jefferson County, Indiana. Died 1920 in Marion County, Indiana. Cora and her husband, Horace are buried in the Greenwood Cemetery in Johnson County, Indiana. Married Horace L Smith 10 October 1883 in Marion.

Cora grew up in Lancaster, Jefferson County, Indiana and as a teenager moved to Johnson County with her parents. She and her husband, Horace were married and lived in Marion County, Indiana all their lives. They had no children but raised her sister, Emily's son, William Conway Love.

Spouse: Horace L Smith.

Son of Andrew Jackson Smith and Sarah Eckels. Born 1862 in Indiana. Died 1928 in Marion County, Indiana (66 years). Married Cora Tripp Conway 10 October 1883 in Marion. Horace was a farmer.

---

19   See Appendix B – Bessie Byfield Suicide.

1283. **Elizabeth Jannette 'Nettie' Conway.** (Emily Byfield-3; Horatio Byfield-2; Abraham H Byfield-1)

Daughter of William Conway and Emily Byfield. Born 18 May 1864 in Lancaster, Jefferson County, Indiana. Died 12 July 1915 in Indianapolis, Marion County, Indiana. Buried in Indianapolis, Marion County, Indiana in the Crown Hill Cemetery. Married Parmenas Collins Jacobs 3 July 1884 in Indianapolis, Marion County, Indiana.

Elizabeth lived in Lancaster, Jefferson County, Indiana as a young girl and moved to Johnson County with her parents as a teenager. She and her husband lived in Marion County.

Spouse: Parmenas Collins Jacobs.

Born 19 June 1857 in Nineveh Township, Johnson County, Indiana. Died 25 January 1949 in Indianapolis, Marion County, Indiana. Married Elizabeth Jannette 'Nettie' Conway 3 July 1884 in Indianapolis, Marion County, Indiana.

Parmenas worked in manufacturing and then as a real estate broker.

Children of Elizabeth Jannette 'Nettie' Conway and Parmenas Collins Jacobs

+ 12831 i.   Mary Hurd Jacobs. Born 17 July 1886 in Browntown (Bluff Creek), White River Township, Johnson County, Indiana. Died 15 May 1971 in Indianapolis, Marion County, Indiana.

+ 12832 ii.   Lawrence Paul Jacobs. Born 5 January 1896 in Irvington, Marion County, Indiana. Died 11 March 1982 in Southfield, Oakland County, Michigan.

+ 12833 iii. Ruth Elizabeth Jacobs. Born 19 October 1897 in Irvington, Marion County, Indiana. Died 17 March 1996 in Clawson, Oakland County, Michigan.

1284. **Mary Mildred Conway.** (Emily Byfield-3; Horatio Byfield-2; Abraham H Byfield-1)

Daughter of William Conway and Emily Byfield. Born 30 November 1866 in Dupont, Jefferson County, Indiana. Died 1937 in Indianapolis, Marion County, Indiana. Buried 30 April 1937 in Indianapolis, Marion County in the Crown Hill Cemetery. Married George McNutt

15 October 1890 in Marion County, Indiana.

Mary grew up in Jefferson County, Indiana and moved to Johnson County with her parents as a teenager. She and her husband lived in Indianapolis.

Spouse: George McNutt.

Born 10 July 1863 in Indiana. Died 20 February 1930 in Marion County, Indiana. Married Mary Mildred Conway 15 October 1890 in Marion County, Indiana.

George worked for the Post Office as a clerk and later a foreman.

Children of Mary Mildred Conway and George McNutt

+ 12841 i. Earl Cowlam McNutt. Born 7 November 1891 in Indiana. Died April 1970 in Grant Park, Kankakee County, Illinois.

12842 ii. Sadie May McNutt. Born June 1893 in Indiana. Died _____ in _____.

+ 12843 iii. Margart E McNutt. Born 23 December 1895 in Indiana. Died January 1963 in Indiana.

12844 iv. Adelaide Dortha McNutt. Born 22 October 1898 in Indiana. Died 1921 in _____.

12845 v. Alice McNutt. Born 26 February 1902 in _____. Died _____ in _____.

+ 12846 vi. Roger T McNutt. Born 1906 in Indiana. Died _____ in _____.

12847 vii. Anna Louise McNutt. Born 16 May 1908 in Indiana. Died 17 February 1998 in Indianapolis, Marion County, Indiana.

1285. **Jessie Adelade Conway.** (Emily Byfield-3; Horatio Byfield-2; Abraham H Byfield-1)

Daughter of William Conway and Emily Byfield. Born 27 March 1870 in Lancaster, Jefferson County, Indiana. Died 31 May 1938 in Detroit, Wayne County, Michigan (68 years, 2 months). Buried 3 June 1938 in Indianapolis, Marion County, Indiana. Married Keller[20] _____ in _____.

---

20 Some speculate that Keller is Albert H Keller, but I have found no solid evidence.

Jessie grew up in Lancaster, Jefferson County, Indiana and moved to Johnson County with her parents as a young girl. In 1900 she was living in Indianapolis with her sister, Emily, who was already a widow, and her sister, Elva. It's uncertain when she married Keller, but her Michigan death certificate proves that she was the daughter of William and Emily and that she was widowed at the time of her death. She is buried near her parents in Indianapolis.

Spouse: Keller.

Born _____ in _____ . Died _____ in _____ . Married Jessie Conway _____ in _____ .

1286.   **Elva Walker Conway.** (Emily Byfield-3; Horatio Byfield-2; Abraham H Byfield-1)

Daughter of William Conway and Emily Byfield. Born 6 July 1872 in Indiana. Died December 1948 in _____ (75 years, 5 months). Buried 27 May 1949 in Indianapolis, Marion County, Indiana at the Crown Hill Cemetery. Married Herman B White 27 September 1906 in Marion County, Indiana.

Elva lived in Johnson County, Indiana with her parents and then moved to Indianapolis as a young woman. She was living in Indianapolis with her sister, Emily and her sister, Jessie in 1900. She and her husband, Herman lived in Indianapolis.

Spouse: Herman B White.

Son of George L White and Kezia Bristol. Born 13 February 1869 in Connecticut. Died _____ in _____ . Married Elva Walker Conway 27 September 1906 in Marion County, Indiana.

Herman worked at a saw mill.

1287.   **Emily 'Emma' Byfield Conway.** (Emily Byfield-3; Horatio Byfield-2; Abraham H Byfield-1)

Daughter of William Conway and Emily Byfield. Born 19 April 1875 in Franklin County, Indiana. Died _____ in _____. Married William C Love 17 August 1897 in Marion County, Indiana.

Emily grew up in Johnson County, Indiana. She probably met and married William C Love in Indianapolis. The couple must have gone to Texas to be near her husband's family who lived in Dallas. She had their son, William Conway Love in 1899 in Texas, but by 1900 she and her son were back in Marion County, Indiana with her parents and she was listed as a widow.

In the 1910 and 1920 censuses her son is living with Emily's sister, Cora. In his World War I draft registration Emily's son says his mother is living in Denver, Colorado, but she may have remarried as no Emily Love or Emily Conway can be found there.

Spouse: William C Love.

Son of William E Love and Jennie Alvida Ewing. Born about 1874 in Mississippi. Died around 1900, probably in Texas. Married Emily 'Emma' Byfield Conway 17 August 1897 in Marion County, Indiana.

Children of Emily 'Emma' Byfield Conway and William C Love

+ 12871 i.   William Conway Love. Born 5 March 1899 in Texas. Died June 1984 in Ann Arbor, Washtenaw County, Michigan.

1291.   **Tanner Walker.** (Elva Byfield-3; Horatio Byfield-2; Abraham H Byfield-1)

Son of Thomas T Walker and Elva Byfield. Born 2 January 1864 in Jefferson County, Indiana. Died 13 September 1864 in Lancaster, Jefferson County, Indiana. Buried in Madison, Jefferson County, Indiana in the Byfield family cemetery on Horatio Byfield's farm.

1292.   **Byfield Walker.** (Elva Byfield-3; Horatio Byfield-2; Abraham H Byfield-1)

Son of Thomas T Walker and Elva Byfield. Born about 1865 in Indiana. Died _____ in _____.

Byfield Walker is with his parents in the 1870 and 1880 censuses but there is no further record of him.

1293.   **William Baxter Walker.** (Elva Byfield-3; Horatio Byfield-2; Abraham H Byfield-1)

Son of Thomas T Walker and Elva Byfield. Born January 1870 in Vernon, Jennings County, Indiana. Died 1 March 1933 in Guthrie, Logan County, Oklahoma (63 years, 2 months). Married Martha Jane 'Mattie' Bartlow 25 March 1896 in _____.

William grew up in Jennings and Tipton Counties in Indiana. He went to Oklahoma which is probably where he met and married his wife, Martha and they settled in Custer County where he worked in the newspaper business. He and Mattie were later found in Guthrie and Seminole counties in Oklahoma where William was a grocer.

Spouse: Martha Jane 'Mattie' Bartlow.

Born 24 September 1872 in Winfield, Cowley County, Kansas. Died 26 June 1945 in Guthrie, Logan County, Oklahoma (72 years, 9 months). Married William Baxter Walker 25 March 1896 in _____.

Children of Martha Jane 'Mattie' Bartlow and William Baxter Walker

+ 12931 i.   Elva Sarah Walker. Born 1897 in Weatherford, Custer County, Oklahoma. Died 1937 in Tonkawa, Kay County, Oklahoma.

+ 12932 ii.   Thomas T Walker. Born 25 September 1900 in Weatherford, Custer County, Oklahoma. Died March 1953 in probably Oklahoma.

1294.   **John Harris Walker.** (Elva Byfield-3; Horatio Byfield-2; Abraham H Byfield-1)

Son of Thomas T Walker and Elva Byfield. Born 24 February 1872 in Indiana. Died 31 May 1904 in Custer County, Oklahoma (32 years, 3 months). Buried in Weatherford, Custer County, Oklahoma in the Greenwood Cemetery.

John also followed his parents to Oklahoma. He died young and was never married.

1295. **James Walker.** (Elva Byfield-3; Horatio Byfield-2; Abraham H Byfield-1)

Son of Thomas T Walker and Elva Byfield. Born about 1874 in Indiana. Died _____ in _____.

James is not found after the 1880 census.

12A1. **Ralph Godman Byfield.** (Whitcomb Byfield-3; Horatio Byfield-2; Abraham H Byfield-1)

Son of Whitcomb Byfield and Margaret Anna Payne. Born about 1870 in Indiana. Died 7 August 1871 in Lancaster, Jefferson County, Indiana (about 1 year, 7 months).

12A2. **Louisa Griffith Byfield.** (Whitcomb Byfield-3; Horatio Byfield-2; Abraham H Byfield-1)

Daughter of Whitcomb Byfield and Margaret Anna Payne. Born 30 July 1872 in Indiana. Died 1 December 1906 in Indianapolis, Indiana (34 years, 4 months). Buried 3 December 1906 in Indianapolis, Marion County, Indiana near her parents in the Crown Hill Cemetery.

Louisa moved with her parents to Hamilton County, Indiana as a young girl. She went to Indianapolis and worked as a bookkeeper until her death at age 34.

12A3. **Harry Whitcomb Byfield.** (Whitcomb Byfield-3; Horatio Byfield-2;

Abraham H Byfield-1)

Son of Whitcomb Byfield and Margaret Anna Payne. Born 18 January 1876 in Indiana. Died 16 June 1930 in Buffalo, Erie County, New York (54 years, 4 months). Buried in Indianapolis, Marion County, Indiana in the Crown Hill Cemetery. Married Cora May Keller 23 July 1900 in Indianapolis, Indiana. Divorced from Cora May Keller before 1910.

Harry was raised in Hamilton County, Indiana and moved to Indianapolis with his parents at a young age. He served in the Spanish American war and also in World War 1. He worked for a printer as a young man. After returning from the Spanish American war he worked as a clerk in a tailor shop where his sister, Louisa, was a bookkeeper. He married in 1900 but was divorced by 1910. He lived in Indianapolis most of his life, but was in Buffalo, New York when he died. He was working as a salesman at that time so he may have been traveling when he died.

Spouse: Cora May Keller.

Daughter of William Keller and Della E. Born 22 November 1879 in Indiana. Died _____ in _____. Married Harry Whitcomb Byfield 23 July 1900 in Indianapolis, Indiana. Later married Henry P Jungclaus 7 February 1920 in Marion County, Indiana.

Children of Cora May Keller and Harry Whitcomb Byfield

+ 12A31 i. Harry Louis Byfield. Born 25 December 1900 in Indianapolis, Marion County, Indiana. Died 27 November 1942 in Indianapolis, Marion County, Indiana.

12B1. **Gavin Lodge Payne.** (Mary Byfield-3; Horatio Byfield-2; Abraham H Byfield-1)

Son of John Godman Payne and Mary Byfield. Born 3 September 1869 in Wirt, Jefferson County, Indiana. Died 12 September 1939 in Indianapolis, Marion County, Indiana. Married Bertha Fahnley 12 December 1904 in Marion County, Indiana. Later married Carolyn Agnes Conde 7 January 1920 in Indianapolis, Marion County,

Indiana.

Gavin grew up in Indianapolis where he got started in the newspaper business. He worked as a reporter for the *Indianapolis Sentinel* then moved to Memphis, Tennessee where he worked at the *Memphis Commercial*, eventually rising to the position of managing editor. He next worked for a while at the *New Delta* newspaper in New Orleans, Louisiana then moved to Kentucky to help edit the *Louisville Commercial*.

In 1893 Gavin came back to Indianapolis and worked as city editor for the *Indianapolis Journal* and the *Indianapolis Press* newspapers. Later he worked in the investment banking business eventually starting his own firm, Gavin L. Payne & Company. There is a biography of him in *The History of Greater Indianapolis*.

Gavin was interested in his ancestry and had traced his father's side of the family to the Revolutionary War and to Stephen Hopkins who arrived on the Mayflower. In 1914 he wrote an article about his grandfather, Horatio Byfield for the *Indiana Past and Present* magazine.[21]

Spouse: Bertha Fahnley.

Born 1874 in Indiana. Died 12 August 1918 in Hot Springs, Bath County, Virginia (44 years, 7 months). Married Gavin Lodge Payne 12 December 1904 in Marion County, Indiana.

Children of Bertha Fahnley and Gavin Lodge Payne

+ 12B11 i.   Ada Payne. Born 28 November 1905 in Indianapolis, Marion County, Indiana. Died 4 May 1965 in Heilbronn, Baden-Württemberg, Germany.

12B12 ii.   Frederick F Payne. Born 1911 in Indianapolis, Marion County, Indiana. Died _____ in _____.

Spouse: Carolyn Agnes Conde.

Daughter of Sanford Cornelius Conde and Agnes Sophia Meeker. Born 19 March 1885 in New York. Died 2 May 1975 in Saint Petersburg, Pinellas County, Florida (90 years, 1 month). Married Gavin Lodge Payne 7 January 1920 in Indianapolis, Marion County,

---

21   See Appendix C for a copy of this article.

Indiana.

12B2.   **Janet P Payne.** (Mary Byfield-3; Horatio Byfield-2; Abraham H Byfield-1)

Daughter of John Godman Payne and Mary Byfield. Born about 1872 in Indianapolis, Marion County, Indiana. Died 20 August 1948 in Indianapolis, Indiana (about 76 years, 7 months). Married Joseph Moore Bowles 22 October 1895 in Marion County, Indiana. Buried in the Crown Hill Cemetery near her mother.

Janet Payne 1887

Janet Payne was an artist, author, and teacher. She grew up in Indianapolis where she met Joseph Bowles. They were both of artistic temperament and were involved in the Arts and Crafts movement. This was a movement in the art world around the turn of the century that promoted recognition of artistry in crafted items as opposed to only the "fine arts" such as painting and sculpture.

Janet's husband published the quarterly, *Modern Art*, which was influential in the Arts and Crafts movement. The magazine was initially published in Indianapolis, but the operation was soon moved to Boston. It was there that Janet became interested in creative metalworking. She met a Russian metalworker who she persuaded to teach her the craft. The Russian was later imprisoned as a suspected spy, but Janet continued her creative work. In her own words:

> *From that time on, I kept at it, working in every sort of shop that would give me a wider training. I even paid for the privilege of working in on shop, where they refused to employ me because I was an apprentice in the trade.*

In 1902 the couple moved to Rye, New York where their daughter, Mira was born and then two years later their son, Jan. In New York she continued to study her craft. Around 1905 the family moved to the artist's community at Helicon Hall near Englewood, New Jersey. This was the community established by the writer Upton Sinclair. They remained there until the facility burned in 1907. They then moved the family to New York City.

In New York City, Janet frequented the Metropolitan Museum of Art where she met the director of the museum, Caspar Perdon Clarke who was enthusiastic about her work. He later introduced her to J. Pierpont Morgan who commissioned her to create several works over the years. In 1912 Janet and Joseph separated, and Janet's brother, Gavin came to New York to bring her and the children back to Indianapolis.

Needing to support herself and the children, Janet got a job as a teacher of metalworking arts at the Shortridge High School. She loved teaching and continued it into her 70s. When she wasn't teaching, she worked on her art. Her pieces won many awards both nationally and internationally. The Indianapolis Museum of Art currently holds 125 of her pieces that were donated by her children after Janet's death.

An excellent biography and overview of Janet Payne Bowles work can be found in the book *The Arts and Crafts Metalwork of Janet Payne Bowles*, produced by the Indiana University Press in conjunction with showings of her work, in 1993, in Indianapolis and Boston.

Spouse: Joseph Moore Bowles.

Son of Thomas H Bowles and Kate Moore. Born 1868 in Indiana. Died _____ in _____. Married Janet Payne 22 October 1895 in Marion County, Indiana.

In Indianapolis, Joseph ran an art store, then worked at Lieber's, which was an art emporium and framing company. He was a member of The Portfolio, an artist's club in Indianapolis established around 1890.

In 1893 Bowles founded *Modern Art*, the first magazine in its field. Originally printed by the Hollenbeck Press in Indianapolis, the magazine, and with it the Bowles family, moved to Boston in 1895.

Children of Janet Payne and Joseph Moore Bowles

12B21 i.   Mira Bowles. Born 8 July 1902 in New York. Died October 1986 in Greenwood, Johnson County, Indiana.

12B22 ii.   Jan Bowles. Born 2 November 1904 in New York. Died 10 October 1974 in Newport Beach, Orange County, California.

12C1.   **Harold Ragsdale Byfield.** (Charles A Byfield-3; Horatio Byfield-2; Abraham H Byfield-1)

Son of Charles A Byfield and Martha 'Mattie' Milhous. Born 21 November 1874 in Indiana. Died 4 February 1921 in Indiana (46 years, 2 months). Married Mary Wyota Kerlin 16 June 1898 in Wisconsin[22].

Harold was a dentist. He grew up in Franklin, Johnson County, Indiana and practiced there for many years, but later moved to Evansville. Harold and Mary divorced.

Spouse: Mary Wyota Kerlin.

Daughter of James Kerlin and Lula Tylor. Born 7 May 1878 in Indiana. Died 21 January 1928 in Fresno, California. Buried in Dinuba, Tulare County, California. Married Harold Ragsdale Byfield 16 June 1898 in Wisconsin.

Children of Mary Wyota Kerlin and Harold Ragsdale Byfield

+ 12C11 i.   Helen Edell Byfield. Born 16 October 1898 in Indiana. Died 8 August 1948 in Columbus, Bartholomew County, Indiana.

12C2.   **Ralph Clermont Byfield.** (Charles A Byfield-3; Horatio Byfield-2; Abraham H Byfield-1)

Son of Charles A Byfield and Martha 'Mattie' Milhous. Born 18 July 1876 in Franklin, Johnson County, Indiana. Died 1933 in _____ (56 years, 5 months). Buried in Franklin, Johnson

---

22 A marriage is recorded for Mary W Kerlin in Milwaukee and Hal R Byfield on this date. It's not clear why they would have married in Wisconsin. In *The Descendants of William Milhous Jr and Martha Vickers*, their marriage is recorded as 29 November 1897.

County, Indiana in the Greenlawn Cemetery. Married Rose M Epstein 14 July 1898 in Johnson County, Indiana. Later Married Mary Emma Clarke 2 November 1918 in Indianapolis, Marion County, Indiana.

Ralph was raised in Franklin, Johnson County, Indiana and lived there for many years as an adult. He was a water company clerk when he married Rose Epstein. By 1910 he was divorced and he and his 11 year old daughter were back living with his mother in Franklin. Ralph was a bookkeeper at that time. He and his second wife lived for a while in Indianapolis but by 1930 he was in Decatur County working in real estate.

Spouse: Rose M Epstein.

Daughter of Samuel Epstein and Emma Epstein. Born November 1877 in Indiana. Died _____ in _____. Married Ralph Clermont Byfield 14 July 1898 in Johnson County, Indiana.

Children of Rose M Epstein and Ralph Clermont Byfield

12C21 i.   Mary M Byfield. Born 26 April 1899 in Johnson, Indiana. Died _____ in _____.

Spouse: Mary Emma Clarke.

Daughter of Alfred Clarke and Minnie Minerva Legg. Born 23 March 1886 in Ohio. Died March 1971 in Franklin County, Indiana (84 years, 11 months). Buried in Franklin, Johnson County, Indiana. Married Ralph Clermont Byfield 2 November 1918 in Indianapolis, Marion County, Indiana.

12C3.   **Charles Augustus Byfield.** (Charles A Byfield-3; Horatio Byfield-2; Abraham H Byfield-1)

Son of Charles A Byfield and Martha 'Mattie' Milhous. Born 15 October 1884 in Franklin, Johnson County, Indiana. Died 24 November 1942 in Indianapolis, Indiana (58 years, 1 month). Buried in Franklin, Johnson County, Indiana in the Greenlawn Cemetery. Married Olive Leona Morris in May 1913 in _____.

Charles worked as a railroad conductor all his life. He grew up in

Franklin, Johnson County, Indiana and lived in Indianapolis as an adult. Later he and his family lived in Lafayette County.

Spouse: Olive Leona Morris.

Daughter of Raymond Morris and Henrietta J Main. Born about 26 May 1893 in Indiana. Died 20 July 1971 in San Francisco, California. Married Charles Augustus Byfield May 1913 in _____. Had previous marriage to Arthur Page 1907 in Indiana.

Children of Olive Leona Morris and Charles Augustus Byfield

12C31 i.   Ralph C Byfield. Born about 1915 in Indiana. Died _____ in _____.

12C4.   **Raymond Frank Byfield.** (Charles A Byfield-3; Horatio Byfield-2; Abraham H Byfield-1)

Son of Charles A Byfield and Martha 'Mattie' Milhous. Born 28 March 1889 in Indiana. Died 20 January 1937 in Kerrville, Kerr County, Texas. Buried 22 January 1937 in Franklin, Johnson County, Indiana. Married Anastasia Mary Ash 25 January 1915 in Indianapolis, Marion County, Indiana.

Raymond was raised in Franklin, Johnson County, Indiana. Raymond and Anastasia were divorced around 1930. Raymond was working as a salesman when he died in Texas. Raymond was a veteran of World War One.

Spouse: Anastasia Mary Ash.

Daughter of John Frank Ash and Anna M Murphy. Born 11 June 1892 in Indiana. Died 6 February 1932 in Indianapolis, Marion County, Indiana. Married Raymond Frank Byfield 25 January 1915 in Indianapolis, Marion County, Indiana. Later married Carl M James 13 February 1931 in Hancock County, Indiana.

Stasia grew up around the Indianapolis area. When she died both of her young daughters went to Texas to live with their aunt (probably one of their mother's sisters)[23].

Children of Anastasia Mary Ash and Raymond Frank Byfield

+ 12C41 i.   Bonnie June Byfield. Born 23 April 1916 in Johnson, Indiana. Died 11 January 1994 in Houston, Harris County, Texas.

+ 12C42 ii.   Dorothy May Byfield. Born 26 November 1919 in Indiana. Died 7 December 2004 in Floresville, Wilson County, Texas.

12C5.   **Bonnie Vivian Byfield.** (Charles A Byfield-3; Horatio Byfield-2; Abraham H Byfield-1)

Daughter of Charles A Byfield and Martha 'Mattie' Milhous. Born 7 August 1895 in Franklin, Johnson County, Indiana. Died 27 December 1978 in San Antonio, Bexar County, Texas (83 years, 4 months). Buried in San Antonio, Bexar County, Texas. Married Howard William Bush 4 May 1918 in Franklin, Johnson County, Indiana. Next married Frank Taylor Charboneau 7 October 1943 in Steuben County, Indiana. Later married Steven Otto Henze 18 January 1945 in _____.

Bonnie was raised in Franklin, Johnson County, Indiana. She was married to her first husband, Howard Bush, in her parents home in Franklin. Bonnie and Howard lived in South Bend, Indiana in 1920, but were in Miami, Florida in 1926. In 1930 they were back in Indianapolis. Bonnie's first husband, Howard died in early 1943 and Bonnie remarried late that year to Frank Charboneau. That marriage was short lived as she married her third husband, Otto Henze in 1945. She and Otto lived in Texas and Bonnie's mother lived with her there for a while. She and Otto are buried together in San Antonio, Texas.

Spouse: Howard William Bush.

Son of Jacob Bush and Gertrude. Born about 1895 in Ohio. Died 25 February 1943 in _____. Married Bonnie Vivian Byfield 4 May 1918 in Indianapolis, Indiana.

Howard worked in the insurance and real estate investment

---

23 Anastasia was in Florida in the 1930 census and was listed with both daughters but not Raymond. In early 1931 there is a marriage record for Anastasia Byfield and Carl James in Indiana.

businesses.

Spouse: Frank Taylor Charboneau.

Born 18 March 1901 in Beloit, Mitchell County, Kansas. Died 17 July 1970 in Wichita, Kansas. Married Bonnie Vivian Byfield 7 October 1943 in Steuben County, Indiana.

Spouse: Steven Otto Henze.

Born 16 February 1900 in _____. Died 9 September 1970 in San Antonio, Texas (70 years). Married Bonnie Vivian Byfield 18 January 1945 in _____.

GRANDCHILDREN OF STELLA HARRIET BYFIELD

1311.   **Stella Ann McGaughey.** (Albert Edwin McGaughey-3; Stella Harriet Byfield-2; Abraham H Byfield-1)

Stella Ann was born on 31 March 1846 in Franklin County, Indiana. She died on 2 January 1917 in Minneapolis, Minnesota at the age of 70 years, 9 months. She was the daughter of Albert Edwin McGaughey and Charlotte B Raymond.

1312.   **Martha Elizabeth McGaughey.** (Albert Edwin McGaughey-3; Stella Harriet Byfield-2; Abraham H Byfield-1)

Martha Elizabeth was born on 15 September 1849 in Indiana. She died on 25 November 1928 in Jefferson County, Montana at the age of 79 years, 2 months. She was buried in Basin, Jefferson County, Montana. She was the daughter of Albert Edwin McGaughey and Charlotte B Raymond. She married John Irwin Armes.

Spouse: John Irwin Armes.

John Irwin was born about 1843 in Ohio. He died in July 1909 in Jefferson County, Montana at the age of about 66 years, 6 months. He was buried in Basin, Jefferson County, Montana. He married Martha Elizabeth McGaughey.

Children of Martha Elizabeth McGaughey and John Irwin Armes

13121 i.   Charles E Armes. Charles E was born about 1868 in Minnesota.

13122 ii.   Mary Charlotte 'Lottie' Armes. Mary Charlotte 'Lottie' was born about 1870 in Minnesota.

13123 iii.   Dora V Armes. Dora V was born about 1879 in Minnesota.

+ 13124 iv.   Albert Irwin Armes. Albert Irwin was born about 1881 in Minnesota. He died on 3 March 1948 in Seattle, King County, Washington.

1313.   **John Henry McGaughey.** (Albert Edwin McGaughey-3; Stella Harriet Byfield-2; Abraham H Byfield-1)

John Henry was born on 15 January 1853 in Indiana. He died on 10

October 1908 in Ortonville, Big Stone County, Minnesota at the age of 55 years, 8 months. He was buried in Ortonville, Big Stone County, Minnesota. He was the son of Albert Edwin McGaughey and Charlotte B Raymond.

1314.   **George E McGaughey.** (Albert Edwin McGaughey-3; Stella Harriet Byfield-2; Abraham H Byfield-1)

George E was born on 11 June 1859 in St Anthony, Hennepin County, Minnesota. He died on 20 February 1934 in Burbank, Los Angeles County, California at the age of 74 years, 8 months. He was the son of Albert Edwin McGaughey and Charlotte B Raymond. He married Elizabeth Addie Barton in 1885.

Spouse: Elizabeth Addie Barton.

Elizabeth Addie was born in August 1869 in Illinois. She married George E McGaughey in 1885.

Children of Elizabeth Addie Barton and George E McGaughey

13141 i.   Harry E McGaughey. Harry E was born in March 1886 in Minnesota.

13142 ii.   William A McGaughey. William A was born in November 1887 in Minnesota.

13143 iii.   Leonard E McGaughey. Leonard E was born in October 1891 in Minnesota.

13144 iv.   George McGaughey. George was born in 1901 in Minnesota.

13145 v.   Wilbur W McGaughey. Wilbur W was born in 1905 in Minnesota.

1315.   **Wiley Allen McGaughey.** (Albert Edwin McGaughey-3; Stella Harriet Byfield-2; Abraham H Byfield-1)

Wiley Allen was born on 15 August 1861 in Minnesota. He died on 4 November 1871 in Minneapolis, Hennepin County, Minnesota at the age of 10 years, 2 months. He was the son of Albert Edwin McGaughey and Charlotte B Raymond.

1331.   **Viola Wynn McGaughey.** (Samuel Newton McGaughey-3; Stella Harriet Byfield-2; Abraham H Byfield-1)

Viola Wynn was born in August 1856 in Leon Township, Goodhue

County, Minnesota. She died on 10 September 1920 in Minneapolis, Hennepin County, Minnesota at the age of 64 years, 1 month. She was buried in Minneapolis, Hennepin County, Minnesota. She was the daughter of Samuel Newton McGaughey and Isabella Wynn. She married Richard Charles Stanley in 1878.

Spouse: Richard Charles Stanley.

Richard Charles was born in June 1850 in Maine. He married Viola Wynn McGaughey in 1878.

Children of Viola Wynn McGaughey and Richard Charles Stanley

13311 i.　　Charles Raymond Stanley. Charles Raymond was born in May 1881 in Minnesota. He died on 4 April 1944 in Minneapolis, Hennepin County, Minnesota.

13312 ii.　　Cora B Stanley. Cora B was born in July 1883 in Minnesota.

13313 iii.　　Lucy Viola Stanley. Lucy Viola was born on 28 May 1890 in Minnesota. She died on 12 January 1961 in Hennepin County, Minnesota.

13314 iv.　　Walter Gleason Stanley. Walter Gleason was born in May 1892 in Minnesota.

1332.　　**Margaret McGaughey.** (Samuel Newton McGaughey-3; Stella Harriet Byfield-2; Abraham H Byfield-1)

Margaret was born on 16 May 1859 in Leon Township, Goodhue County, Minnesota. She died on 18 April 1916 in Florida at the age of 56 years, 11 months. She was buried in Bartow, Polk County, Florida. She was the daughter of Samuel Newton McGaughey and Isabella Wynn. She married Samuel Fuller Heath on 11 April 1882 in Minneapolis, Hennepin County, Minnesota.

Spouse: Samuel Fuller Heath.

Samuel Fuller was born on 7 March 1857 in Wisconsin. He died on 24 October 1917 in Florida at the age of 60 years, 7 months. He married Margaret McGaughey on 11 April 1882 in Minneapolis, Hennepin County, Minnesota.

Children of Margaret McGaughey and Samuel Fuller Heath

13321 i.　　Mark Warren Heath. Mark Warren was born on 10 March 1883 in Minneapolis, Hennepin County, Minnesota. He died on 9 December 1971 in

Tucson, Pima County, Arizona.

13322 ii.   Harold Fuller Heath. Harold Fuller was born on 17 November 1884 in Minnesota.

13323 iii.   Samuel Clark Heath. Samuel Clark was born on 12 August 1886 in Minnesota. He died in October 1965 in Massachusetts.

13324 iv.   Margaret Isabel Heath. Margaret Isabel was born on 10 July 1889 in Minneapolis, Hennepin County, Minnesota.

13325 v.   Lawrence Rockwell Heath. Lawrence Rockwell was born on 20 September 1891 in Minneapolis, Hennepin County, Minnesota. He died on 21 March 1971 in Clearwater, Pinellas County, Florida.

13326 vi.   Marion Lovina Heath. Marion Lovina was born on 20 September 1891 in Minneapolis, Hennepin County, Minnesota.

13327 vii.   Hume Crandall Heath. Hume Crandall was born on 31 August 1897 in Minneapolis, Hennepin County, Minnesota. He died on 6 January 1989 in Tallahassee, Leon, Florida.

1333.   **Cora Ellen McGaughey.** (Samuel Newton McGaughey-3; Stella Harriet Byfield-2; Abraham H Byfield-1)

Cora Ellen was born about 1862 in Minnesota. She died on 8 May 1943 in Hennepin County, Minnesota at the age of about 81 years, 4 months. She was the daughter of Samuel Newton McGaughey and Isabella Wynn. She married John Wesley Washburn.

Spouse: John Wesley Washburn.

John Wesley was born in 1858 in New York. He married Cora Ellen McGaughey.

Children of Cora Ellen McGaughey and John Wesley Washburn

13331 i.   Arthur Leslie Washburn. Arthur Leslie was born on 30 June 1894 in Minneapolis, Hennepin County, Minnesota.

13332 ii.   Carl H Washburn. Carl H was born in 1896 in Minnesota.

13333 iii.   Cora May Washburn. Cora May was born on 30 March 1900 in Minneapolis, Hennepin County, Minnesota.

1351.   **Stella A Shafer.** (Catherine R McGaughey-3; Stella Harriet Byfield-2; Abraham H Byfield-1)

Daughter of David Shafer and Catherine R McGaughey. Born 19 August 1850 in Indiana. Died 17 July 1882 in Richland, Indiana (31 years, 10 months). Buried in Olney, Richland County, Illinois. Married Nathan W Coggburn 6 February 1868 in Decatur County, Indiana.

Spouse: Nathan W Coggburn.

Born 16 March 1844 in Greene County, Tennessee. Died 5 August 1911 in Richland County, Illinois, (67 years, 4 months). Buried in Olney, Richland County, Illinois. Married Stella A Shafer 6 February 1868 in Decatur County, Indiana.

Children of Stella A Shafer and Nathan W Coggburn

13511 i.   Mary Emmaline Coggburn. Born 21 March 1870 in Decatur County, Illinois. Died 17 July 1935 in Madison, Richland County, Illinois.

13512 ii.   William D Coggburn. Born 7 April 1872 in Decatur County, Indiana. Died 20 December 1951 in Richland County, Illinois.

13513 iii.   Lillie Catherine Coggburn. Born 7 April 1872 in Decatur County, Indiana. Died 7 March 1953 in Olney, Richland County, Illinois.

13514 iv.   Hiram Frank Coggburn. Born 06 June 1874 in Indiana. Died 9 April 1938 in Madison, Richland County, Illinois.

1352.   **Mary C Shafer.** (Catherine R McGaughey-3; Stella Harriet Byfield-2; Abraham H Byfield-1)

Daughter of David Shafer and Catherine R McGaughey. Born about 1853 in Indiana. Died _____ in _____. Married Jesse D Hern 30 April 1871 in Decatur County, Indiana.

Spouse: Jesse D Hern.

Son of Larkin Hern and Mary Jane Stevens. Born about 1849 in Indiana. Died 3 September 1887 in Decatur County, Indiana. Married Mary C Shafer 30 April 1871 in Decatur County, Indiana.

Children of Mary C Shafer and Jesse D Hern

13521 i.   David Edward Hern. Born about 1872 in Indiana. Died 18 September 1958 in Decatur County, Indiana.

+ 13522 ii.   Charles Shafer Hern. Born 5 May 1880 in Indiana. Died 20 July 1971 in New Castle, Henry County, Indiana.

13523 iii.   Mary Hern. Born about 1880 in Indiana. Died _____ in _____.

1353.   **Horatio W Shafer.** (Catherine R McGaughey-3; Stella Harriet Byfield-2; Abraham H Byfield-1)

Son of David Shafer and Catherine R McGaughey. Born April 1855 in Indiana. Died _____ in _____. Married Nora E Talkington _____ in _____.

Spouse: Nora E Talkington.

Daughter of Jesse Talkington and Margaret M. Born 8 October 1860 in Alert, Decatur County, Indiana. Died _____ in _____. Married Horatio W Shafer _____ in _____.

Children of Nora E Talkington and Horatio W Shafer

13531 i.   Dessie M Shafer. Born about 1878 in Indiana. Died _____ in _____.

13532 ii.   Harry M Shafer. Born April 1880 in Indiana. Died _____ in _____.

13533 iii.   Jesse O Shafer. Born October 1883 in Indiana. Died _____ in _____.

13534 iv.   George Shafer. Born May 1885 in Indiana. Died _____ in _____.

13535 v.   Margaret E Shafer. Born June 1888 in Indiana. Died _____ in _____.

13536 vi.   Monta H Shafer. Born November 1891 in Indiana. Died _____ in _____.

13537 vii.   Mamie I Shafer. Born February 1898 in Indiana. Died _____ in _____.

13538 viii.   Otis Shafer. Born about 1902 in Indiana. Died _____ in _____.

13539 ix.   Verlin L Shafer. Born about 1905 in Indiana. Died _____ in _____.

1354.   **Addie E Shafer.** (Catherine R McGaughey-3; Stella Harriet Byfield-2; Abraham H Byfield-1)

Daughter of David Shafer and Catherine R McGaughey. Born 26 June 1855 in Indiana. Died 17 September 1922 in _____. Buried in Westport Cemetery, Westport, Decatur County, Indiana. Married James Frank Talkington 10 August 1876 in Decatur County, Indiana.

Spouse: James Frank Talkington.

Son of Jesse Talkington and Margaret M. Born 1 February 1855 in Alert, Decatur County, Indiana. Died 15 June 1942 in Westport, Decatur County, Indiana. Buried in Westport, Decatur County, Indiana. Married Addie E Shafer 10 August 1876 in Decatur County, Indiana.

Children of Addie E Shafer and James Frank Talkington

+ 13541 i.   Fannie Belle Talkington. Born 29 July 1878 in Alert, Decatur County, Indiana. Died 18 February 1947 in Greeley, Weld County, Colorado.

13542 ii.   Maunte M Talkington. Born about 1879 in Indiana. Died _____ in _____.

13543 iii.   David Talkington. Born July 1880 in Indiana. Died 3 July 2009 in _____.

13544 iv.   Ottis Franklin Talkington. Born September 1884 in Indiana. Died January 1963 in Colorado.

13545 v.   Paul Spencer. Born about 1908 in Indiana. Died _____ in _____.

1355.   **Harriet Shafer.** (Catherine R McGaughey-3; Stella Harriet Byfield-2; Abraham H Byfield-1)

Daughter of David Shafer and Catherine R McGaughey. Born about 1861 in Indiana. Died _____ in _____.

1356.   **Sarah E Shafer.** (Catherine R McGaughey-3; Stella Harriet Byfield-2; Abraham H Byfield-1)

Daughter of David Shafer and Catherine R McGaughey. Born December 1862 in Indiana. Died 1944 in Bartholomew County, Indiana (81 years, 1 month). Married Jeremiah Sater 6 March 1901 in Decatur County, Indiana, USA.

Spouse: Jeremiah Sater.

Born 5 January 1842 in Franklin County, Ohio. Died 5 September 1919 in Bartholomew County, Indiana (77 years, 8 months). Married Sarah E Shafer 6 March 1901 in Decatur County, Indiana.

1357.   **David Nelson Shafer.** (Catherine R McGaughey-3; Stella Harriet Byfield-2; Abraham H Byfield-1)

Son of David Shafer and Catherine R McGaughey. Born about 1869 in Indiana. Died _____ in _____.

1361.   **William A McGaughey.** (George Calvin McGaughey-3; Stella Harriet Byfield-2; Abraham H Byfield-1)

William A was born July 1885 in Arkansas. He was the son of George Calvin McGaughey and Julia Ann Allen.

1362.   **Clarissa E McGaughey.** (George Calvin McGaughey-3; Stella Harriet Byfield-2; Abraham H Byfield-1)

Clarissa E was born about 1852 in Indiana. She was the daughter of George Calvin McGaughey and Elizabeth Henderson.

1363.   **Mary S L McGaughey.** (George Calvin McGaughey-3; Stella Harriet Byfield-2; Abraham H Byfield-1)

Mary S L was born about 1854 in Indiana. She was the daughter of George Calvin McGaughey and Elizabeth Henderson.

1364.   **Hariett McGaughey.** (George Calvin McGaughey-3; Stella Harriet Byfield-2; Abraham H Byfield-1)

Hariett was born in 1857 in Goodhue County, Minnesota. She was the daughter of George Calvin McGaughey and Elizabeth Henderson.

1365. **James T McGaughey.** (George Calvin McGaughey-3; Stella Harriet Byfield-2; Abraham H Byfield-1)

James T was born about 1857 in Minnesota. He was the son of George Calvin McGaughey and Elizabeth Henderson.

1366. **Horatio Edward McGaughey.** (George Calvin McGaughey-3; Stella Harriet Byfield-2; Abraham H Byfield-1)

Horatio Edward was born about 1864 in Minnesota. He was the son of George Calvin McGaughey and Elizabeth Henderson. He married Emma Halbert on 6 March 1892 in Pulaski County, Arkansas.

Spouse: Emma Halbert.

Emma was born in August 1873 in Tennessee. She married Horatio Edward McGaughey on 6 March 1892 in Pulaski County, Arkansas.

1367. **Lucinda McGaughey.** (George Calvin McGaughey-3; Stella Harriet Byfield-2; Abraham H Byfield-1)

Lucinda was born about 1868 in Minnesota. She was the daughter of George Calvin McGaughey and Elizabeth Henderson.

1381. **Franklin E Davis.** (Mary P McGaughey-3; Stella Harriet Byfield-2; Abraham H Byfield-1)

Franklin E was born in May 1864 in Minnesota. He was the son of Benjamin F Davis and Mary P McGaughey. He married Jannie S Smithson on 17 December 1890 in Goodhue County, Minnesota.

Spouse: Jannie S Smithson.

Jannie S was born in October 1860 in Minnesota. She married Franklin E Davis on 17 December 1890 in Goodhue County, Minnesota.

Children of Jannie S Smithson and Franklin E Davis

13811 i.   Ruth E Davis. Ruth E was born in November 1891 in Minnesota.

13812 ii.   Harvey Davis. Harvey was born about 1912 in Minnesota.

1382.   **Harriet E Davis.** (Mary P McGaughey-3; Stella Harriet Byfield-2; Abraham H Byfield-1)

Harriet E was born on 27 November 1865 in Goodhue County, Minnesota. She died on 8 June 1924 in Goodhue County, Minnesota at the age of 58 years, 6 months. She was buried in Cannon Falls, Goodhue County, Minnesota. She was the daughter of Benjamin F Davis and Mary P McGaughey. She married Charles Albert Nelson on 9 February 1887 in Goodhue County, Minnesota.

Spouse: Charles Albert Nelson.

Charles Albert was born on 5 September 1862 in Minnesota. He died on 7 July 1908 in Goodhue County, Minnesota at the age of 45 years, 10 months. He was buried in Cannon Falls, Goodhue County, Minnesota. He was the son of S P Nelson and Lizzie. He married Harriet E Davis on 9 February 1887 in Goodhue County, Minnesota.

Children of Harriet E Davis and Charles Albert Nelson

13821 i.   Lloyd Franklin Nelson. Lloyd Franklin was born in July 1888 in Goodhue County, Minnesota.

13822 ii.   Roy B Nelson. Roy B was born in October 1889 in Goodhue County, Minnesota.

13823 iii.   Lester W Nelson. Lester W was born in March 1896 in Goodhue County, Minnesota.

1383.   **Bertram E Davis.** (Mary P McGaughey-3; Stella Harriet Byfield-2; Abraham H Byfield-1)

Bertram E was born about 1867 in Minnesota. He was the son of Benjamin F Davis and Mary P McGaughey. He married Mary R Martin.

Spouse: Mary R Martin.

Mary R was born about 1888 in Minnesota. She married Bertram E Davis.

Children of Mary R Martin and Bertram E Davis

13831 i.   Geraldine Martin. Geraldine was born about 1923 in Minnesota.

1384.   **William E Davis.** (Mary P McGaughey-3; Stella Harriet Byfield-2; Abraham H Byfield-1)

William E was born about 1872 in Minnesota. He was the son of Benjamin F Davis and Mary P McGaughey.

1391.   **Frank McGaughey.** (Horatio M McGaughey-3; Stella Harriet Byfield-2; Abraham H Byfield-1)

Frank was born on 14 January 1877 in Minnesota. He died on 19 October 1929 in Carthage, Jasper County, Missouri at the age of 52 years, 9 months. He was buried in Carthage, Jasper County, Missouri. He was the son of Horatio M McGaughey and Eliza Ann Shafer. He married Lillie M Grimes on 9 March 1901 in Benton, Arkansas.

Spouse: Lillie M Grimes.

Lillie M was born in 1878 in Arkansas. She married Frank McGaughey on 9 March 1901 in Benton, Arkansas.

Children of Lillie M Grimes and Frank McGaughey

13911 i.   Victor O McGaughey. Victor O was born in 1902 in Arkansas.

13912 ii.   Max L McGaughey. Max L was born in 1905 in Arkansas.

13913 iii.   Otis D McGaughey. Otis D was born in 1908 in Arkansas.

13914 iv.   Irene M McGaughey. Irene M was born about 1914 in Missouri.

13915 v.   Glen E McGaughey. Glen E was born about 1916 in Missouri.

13916 vi.   Helen E McGaughey. Helen E was born about 1918 in Missouri.

1392.   **Cora I McGaughey.** (Horatio M McGaughey-3; Stella Harriet Byfield-2; Abraham H Byfield-1)

Cora I was born on 25 July 1878 in Cottonwood County, Minnesota. She died on 19 August 1967 in Contra Costa County, California at the age of 89 years, 25 days. She was the daughter of Horatio M McGaughey and Eliza Ann Shafer. She married Jay B Iden on 25 August 1907 in Benton, Arkansas.

Spouse: Jay B Iden.

Jay B was born about 1887 in Iowa. He married Cora I McGaughey on 25 August 1907 in Benton, Arkansas.

Children of Cora I McGaughey and Jay B Iden

13921 i. Margaret B Iden. Margaret B was born about 1916 in Arkansas.

13922 ii. Mary Joe Iden. Mary Joe was born about 1919 in Missouri.

GRANDCHILDREN OF HOLMES BYFIELD

1421. **James Byfield.** (James Byfield-3; Holmes Byfield-2; Abraham H Byfield-1)

James was born in 1869 in Goliad, Goliad County, Texas. He died before 1880 at the age of less than 11 years. He was the son of James Byfield and Elizabeth Hines.

1422. **Columbus H. 'Lum' Byfield.** (James Byfield-3; Holmes Byfield-2; Abraham H Byfield-1)

Columbus H. 'Lum' was born in September 1872 in Texas. He died on 6 February 1931 in Gila, Arizona at the age of 58 years, 5 months. He was the son of James Byfield and Elizabeth Hines. He married Virginia May Daves.

Spouse: Virginia May Daves.

Virginia May was born on 24 October 1892 in Santo, Palo Pinto County, Texas. She died on 4 February 1947 in El Paso, Texas at the age of 54 years, 3 months. She was buried on 7 February 1947 in El Paso, El Paso County, Texas. She was the daughter of Ben L Daves and Rosalie Bell. She married Columbus H. 'Lum' Byfield.

Children of Virginia May Daves and Columbus H. 'Lum' Byfield

14221 i.   Ada Alice Byfield. Ada Alice was born on 17 February 1908 in New Mexico. She died on 3 January 1986 in Kern County, California.

14222 ii.   Benjamin D Byfield. Benjamin D was born in 1910 in New Mexico.

14223 iii.   Virginia H Byfield. Virginia H was born about 1912 in New Mexico.

14224 iv.   Lincoln Jesse 'Link' Byfield. Lincoln Jesse 'Link' was born on 30 April 1915 in New Mexico. He died on 15 November 1983 in San Diego.

+ 14225 v.   Drexdell Byfield. Drexdell was born about 1920 in New Mexico. She died in July 1986 in Ruidoso, Lincoln, New Mexico.

1423. **Sarah Alice Byfield.** (James Byfield-3; Holmes Byfield-2; Abraham H Byfield-1)

Sarah Alice was born on 18 August 1876 in Texas. She died on 28 February 1941 in Gila, Arizona at the age of 64 years, 6 months. She was buried in Central Heights, Gila County, Arizona. She was the daughter of James Byfield and Elizabeth Hines. She married Emmett C Barton.

Spouse: Emmett C Barton.

Emmett C was born about 1872 in Texas. He married Sarah Alice Byfield.

Children of Sarah Alice Byfield and Emmett C Barton

14231 i.   Beatrice Barton. Beatrice was born about 1906 in New Mexico.

14232 ii.   Elizabeth Holmes Barton. Elizabeth Holmes was born about 1908 in New Mexico.

14233 iii.   Clara Barton. Clara was born about 1911 in Arizona.

14234 iv.   William C Barton. William C was born about 1912 in Arizona.

1441.   **Holmes Ferguson.** (Elizabeth Byfield-3; Holmes Byfield-2; Abraham H Byfield-1)

Holmes was born on 5 January 1859 in Shelby County, Texas. He died on 28 January 1923 in Edwards County, Texas at the age of 64 years, 23 days. He was the son of Lea Ferguson and Elizabeth Byfield. He married Margaret Olive A Janes on 5 July 1889 in Edwards County, Texas.

Spouse: Margaret Olive A Janes.

Margaret Olive A was born on 24 October 1870 in Gillespie County, Texas. She died on 7 January 1891 in Edwards County, Texas at the age of 20 years, 2 months. She married Holmes Ferguson on 5 July 1889 in Edwards County, Texas.

Children of Margaret Olive A Janes and Holmes Ferguson

14411 i.   Oma Mae Ferguson. Oma Mae was born on 16 December 1890 in Leaky, Real County, Texas. She died on 8 July 1995 in Bakersfield, Kern County, California, Buried in Odd Fellows Cemetery, Fresno County, California.

1451.   **Cicero Loe.** (Martha Jane 'Jenny' Byfield-3; Holmes Byfield-2;

Abraham H Byfield-1)

Cicero was born on 19 December 1878 in Goliad County, Texas. He died in 1939 in Tempe, Maricopa County, Arizona at the age of 60 years, 13 days. He was the son of Benjamin Franklin Loe and Martha Jane 'Jenny' Byfield. He married Martha May.

Spouse: Martha May.

Martha was born in August 1879 in Texas. She married Cicero Loe. She also married George Helincamp.

Children of Martha May and Cicero Loe

+ 14511 i.   Edna Alvina Loe. Edna Alvina was born in 1899 in Texas.

1452.   **Alice Loe.** (Martha Jane 'Jenny' Byfield-3; Holmes Byfield-2; Abraham H Byfield-1)

Alice was born on 13 August 1880 in Llano County, Texas. She died on 1 March 1962 in Buried in Llano City Cemetery, Llano County, Texas at the age of 81 years, 6 months. She was buried in Llano, Llano County, Texas. She was the daughter of Benjamin Franklin Loe and Martha Jane 'Jenny' Byfield. She married Jerry Gilmer Allred.

Spouse: Jerry Gilmer Allred.

Jerry Gilmer was born on 23 May 1867 in North Carolina. He died on 13 August 1952 in Llano, Texas at the age of 85 years, 2 months. He married Alice Loe.

Children of Alice Loe and Jerry Gilmer Allred

14521 i.   Roy Allred. Roy was born about 1903 in Texas.

14522 ii.   Winnie Davis Allred. Winnie Davis was born on 19 January 1912 in Llano, Llano County, Texas. She died on 8 December 2008 in Austin, Travis County, Texas.

1453.   **Elizabeth 'Bettie' Loe.** (Martha Jane 'Jenny' Byfield-3; Holmes Byfield-2; Abraham H Byfield-1)

Elizabeth 'Bettie' was born on 12 March 1882 in Llano County, Texas. She died on 3 May 1959 in San Antonio, Bexar County, Texas,

Buried in Mission Burial Park at the age of 77 years, 1 month. She was the daughter of Benjamin Franklin Loe and Martha Jane 'Jenny' Byfield. She married Celestine Cornelius 'Charlie' Farque about 1930.

Spouse: Celestine Cornelius 'Charlie' Farque.

Celestine Cornelius 'Charlie' was born on 25 September 1880 in Lake Charles, Ward 3, Calcasieu Parrish, Louisiana. He died on 30 October 1947 in San Antonio, Bexar County, Texas at the age of 67 years, 1 month. He married Elizabeth 'Bettie' Loe about 1930.

1461.   **Ovid Vance Byfield.** (Benjamin Franklin Byfield-3; Holmes Byfield-2; Abraham H Byfield-1)

Ovid Vance was born on 14 March 1890 in Llano, Texas. He died on 2 January 1970 in Dallas, Texas at the age of 79 years, 9 months. He was the son of Benjamin Franklin Byfield and Kentucky C Toland. He married Helen Marcia Curtis in 1907. He also married Alene Smith on 1 August 1931 in Durant, Bryan County, Oklahoma.

Spouse: Helen Marcia Curtis.

Helen Marcia was born on 12 July 1890 in Rochester, Monroe County, New York. She married Ovid Vance Byfield in 1907.

Children of Helen Marcia Curtis and Ovid Vance Byfield

14611 i.   Evelyn Byfield. Evelyn was born on 27 July 1908 in Atlanta, Fulton County, Georgia. She died on 27 December 1935 in Atlanta, Fulton, Georgia.

Spouse: Alene Smith.

Alene was born on 6 June 1905 in Texas. She died on 21 March 1987 in Dallas, Texas at the age of 81 years, 9 months. She was the daughter of Walter A Smith and Anna S Smith. She married Ovid Vance Byfield on 1 August 1931 in Durant, Bryan County, Oklahoma. She also married Harrison.

1462.   **Ibera 'Bera' Byfield.** (Benjamin Franklin Byfield-3; Holmes Byfield-

2; Abraham H Byfield-1)

Daughter of Benjamin Franklin Byfield and Lula E Donahoe. Born 21 August 1892 in Texas. Died 3 March 1945 in Fulton County, Georgia. Buried in Forest Park, Clayton County, Georgia. Married James Augustus Mabry 11 January 1915 in Fulton, Georgia.

Spouse: James Augustus Mabry.

Son of Thomas Alfred Mabry and Fannie Parham. Born 29 November 1886 in Georgia. Died 22 April 1928 in Georgia. Buried in Forest Park, Clayton County, Georgia. Married Ibera 'Bera' Byfield 11 January 1915 in Fulton, Georgia.

Children of Ibera 'Bera' Byfield and James Augustus Mabry

14611 i.   B F Mabry. Born about 1916 in Georgia. Died _____ in _____.

14612 ii.   Francis C Mabry. Born 16 July 1917 in Fulton County, Georgia. Died 10 March 1998 in _____.

1463.   **Clyde King Byfield.** (Benjamin Franklin Byfield-3; Holmes Byfield-2; Abraham H Byfield-1)

Son of Benjamin Franklin Byfield and Lula E Donahoe. Born 15 October 1894 in Atlanta, Georgia. Died 12 May 1952 in Dallas, Texas (57 years, 6 months). Married Sarah Geraldine Gillespie 9 June 1919 in Atlanta, Georgia. Also married Birdie L 1928 in _____.

Clyde King Byfield

Clyde Byfield served in World War I, reaching the rank of Sergeant Major. After the war, he returned home to Atlanta and married Sarah Gillespie. Clyde became a dealer for Apperson automobiles – a car that was manufactured in Indiana during the early 1920s.

He and Sarah were interested in horse racing and through that social group came to know Walter Chandler, son of the Coca-Cola magnate, Asa Chandler. In 1922, Walter Chandler invited the Byfields to accompany him on a cruise to Europe. Sarah and Clyde accused Walter Chandler of assaulting Sarah in her stateroom. The Byfields sued Chandler and gained national media attention.[24]

Clyde and Sarah divorced in July of 1926. In 1928, Clyde married Birdie. Clyde and Birdie lived in Atlanta for many years. In 1932 Clyde is listed as president of B & C Auto Sales, a Pierce-Arrow dealer. His mother is listed as treasurer of the company. In 1940 Clyde and Birdie are listed in the U. S. Census in Los Angeles, California where Clyde is selling auto parts.

Spouse: Sarah Geraldine Gillespie.

Daughter of Benjamin P Gillaspie and Cordelia Beulah 'Cordie' Wilson. Born 1 May 1901 in Georgia. Died 17 May 1953 in Dekalb County, Georgia (52 years, 16 days). Married Clyde King Byfield 9 June 1919 in Atlanta, Georgia. Also married Cheney _____ in _____.

Sarah Gillespie

Spouse: Birdie L.

Born about 1907 in Atlanta, Fulton, Georgia,. Died _____ in _____. Married Clyde King Byfield 1928 in _____.

1471.   **Raymond Anderson Byfield.** (George Washington 'Link' Byfield-3; Holmes Byfield-2; Abraham H Byfield-1)

Raymond Anderson was born on 6 November 1885 in Texas. He died on 20 May 1947 in Llano County, Texas at the age of 61 years, 6 months. He was buried in Llano, Llano County, Texas. He was the son of George Washington 'Link' Byfield and Mary Siambra Barnett. He married Ila F Mayes in Llano County, Texas.

Spouse: Ila F Mayes.

---

24 See Appendix E for newspaper clippings describing the scandal.

Ila F was born in 1896 in Texas. She died on 25 December 1988 in Llano County, Texas at the age of 92 years, 11 months. She married Raymond Anderson Byfield in Llano County, Texas.

Children of Ila F Mayes and Raymond Anderson Byfield

+ 14711 i.　Frances Brown 'Brownie' Byfield. Frances Brown 'Brownie' was born on 21 January 1914 in Llano, Texas. She died on 5 August 1985 in Bexar County, Texas.

+ 14712 ii.　Nonie Louise Byfield. Nonie Louise was born on 30 December 1916 in Llano County, Texas.

+ 14713 iii.　Ila Marie Byfield. Ila Marie was born on 9 February 1918 in Texas. She died on 23 September 2000 in Llano, Llano County, Texas.

+ 14714 iv.　Molly Jeane Byfield. Molly Jeane was born on 12 January 1928 in Llano, Texas. She died on 4 December 2005 in Bossier City, Bossier Parish, Louisiana.

1472.　**Zora Ann Byfield.** (George Washington 'Link' Byfield-3; Holmes Byfield-2; Abraham H Byfield-1)

Zora Ann was born 12 March 1886 in Texas. She died 10 April 1965 in Harris, Texas. She was buried in Llano, Llano County, Texas. She was the daughter of George Washington 'Link' Byfield and Mary Siambra Barnett.

1473.　**Augusta Lucinda 'Gussie' Byfield.** (George Washington 'Link' Byfield-3; Holmes Byfield-2; Abraham H Byfield-1)

Augusta Lucinda 'Gussie' was born 27 October 1888 in Texas. She died on 17 May 1981 in Travis, Texas. She was buried in Austin, Travis County, Texas. She was the daughter of George Washington 'Link' Byfield and Mary Siambra Barnett. She married Arthur Byron Smith.

Spouse: Arthur Byron Smith.

Arthur Byron was born about 1895 in Texas. He married Augusta Lucinda 'Gussie' Byfield.

Children of Augusta Lucinda 'Gussie' Byfield and Arthur Byron Smith

14731 i.　Augusta Athena Smith. Augusta Athena was born on 23 September 1916 in Austin, Travis County, Texas.

14732 ii.   Harriet Josephine Smith. Harriet Josephine was born about 1919 in Texas.

14733 iii.   Marjorie Smith. Marjorie was born about 1926 in Texas.

1474.   **Holmes Barnett Byfield.** (George Washington 'Link' Byfield-3; Holmes Byfield-2; Abraham H Byfield-1)

Holmes Barnett was born on 6 February 1890 in Texas. He died on 10 January 1891 in Texas at the age of 11 months, 4 days. He was the son of George Washington 'Link' Byfield and Mary Siambra Barnett.

1475.   **Callie Byfield.** (George Washington 'Link' Byfield-3; Holmes Byfield-2; Abraham H Byfield-1)

Callie was born on 10 December 1892 in Texas. She died 20 January 1981 in Houston, Harris County, Texas. She was buried in Houston, Harris County, Texas. She was the daughter of George Washington 'Link' Byfield and Mary Siambra Barnett. She married Ernest Taylor on 2 September 1922 in Texas.

Spouse: Ernest Taylor.

Ernest was born about 1896 in Texas. He married Callie Byfield on 2 September 1922 in Texas.

Children of Callie Byfield and Ernest Taylor

14751 i.   Ernest Byfield Taylor. Ernest Byfield was born on 25 April 1926 in Taylor County, Texas.

1476.   **Frankie Byfield.** (George Washington 'Link' Byfield-3; Holmes Byfield-2; Abraham H Byfield-1)

Frankie was born on 22 July 1895 in Llano, Texas. She died on 19 December 1970 in Houston, Harris County, Texas at the age of 75 years, 4 months. She was the daughter of George Washington 'Link' Byfield and Mary Siambra Barnett. She married Joseph J Backues.

Spouse: Joseph J Backues.

Joseph J was born about 1897 in Texas. He married Frankie Byfield.

Children of Frankie Byfield and Joseph J Backues

14761 i.   Mary Backues. Mary was born about 1917 in Texas.

14762 ii.   Jim Link Backues. Jim Link was born in 1919 in Texas. He died on 8 February 1920 in Louise, Wharton, Texas.

14763 iii.   Joseph Raymond Backues. Joseph Raymond was born on 27 February 1924 in Llano, Texas. He died on 21 June 1966 in Houston, Harris County, Texas.

1477.   **Dixie Fay Byfield.** (George Washington 'Link' Byfield-3; Holmes Byfield-2; Abraham H Byfield-1)

Dixie Fay was born 10 April 1897 in Texas. She died 5 April 1997. She was buried in Altus, Jackson County, Oklahoma. She was the daughter of George Washington 'Link' Byfield and Mary Siambra Barnett. She married Charles Emory Aldridge on 6 July 1923 in Texas.

Spouse: Charles Emory Aldridge.

Charles Emory was born about 1898 in Texas. He married Dixie Fay Byfield on 6 July 1923 in Texas.

Children of Dixie Fay Byfield and Charles Emory Aldridge

14771 i.   Mary Fay Aldridge. Mary Fay was born about 1925 in Texas.

14772 ii.   George Alexander Aldridge. George Alexander was born on 22 February 1937 in Nueces County, Texas.

1478.   **George W Byfield.** (George Washington 'Link' Byfield-3; Holmes Byfield-2; Abraham H Byfield-1)

George W was born on 21 September 1899 in Llano County, Texas. He died on 12 July 1939 in Llano County, Texas at the age of 39 years, 9 months. He was buried in Llano, Llano County, Texas. He was the son of George Washington 'Link' Byfield and Mary Siambra Barnett. He married Irene Dorman about 1921 in Texas.

Spouse: Irene Dorman.

Irene was born on 11 December 1900 in Wharton County, Texas. She died on 16 April 1982 in Nueces County, Texas at the age of 81 years, 4 months. She married George W Byfield about 1921 in Texas.

Children of Irene Dorman and George W Byfield

+ 14781 i.   George Daniel Byfield. George Daniel was born 6 November 1922 in Travis County, Texas. He died on 28 July 1979 in Travis County, Texas.

+ 14782 ii.   June Elizabeth Byfield. June Elizabeth was born on 1 June 1926 in San Antonio, Bexar County, Texas. She died on 25 December 2011 in Houston, Harris County, Texas.

1479.   **James Finley Byfield.** (George Washington 'Link' Byfield-3; Holmes Byfield-2; Abraham H Byfield-1)

James Finley was born on 14 August 1901 in Texas. He died on 7 May 1967 in Austin, Travis County, Texas of America at the age of 65 years, 8 months. He was buried in Llano, Llano County, Texas. He was the son of George Washington 'Link' Byfield and Mary Siambra Barnett.

1481.   **Mary Ann Moss.** (Sarah 'Sallie' Byfield-3; Holmes Byfield-2; Abraham H Byfield-1)

Mary Ann was born on 15 May 1883 in Llano, Llano County, Texas. She died on 21 April 1891 in Llano, Llano County, Texas at the age of 7 years, 11 months. She was the daughter of Charles Tate Moss and Sarah 'Sallie' Byfield.

1482.   **Holmes Moss.** (Sarah 'Sallie' Byfield-3; Holmes Byfield-2; Abraham H Byfield-1)

Holmes was born on 11 February 1885 in Llano, Llano County, Texas. He died on 20 August 1956 in Gillespie, Texas at the age of 71 years, 6 months. He was the son of Charles Tate Moss and Sarah 'Sallie' Byfield.

1483.   **Carlos Smith Moss.** (Sarah 'Sallie' Byfield-3; Holmes Byfield-2; Abraham H Byfield-1)

Carlos Smith was born on 28 September 1887 in Llano, Llano County, Texas. He died on 16 September 1952 in Llano, Llano County, Texas at the age of 64 years, 11 months. He was the son of Charles Tate Moss and Sarah 'Sallie' Byfield.

1484.   **Dale Moss.** (Sarah 'Sallie' Byfield-3; Holmes Byfield-2; Abraham H Byfield-1)

Dale was born on 8 July 1890 in Llano, Llano County, Texas. He died on 26 March 1892 in Llano, Llano County, Texas at the age of 1 year, 8 months. He was the son of Charles Tate Moss and Sarah 'Sallie' Byfield.

1485. **Maud Moss.** (Sarah 'Sallie' Byfield-3; Holmes Byfield-2; Abraham H Byfield-1)

Maud was born on 2 April 1892 in Llano, Llano County, Texas. She died on 2 May 1981 in San Antonio, Bexar County, Texas at the age of 89 years, 1 month. She was the daughter of Charles Tate Moss and Sarah 'Sallie' Byfield.

1486. **Cash Moss.** (Sarah 'Sallie' Byfield-3; Holmes Byfield-2; Abraham H Byfield-1)

Cash was born on 4 May 1894 in Llano, Llano County, Texas. He died on 17 October 1971 in San Angelo, Tom Green, Texas at the age of 77 years, 5 months. He was buried in Llano County, Texas. He was the son of Charles Tate Moss and Sarah 'Sallie' Byfield. He married Eula Irene Garrett on 1 June 1916 in Llano, Texas.

Spouse: Eula Irene Garrett.

Eula Irene was born on 13 November 1897 in Oxford, Llano County, Texas. She died on 7 April 1989 in Llano, Texas at the age of 91 years, 4 months. She married Cash Moss on 1 June 1916 in Llano, Texas.

Children of Eula Irene Garrett and Cash Moss

14861 i.   Taylor J Moss. Taylor J was born on 8 September 1917 in Llano, Texas. He died on 26 January 1918 in Llano, Texas.

14862 ii.   Matthew Firmon Moss. Matthew Firmon was born on 10 April 1919 in Llano, Texas. He died on 15 May 1995 in Fort Worth, Tarrant County, Texas.

14863 iii.   Ada Lee Moss. Ada Lee was born about 1922 in Texas.

14864 iv.   James Cash Moss. James Cash was born on 20 January 1924 in Llano, Texas. He died on 18 May 1997 in Tulsa, Tulsa County, Oklahoma.

1487. **Charles Tate Moss.** (Sarah 'Sallie' Byfield-3; Holmes Byfield-2; Abraham H Byfield-1)

Charles Tate was born on 14 September 1898 in Llano, Llano County, Texas. He died on 18 December 1955 in Llano, Llano County, Texas at the age of 57 years, 3 months. He was buried in Llano County, Texas. He was the son of Charles Tate Moss and Sarah 'Sallie' Byfield. He married Maurine Berry.

Spouse: Maurine Berry.

Maurine was born about 1902 in Texas. She married Charles Tate Moss.

Children of Maurine Berry and Charles Tate Moss

14871 i.   Charles T Moss. Charles T was born about 1923 in Texas.

14872 ii.   June Moss. June was born about 1926 in Texas.

1491.   **Charles Vernon Wilson.** (Nancy Caroline Byfield-3; Holmes Byfield-2; Abraham H Byfield-1)

Charles Vernon was born on 29 May 1889 in Click, Llano County, Texas. He died on 7 April 1932 in Temple, Bell County, Texas at the age of 42 years, 10 months. He was buried in Llano, Llano County, Texas. He was the son of Robert E Lee Wilson and Nancy Caroline Byfield. He married Beulah L Click.

Spouse: Beulah L Click.

Beulah L was born about 1894 in Texas. She married Charles Vernon Wilson.

Children of Beulah L Click and Charles Vernon Wilson

14911 i.   Thomas W Wilson. Thomas W was born about 1914 in Texas.

14912 ii.   Imogene Wilson. Imogene was born about 1918 in Texas.

1492.   **Ora Wilson.** (Nancy Caroline Byfield-3; Holmes Byfield-2; Abraham H Byfield-1)

Ora was born in July 1891 in Texas. She died in 1945 in Llano County, Texas at the age of 53 years, 6 months. She was buried in Llano, Llano County, Texas. She was the daughter of Robert E Lee Wilson and Nancy Caroline Byfield. She married G W Nullmeyer on 4 October 1933 in Burnet, Texas.

Spouse: G W Nullmeyer.

G W was born about 1872 in Missouri. He married Ora Wilson on 4 October 1933 in Burnet, Texas.

1493. **Hester 'Hettie' Wilson.** (Nancy Caroline Byfield-3; Holmes Byfield-2; Abraham H Byfield-1)

Hester 'Hettie' was born on 31 July 1893 in Oxford, Llano County, Texas. She died on 5 October 1974 in Hillsboro, Hill County, Texas at the age of 81 years, 2 months. She was the daughter of Robert E Lee Wilson and Nancy Caroline Byfield. She married Cone.

Spouse: Cone.

He married Hester 'Hettie' Wilson.

1494. **Ruth Wilson.** (Nancy Caroline Byfield-3; Holmes Byfield-2; Abraham H Byfield-1)

Ruth was born November 27, 1900 in Llano, Llano County, Texas. She died October 24, 1976 in Atlanta, Fulton, Georgia. She was buried in Llano, Llano County, Texas. She was the daughter of Robert E Lee Wilson and Nancy Caroline Byfield. She married Homer Scott Patterson.

Spouse: Homer Scott Patterson.

Homer Scott was born September 22, 1898 in Dawson County, Georgia. He died about 1950 in Atlanta, Fulton, Georgia. He married Ruth Wilson.

Children of Ruth Wilson and Homer Scott Patterson

14941 i.   Homer S Patterson Junior. Homer S was born about 1932 in Washington, District of Columbia.

GRANDCHILDREN OF MASSIA BYFIELD

1511.   **Thomas Delmar Byfield.** (Benjamin F Byfield-3; Massia Byfield-2; Abraham H Byfield-1)

Son of Benjamin F Byfield and Elizabeth Mary Rector. Born 25 October 1849 in Jennings County, Indiana. Died 6 October 1864 in Montgomery, Jennings County, Indiana. Buried in Hopewell Cemetery, Commiskey, Jennings County, Indiana. Thomas was just 14 years old when he died.

1512.   **Lester Rector Byfield.** (Benjamin F Byfield-3; Massia Byfield-2; Abraham H Byfield-1)

Son of Benjamin F Byfield and Elizabeth Mary Rector. Born 9 March 1853 in Jennings County, Indiana. Died 19 December 1929 in Greene County, Missouri. Buried in Hazelwood Cemetery, Springfield, Greene County, Missouri. Married Annie Belle Glenn 2 August 1876 in Jennings County, Indiana.

Lester and Annie moved their family from Indiana to the Springfield, Missouri area around 1885. Lester bought 40 acres in the southeast corner of Section 11 in the Brookline Township of Greene County, just a few miles southwest of Springfield. They were the first of the Byfields to settle in southwest Missouri though others would follow including several of Lester's cousins.

Many of Lester and Annie's children stayed around the Springfield and Joplin areas of Missouri. A few ended up around East Saint Louis and a couple migrated to northeastern Oklahoma.

Spouse: Annie Belle Glenn.

Daughter of Johannis Glenn and Melissa Jane Biggs. Born 6 July 1858 in North Vernon, Jennings County, Indiana. Died 12 May 1942 in Tulsa, Tulsa County, Oklahoma. Buried in Springfield, Greene County, Missouri. Married Lester Rector Byfield 2 August 1876 in

Jennings County, Indiana.

After her husband's death, Annie was living with her oldest son, Leroy. At the time of her death she was probably living with her son, Bruce in Tulsa, Oklahoma.

Children of Annie Belle Glenn and Lester Rector Byfield

+ 15121 i.   Leroy 'Roy' Byfield. Born 2 February 1877 in Indiana. Died 20 September 1931 in Brookline, Greene County, Missouri.

15122 ii.   Leora Byfield. Born 27 June 1878 in Indiana. Died 4 August 1879 in Indiana.

+ 15123 iii.   Hugh Kenneth Byfield. Born 4 September 1879 in Indiana. Died 2 November 1930 in Missouri.

15124 iv.   Corwin R Byfield. Born 11 February 1882 in Indiana. Died 1 June 1924 in Missouri.

+ 15125 v.   Elmyra 'Myra' Byfield. Born 22 July 1884 in Indiana. Died 4 July 1953 in East Saint Louis, Saint Clair County, Illinois.

+ 15126 vi.   Delmer Byfield. Born 29 June 1887 in Brookline, Greene County, Missouri. Died 13 May 1941 in San Diego.

15127 vii.   Elizabeth Mary 'Lizzy' Byfield. Born 17 July 1889 in Brookline, Greene County, Missouri. Died 29 August 1974 in Collinsville, Madison County, Illinois.

+ 15128 viii.   Bruce Byfield. Born 31 August 1891 in Missouri. Died 1 April 1959 in Tulsa, Tulsa County, Oklahoma.

15129 ix.   Mabel Byfield. Born 20 February 1894 in Brookline, Greene County, Missouri. Died 13 September 1987 in Tulsa, Tulsa County, Oklahoma.

+ 1512A x.   Maurice Byfield. Born 7 July 1896 in Brookline, Greene County, Missouri. Died 21 October 1981 in Lakeland, Polk County, Florida.

+ 1512B xi.   Louella Marie Byfield. Born 9 November 1901 in Green City, Hickory, Missouri. Died 27 October 1974 in Tulsa, Osage County, Oklahoma.

1513.   **Sardius[25] Henry Byfield.** (Benjamin F Byfield-3; Massia Byfield-2; Abraham H Byfield-1)

Son of Benjamin F Byfield and Elizabeth Mary Rector. Born 19 April

---

25 Sometimes recorded as Sardus or Sardis. Sardinian mythology included a hero named "Sardus". Sardius is a red stone also known as carnelian – one of the precious stones recorded in the Bible. "Sardis" was the name of the capitol of Lydia and is one of seven churches mentioned in the Biblical book of Revelations.

1855 in Jennings County, Indiana. Died 1924 in Indiana (68 years, 8 months). Married Deborah C Young 13 May 1875 in Scott County, Indiana. Married Mary E 'Polly' Hutchinson 2 October 1881 in Jennings County, Indiana.

Sardius married his second cousin, Deborah Young. She died when the couple had been married only five years. A few years after his first wife's death he married Polly Hutchinson. Sardius and Polly moved from Jennings County to Boone County in 1888 and remained there for the rest of their lives.

Spouse: Deborah C Young.

Ref: 1146. Deborah C Young

Children of Deborah C Young and Sardius Henry Byfield

15131 i.   Flora Byfield. Born about 1875 in Indiana. Died _____ in _____.

+ 15132 ii.   Maude Marier Byfield. Born February 1876 in Lebanon, Boone County, Indiana. Died 10 September 1940 in Boone County, Indiana.

+ 15133 iii.   Claude Clement Byfield. Born 15 January 1878 in Indiana. Died *20 July 1949* in *Indiana*.

Spouse: Mary E 'Polly' Hutchinson.

Daughter of Joseph Isaac Hutchinson and Phebe A Wells[26]. Born December 1859 in Indiana. Died _____ in _____.
She married Duncan Blake 19 January 1879 in Jefferson County, Indiana. Married Sardius Henry Byfield 2 October 1881 in Jennings County, Indiana. In 1930, at age 70, she was living with her step-daughter, Maude, in Boone County, Indiana.

Children of Mary E 'Polly' Hutchinson and Sardius Henry Byfield

15134 i.   Carrie Belle Byfield. Born June 1882 in Indiana. Died 25 November 1901 in Center Township, Boone County, Indiana.

+ 15135 ii.   Lester Byfield. Born 4 August 1899 in Boon County, Indiana. Died

---

26   Mary was a Blake when she married Sardius Byfield. Her son, Lester, gave his mother's maiden name as Hutchinson in his marriage license record. There is a Mary E Hutchison that married a Duncan Blake in early 1879 in Jefferson County. Duncan Blake is remarried around 1890 so it's possible the first marriage ended in divorce. Phebe and Joseph Hutchison lived in Jefferson County and had a daughter Mary of the right age. This connection is pretty circumstantial. Really need to find some record to positively identify the Mary that was the second wife of Sardius Byfield.

August 1972 in Indianapolis, Marion County, Indiana.

1514.   **Marietta Byfield.** (Benjamin F Byfield-3; Massia Byfield-2; Abraham H Byfield-1)

Daughter of Benjamin F Byfield and Elizabeth Mary Rector. Born 17 March 1858 in Jennings County, Indiana. Died 2 March 1935 in Pacific, Franklin, Missouri. Buried in Lonesome Hill Cemetery, Phillipsburg, Laclede County, Missouri. Married William Webster Johnson 1878 in _____.   Marietta and William moved from Indiana to Missouri around 1883.

Spouse: William Webster Johnson.

Son of John B Johnson and Nancy Fowler. Born 16 September 1857 in Jennings County, Indiana. Died 31 March 1930 in Union, Laclede County, Missouri. Buried in Lonesome Hill Cemetery, Phillipsburg, Laclede County, Missouri. Married Marietta Byfield 1878 in _____.

Children of Marietta Byfield and William Webster Johnson

+ 15141 i.   Jennie Pearl Johnson. Born 8 September 1877 in Jennings County, Indiana. Died 14 September 1949 in Lebanon, Laclede County, Missouri.

15142 ii.   Elizabeth Johnson. Born 17 November 1879 in Indiana. Died _____ in _____.

+ 15143 iii.   Rutherford Benjamin Johnson. Born 18 November 1882 in Indiana. Died 3 November 1958 in Springfield, Greene County, Missouri.

+ 15144 iv.   Orlando Oliver Vincent Johnson. Born 14 August 1884 in Phillipsburg, Missouri. Died 10 February 1963 in _____.

15145 v.   Wilbert Johnson. Born March 1888 in Missouri. Died _____ in _____.

+ 15146 vi.   Marietha Johnson. Born 29 July 1891 in Missouri. Died 30 May 1979 in _____.

+ 15147 vii.   Naomi Johnson. Born 24 July 1894 in Missouri. Died 22 October 1974 in Springfield, Greene County, Missouri.

15148 viii.   Johnnie Johnson. Born 14 March 1898 in _____. Died 19 March 1898 in _____.

15149 ix.   Sherman Johnson. Born November 1899 in Missouri. Died _____ in _____.

1521.   **Charles Harrison Imel.** (Mary Ann Byfield-3; Massia Byfield-2; Abraham H Byfield-1)

Son of William Henry Imel and Mary Ann Byfield. Born 21 September 1857 in Indian Point, Knox County, Illinois. Died 29 January 1944 in Foster, Bates County, Missouri, (86 years, 4 months). Buried in Woodfin Cemetery, Bates County, Missouri, according to his death certificate. Married Irene Emmeline Woodfin 2 April 1882 in Bates County, Missouri.   Charles' father died when he was young so Charles was raised by Mary Ann's second husband, Jesse Mullies. In the 1870 census, Charles was listed as a Mullies rather than as an Imel.

Spouse: Irene Emmeline Woodfin.

Daughter of John Woodfin and Emily Brians. Born 9 August 1862 in Walnut, Bates County, Missouri. Died 12 April 1946 in Walnut, Bates County, Missouri, (83 years, 8 months). Buried in Woodfin Cemetery, Bates County, Missouri. Married Charles Harrison Imel 2 April 1882 in Bates County, Missouri.

Children of Irene Emmeline Woodfin and Charles Harrison Imel

15211 i.   Anna Pearl Imel. Born 2 September 1882 in LeRoy, Coffey, Kansas. Died 11 July 1973 in Pittsburg, Crawford County, Kansas.

15212 ii.   Aubrey Imel. Born 26 March 1884 in Walnut, Bates County, Missouri. Died 18 October 1885 in Walnut, Bates County, Missouri.

+ 15213 iii.   William Harley Imel. Born 31 August 1886 in Walnut, Bates County, Missouri. Died 1 April 1947 in Webb City, Jasper County, Missouri.

1522.   **M Westfall Imel.** (Mary Ann Byfield-3; Massia Byfield-2; Abraham H Byfield-1)

Son of William Henry Imel and Mary Ann Byfield. Born May 1859 in Illinois. Died _____ in _____.   Westfall Imel shows up with his mother and father in the 1860 census in Illinois and then with his mother and step-father (Jesse Mullies) in the 1870 census in Missouri.   He is likely in Leadville, Colorado in 1880 as there is a census listing M W Imel, a 20 year old miner, parents both born in Indiana.   Two lines down from this listing is John Mulis, a 27 year old miner, who could possibly be Westfall's step-brother. No further records of Westfall Imel have been found.

1523. **Henry Mason Mullies.** (Mary Ann Byfield-3; Massia Byfield-2; Abraham H Byfield-1)

Son of Jesse Mullies and Mary Ann Byfield. Born 4 February 1865 in Knox County, Illinois. Died 21 December 1944 in Polk County, Arkansas (79 years, 10 months). Married Nina Knowles 19 April 1919 in Miller, Arkansas.

Spouse: Nina Knowles.

Daughter of Reuben Jasper Knowles and Cassie Anderson. Born 18 April 1871 in Texas. Died 23 September 1955 in Arkansas City, Arkansas County, Arkansas (84 years, 5 months). Married Henry Mason Mullies 19 April 1919 in Miller, Arkansas. Previously married William Eli Coyle 24 January 1889 in Camp, Texas.

1524. **Elfreda Florence Mullies.** (Mary Ann Byfield-3; Massia Byfield-2; Abraham H Byfield-1)

Daughter of Jesse Mullies and Mary Ann Byfield. Born 11 November 1866 in Mound City, Linn County, Kansas. Died 21 April 1956 in Nevada, Vernon County, Missouri, (89 years, 5 months). Buried in McKill Cemetery, Vernon County, Missouri. Married Samuel J Titus 18 January 1899 in Vernon County, Missouri.

Spouse: Samuel J Titus.

Son of Harmon Riley Titus and Minerva Nelson. Born 15 April 1862 in Indiana. Died 29 January 1929 in Harrison, Vernon County, Missouri, (66 years, 9 months). Buried in McKill Cemetery, Vernon County, Missouri. Married Elfreda Florence Mullies 18 January 1899 in Vernon County, Missouri.

Children of Elfreda Florence Mullies and Samuel J Titus

15241 i.   Harvey Massy Titus. Born 8 November 1900 in Missouri. Died May

1928 in Pittsburg, Crawford County, Kansas.

+ 15242 ii.　　Charles Duke Titus. Born 8 May 1902 in Bronaugh, Vernon County, Missouri. Died 12 March 1959 in El Dorado Springs, Cedar County, Missouri.

1531.　　**Harriett B 'Hattie' Imel.** (Julia Ann Byfield-3; Massia Byfield-2; Abraham H Byfield-1)

Daughter of Peche Harrison Imel and Julia Ann Byfield. Born January 1856 in Illinois. Died about 1929 in Linn County, Kansas (about 73 years). Married Oscar C Spurgeon 6 November 1874 in Coffey County, Kansas. This marriage seem to have not lasted long as Julia remarried just a few years later and Oscar was listed as a prison inmate in the 1880 census. Married George Gilbert Holmes 22 June 1878 in Coffey County, Kansas.

Spouse: Oscar C Spurgeon.

Son of Daniel C Spurgeon and Mary A. Born 1850 in Ohio. Died _____ in _____. Married Harriett B 'Hattie' Imel 6 November 1874 in Coffey County, Kansas.

Children of Harriett B 'Hattie' Imel and Oscar C Spurgeon

15311 i.　　Addie Spurgeon. Born about 1876 in Kansas. Died _____ in _____.

Spouse: George Gilbert Holmes.

Son of James Holmes and Mary Williams. Born 19 March 1855 in Indiana. Died 8 March 1903 in Linn County, Kansas (47 years, 11 months). Married Harriett B 'Hattie' Imel 22 June 1878 in Coffey County, Kansas.

Children of Harriett B 'Hattie' Imel and George Gilbert Holmes

+ 15312 i.　　Charles C Holmes. Born October 1878 in Kansas. Died 14 November 1916 in Mound City, Linn County, Kansas.

+ 15313 ii.　　Albert James Holmes. Born 13 September 1882 in Kansas. Died _____ in _____.

+ 15314 iii.　　Paul M Holmes. Born 12 February 1885 in LeRoy, Coffey, Kansas. Died 12 June 1965 in Missoula, Montana.

1532.   **Clara May Imel.** (Julia Ann Byfield-3; Massia Byfield-2; Abraham H Byfield-1)

Daughter of Peche Harrison Imel and Julia Ann Byfield. Born about 1858 in Illinois. Clara May is listed in the censuses through 1875. Died _____ in _____.

1533.   **Mary Lincoln Imel.** (Julia Ann Byfield-3; Massia Byfield-2; Abraham H Byfield-1)

Daughter of Peche Harrison Imel and Julia Ann Byfield. Born 30 May 1863 in Kansas. Died 17 February 1869 in Kansas (5 years, 8 months).

1534.   **Louisa Imel.** (Julia Ann Byfield-3; Massia Byfield-2; Abraham H Byfield-1)

Daughter of Peche Harrison Imel and Julia Ann Byfield. Twin sister of Lewis Imel who died young. Born 6 May 1867 in Kansas. Died 1935 in Baldwin City, Douglas County, Kansas (67 years, 8 months). Buried in Baldwin City, Douglas County, Kansas. Married Frank C Shiffer 4 January 1893 in Coffey County, Kansas.

Spouse: Frank C Shiffer.

Born March 1860 in New York. Died _____ in _____. Married Louisa Imel 4 January 1893 in Coffey County, Kansas.

Children of Louisa Imel and Frank C Shiffer

15331 i.   Frances L Shiffer. Born about 1915 in Kansas. Died _____ in _____.

1535.   **Lewis Imel.** (Julia Ann Byfield-3; Massia Byfield-2; Abraham H Byfield-1)

Son of Peche Harrison Imel and Julia Ann Byfield. Born 6 May 1867 in Kansas. Died 8 April 1869 in Kansas (1 year, 11 months).

1541.   **William Albert Byfield.** (Vermilion Wright Byfield-3; Massia Byfield-2; Abraham H Byfield-1)

Son of Vermilion Wright Byfield and Mary Elizebeth Imel. Born 24 November 1860 in Illinois. Died 17 January 1929 in Rural Colony, Anderson County, Kansas (68 years, 1 month). Buried in Cedar Vale Cemetery, Neosho Falls, Kansas. Married Isadora Jones 13 October 1886 in Woodson County, Kansas.

William Albert farmed around the Neosho Falls area his entire life.

Spouse: Isadora Jones.

Daughter of Jeffery Jones and Margarett Elda Cunningham. Born 1 August 1868 in Rossville, Clinton County, Indiana. Died 25 February 1957 in Neosho Falls, Woodson County, Kansas (88 years, 6 months). Buried 28 February 1957 in the Cedar Vale Cemetery, Neosho Falls, Kansas. Married William Albert Byfield 13 October 1886 in Woodson, Kansas.

Isadora Jones

Children of Isadora Jones and William Albert Byfield

+ 15411 i.   Artie Belle Byfield. Born 17 September 1887 in Colony, Anderson County, Kansas. Died 7 December 1967 in Iola, Allen County, Kansas.

+ 15412 ii.   Wessie Arlington Byfield. Born 2 April 1889 in North Cot, Anderson County, Kansas. Died 30 December 1966 in Yates Center, Woodson County, Kansas.

+ 15413 iii.   Nina Edith Byfield. Born 4 November 1890 in Anderson County, Kansas. Died 15 June 1988 in Iola, Allen, Kansas.

+ 15414 iv.   Winona Mae Byfield. Born 31 August 1892 in Coffey County, Kansas. Died 29 March 1970 in Boise, Idaho.

+ 15415 v.   Margaret Elizabeth Byfield. Born 26 September 1894 in Coffey County, Kansas. Died 29 July 1984 in Iola, Allen, Kansas.

+ 15416 vi.   William Leo Byfield. Born 20 December 1899 in Coffey County, Kansas. Died January 1978 in Shawnee Mission, Johnson, Kansas.

+ 15417 vii.   Beulah Beatrice Byfield. Born 15 September 1905 in Coffey County, Kansas. Died 8 August 1991 in Iola, Allen, Kansas.

+ 15418 viii.   Milton Ray Byfield. Born 27 November 1909 in Coffey County, Kansas. Died 10 December 1961 in Kansas City, Missouri.

1542.   **Emma Frances Byfield.** (Vermilion Wright Byfield-3; Massia

Byfield-2; Abraham H Byfield-1)

Daughter of Vermilion Wright Byfield and Mary Elizebeth Imel. Born 28 September 1863 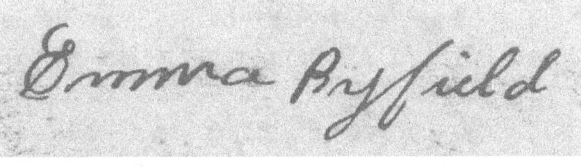 in Illinois. Died 24 December 1916 in Neosho Falls, Woodson County, Kansas (53 years, 2 months). Married Louis August Godfrey Weiland 19 March 1892 in Geneva, Allen, Kansas.

Spouse: Louis August Godfrey Weiland.

Son of August Louis Weiland and Caroline Frederick. Born 23 September 1866 in Bethel, Marion County, Indiana. Died 27 March 1932 in Coffeyville, Montgomery County, Kansas, (65 years, 6 months). Married Emma Frances Byfield 19 March 1892 in Geneva, Allen, Kansas.

Children of Emma Frances Byfield and Louis August Godfrey Weiland

+ 15421 i.   Lovela Ethel Weiland. Born 9 February 1893 in Neosho Falls, Woodson, Kansas. Died 14 October 1918 in Neosho Falls, Woodson, Kansas.

+ 15422 ii.   Vermilion Lee Weiland. Born 8 April 1898 in Neosho Falls, Woodson, Kansas. Died 7 March 1971 in Coffeyville, Montgomery County, Kansas.

1543.   **Olive May Byfield.** (Vermilion Wright Byfield-3; Massia Byfield-2; Abraham H Byfield-1)

Daughter of Vermilion Wright Byfield and Mary Elizebeth Imel. Born 14 June 1869 in Kansas. Died 1962 in Neosho Falls, Woodson County, Kansas (92 years, 6 months). Buried in 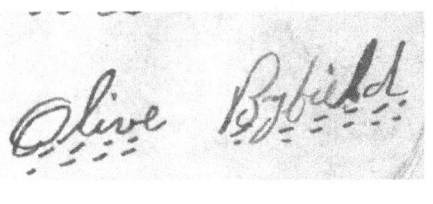 Neosho Falls, Woodson County, Kansas. Married George F Weiland 12 December 1897 in _____. They had no children.

Spouse: George F Weiland.

Born February 1874 in Indiana. Died 1936 in _____ (61 years, 11 months). Married Olive May Byfield 12 December 1897 in _____.

1544.   **Charles Alfred Byfield.** (Vermilion Wright Byfield-3; Massia Byfield-2; Abraham H Byfield-1)

Son of Vermilion Wright Byfield and Mary Elizebeth Imel. Born 8 September 1872 in Kansas. Died 1 March 1940 in Neosho Falls, Woodson County, Kansas (67 years, 5 months). Buried in Cedar Vale Cemetery, Neosho Falls, Kansas. Married Mary Elizebeth Titas 22 June 1898 in Allen County, Kansas.

Spouse: Mary Elizebeth Titas.

Born 27 August 1878 in Nebraska. Died 30 July 1946 in Neosho Falls, Woodson County, Kansas (67 years, 11 months). Buried in Cedar Vale Cemetery, Neosho Falls, Kansas. Married Charles Alfred Byfield 22 June 1898 in Allen County, Kansas.

Children of Mary Elizebeth Titas and Charles Alfred Byfield

+ 15441 i.   Reva E Byfield. Born 11 September 1899 in Kansas. Died 10 February 1992 in Kansas.

15442 ii.   Velma F Byfield. Born 2 July 1901 in Kansas. Died 8 September 1994 in Yates Center, Woodson, Kansas.

1545.   **Sara Florance Byfield.** (Vermilion Wright Byfield-3; Massia Byfield-2; Abraham H Byfield-1)

Daughter of Vermilion Wright Byfield and Mary Elizebeth Imel. Born 2 October 1875 in Kansas. Died 22 April 1903 in Neosho Falls, Woodson County, Kansas (27 years, 6 months). Married George N Dulinsky 27 August 1901 in _____. Sara and George had no children.

Spouse: George N Dulinsky.

Son of William M Dulinsky and Alice H Bryan. Born January 1884 in Kansas. Died _____ in _____. Married Sara Florance Byfield 27 August 1901 in _____.

1546.   **Leonard Lee Byfield.** (Vermilion Wright Byfield-3; Massia Byfield-2; Abraham H Byfield-1)

Son of Vermilion Wright Byfield and Mary Elizebeth Imel. Born 4 August 1877 in Kansas. Died September 1960 in Neosho Falls, Woodson County, Kansas (83 years, 28 days). Buried in Cedar Vale Cemetery, Neosho Falls, Kansas. Married June Nettie Duncan 23 December 1902 in _____ .

Spouse: June Nettie Duncan.[27]

Born 1879 in Lincoln County, Kansas Died 1955 in Kansas (76 years). Buried in Cedar Vale Cemetery, Neosho Falls, Kansas. Married Leonard Lee Byfield 23 December 1902 in _____ .

Children of June Nettie Duncan and Leonard Lee Byfield

15461 i. Nellie F Byfield. Born about 1905 in Coffey County, Kansas. Died _____ in _____ .

+ 15462 ii. Lyle L Byfield. Born 16 December 1906 in Allen County, Kansas. Died February 1983 in Wakita, Grant, Oklahoma.

+ 15463 iii. Charles L Byfield. Born 15 April 1911 in Woodson County, Kansas. Died October 1985 in Wichita, Sedgwick County, Kansas.

+ 15464 iv. Saddie O Byfield. Born 25 October 1914 in Woodson County Died 12 April 2002 in Yates Center, Woodson, Kansas.

1547. **Thomas Westfall Byfield.** (Vermilion Wright Byfield-3; Massia Byfield-2; Abraham H Byfield-1)

Son of Vermilion Wright Byfield and Mary Elizebeth Imel. Born 29 May 1881 in Kansas. Died 19 April 1946 in Los Angeles, California (64 years, 10 months). Married Letha Tressa Mae Gillette 13 June 1915 in Woodson County, Kansas.

Spouse: Letha Tressa Mae Gillette.

Daughter of Enos N Gillette and Mary E Gillette. Born 1 May 1895 in Kansas. Died 11 July 1979 in Coffey, Kansas, (84 years, 2 months). Married Thomas Westfall Byfield 13 June 1915 in Woodson County, Kansas.

Children of Letha Tressa Mae Gillette and Thomas Westfall Byfield

+ 15471 i. Thomas Wright Byfield. Born 3 June 1916 in Leroy, Coffey, Kansas. Died 8 June 1973 in Sepulveda, Los Angeles County, California.

---

27 Also found listed as J. M. Dunton and Junetta Jane Dunton.

+ 15472 ii.   Mary Frances Byfield. Born 3 January 1929 in Kansas. Died
               _____ in _____.

1551.   **Willard Elmer Baldwin.** (Jennette Byfield-3; Massia Byfield-2;
         Abraham H Byfield-1)

Son of Martin Varner Baldwin and Jennette
Byfield. Born 29 September 1867 in Missouri.
Died 22 December 1953 in _____.
Buried in Okmulgee, Okmulgee County,
Oklahoma. Married Mary Christena Jacobson
1897 in _____.

Spouse: Mary Christena Jacobson.

Born 18 December 1868 in Gilford, Nodaway
County, Missouri. Died 11 January 1934 in
Severa, Okmulgee County Oklahoma (65 years,
24 days). Married Willard Elmer Baldwin 1897 in

_____.

*Willard Elmer
Baldwin*

Children of Mary Christena Jacobson and Willard E Baldwin

15511 i.   Myrtle E Baldwin. Born 12 July 1898 in Missouri. Died June 1980 in
            Okmulgee, Okmulgee County, Oklahoma.

15512 ii.   Jessie Frances Baldwin. Born 5 August 1901 in Guilford, Nodaway
            County, Missouri. Died 29 December 1970 in Okmulgee, Okmulgee County,
            Oklahoma.

15513 iii. Willard Elmer Jr Baldwin. Born 10 February 1904 in Kansas. Died 5
            February 1921 in _____.

15514 iv.   Helen C Baldwin. Born 27 February 1906 in Missouri. Died 12
            November 1987 in Okmulgee, Okmulgee, County Oklahoma.

15515 v.   Baldwin. Born 1909 in Oklahoma. Died _____ in
            _____.

15516 vi.   Eveline Baldwin. Born 27 April 1909 in Missouri. Died 20 March
            1967 in Okmulgee Oklahoma.

1552.   **Rosa Emily Baldwin.** (Jennette Byfield-3; Massia Byfield-2;
         Abraham H Byfield-1)

Daughter of Martin Varner Baldwin and Jennette Byfield. Born March 1870 in Kansas. Died 11 May 1957 in Kansas City, Wyandotte County, Kansas (87 years, 2 months). Buried in Kansas City, Wyandotte County, Kansas. Married Jarrett Tribble Miller 29 August 1885 in Buchanan, Missouri.

Spouse: Jarrett Tribble Miller.

Born March 1859 in Wathena, Doniphan, Kansas. Died 14 February 1948 in Kansas City, Kansas (88 years, 11 months). Married Rosa Emily Baldwin 29 August 1885 in Buchanan, Missouri.

Children of Rosa Emily Baldwin and Jarrett Tribble Miller

15521 i.   Maggie Miller. Born October 1887 in Doniphan, Kansas. Died _____ in _____ .

15522 ii.   William H Miller. Born August 1889 in Doniphan, Kansas. Died _____ in _____ .

15523 iii.   Bessie Naomie Miller. Born 2 September 1891 in Troy, Doniphan, Kansas. Died 30 May 1958 in Kansas City, Wyandotte County, Kansas.

15524 iv.   Clarence Miller. Born 1894 in Kansas. Died _____ in _____ .

15525 v.   Charles Miller. Born November 1897 in Doniphan, Kansas. Died _____ in _____ .

15526 vi.   Lola R Miller. Born 1902 in Kansas. Died _____ in _____ .

15527 vii.   Lura Lucille Miller. Born 21 June 1908 in Clay, Missouri. Died 28 September 1989 in Kansas City, Wyandotte County, Kansas.

15528 viii.   Nora Miller. Born about 1909 in Missouri. Died _____ in _____ .

15529 ix.   Irene B Miller. Born about 1910 in Missouri. Died _____ in _____ .

1552A x.   Carl Miller. Born about 1914 in Kansas. Died _____ in _____ .

1553.   **Mary E Baldwin.** (Jennette Byfield-3; Massia Byfield-2; Abraham H Byfield-1)

Daughter of Martin Varner Baldwin and Jennette Byfield. Born 30

May 1872 in Linn County, Kansas. Died 1 August 1873 in Linn County, Kansas (1 year, 2 months).

1554.   **Martin E Baldwin.** (Jennette Byfield-3; Massia Byfield-2; Abraham H Byfield-1)

Son of Martin Varner Baldwin and Jennette Byfield. Born about 1874 in Kansas. Died _____ in _____.

1555.   **Louisa Baldwin.** (Jennette Byfield-3; Massia Byfield-2; Abraham H Byfield-1)

Daughter of Martin Varner Baldwin and Jennette Byfield. Born about 1876 in Kansas. Died _____ in _____.

1556.   **Minnie Imel.** (Jennette Byfield-3; Massia Byfield-2; Abraham H Byfield-1)

Daughter of Peche Harrison Imel and Jennette Byfield. Born about 1878 in Kansas. Died _____ in _____.

1557.   **Maude M Imel.** (Jennette Byfield-3; Massia Byfield-2; Abraham H Byfield-1)

Daughter of Peche Harrison Imel and Jennette Byfield. Born about 1882 in Kansas. Died _____ in _____.   In 1910 Maude and her mother, Jennette, are listed together in the census for Saint Joseph, Missouri. They are both listed with the last name Baldwin. They are both working as laundresses.

1561.   **Hattie Etora Byfield.** (Marion Josephus Byfield-3; Massia Byfield-2; Abraham H Byfield-1)

Daughter of Marion Josephus Byfield and Susan Angeline Biers. Born 30 April 1871 in Leroy, Coffey, Kansas. Died 28 January 1957 in Boise, Ada County, Idaho (85 years, 8 months). Buried in Boise, Ada County, Idaho. Married Charles G Massey 16 November 1919 in Boise, Ada County, Idaho. Also married Ira J Gardner 1893 in _____.

Spouse: Charles G Massey.

Born 10 May 1868 in Duart, Kent, Ontario, Canada. Died 21 December 1942 in Boise, Ada County, Idaho (74 years, 7 months). Married Hattie Etora Byfield 16 November 1919 in Boise, Ada County, Idaho.

Spouse: Ira J Gardner.

Son of Charles Gardner and Ann Dodsworth. Born June 1869 in Iowa. Died 1934 in Idaho (64 years, 7 months). Buried in Nampa, Canyon County, Idaho. Married Hattie Etora Byfield 1893 in _____.

Children of Hattie Etora Byfield and Ira J Gardner

15611 i.   Charles L Gardner. Born 1893 in Missouri. Died _____ in _____.

+ 15612 ii.   Lottie Leora Gardner. Born 30 May 1894 in Missouri. Died 4 March 1981 in Boise, Ada County, Idaho.

1562.   **Mary Etta Byfield.** (Marion Josephus Byfield-3; Massia Byfield-2; Abraham H Byfield-1)

Daughter of Marion Josephus Byfield and Susan Angeline Biers. Born 19 September 1872 in Leroy, Coffey, Kansas. Died 8 September 1950 in Nampa, Canyon, Idaho (77 years, 11 months). Married William Henry Adams 29 September 1898 in Boise, Ada County, Idaho.

Spouse: William Henry Adams.

Son of Charles Adams and Elizabeth Amanda Gardner. Born 1 December 1876 in Boise, Ada County, Idaho. Died 4 March 1941 in Nampa, Canyon County, Idaho, (64 years, 3 months). Buried in Nampa, Canyon County, Idaho. Married Mary Etta Byfield 29

September 1898 in Boise, Ada County, Idaho.

Children of Mary Etta Byfield and William Henry Adams

15621 i.   John Howard Adams. Born 8 February 1900 in Silver City, Owyhee County, Idaho. Died 1 May 1975 in Fairbanks, Fairbanks North Star County, Alaska.

15622 ii.   Harry Fay Adams. Born 12 February 1902 in Silver City, Owyhee County, Idaho. Died 7 August 1957 in Nampa, Canyon County, Idaho.

+ 15623 iii. Willa Leora Adams. Born 7 December 1908 in Reynolds, Owyhee County, Idaho. Died 15 September 1985 in Nampa, Canyon County, Idaho.

1563.   **Bernice Blanche Byfield.** (Marion Josephus Byfield-3; Massia Byfield-2; Abraham H Byfield-1)

Daughter of Marion Josephus Byfield and Susan Angeline Biers. Born 14 February 1875 in Leroy, Coffey, Kansas. Died 31 May 1892 in Walnut, Bates County, Missouri (17 years, 3 months).

1564.   **Arley Oliver Byfield.** (Marion Josephus Byfield-3; Massia Byfield-2; Abraham H Byfield-1)

Son of Marion Josephus Byfield and Susan Angeline Biers. Born 2 February 1877 in Leroy, Coffey, Kansas. Died 3 December 1946 in Union, Union, Oregon (69 years, 10 months). Buried in Union Cemetery, Union County, Oregon. Married Nellie Mitchell 10 April 1905 in Jackson, Missouri.   In the marriage records, Arley Byfield is recorded as residing in Owahee County, Oregon.   His wife, Nellie Mitchell, is recorded as residing in New York, New York. Interesting that the marriage was in Kansas City.

Spouse: Nellie Mitchell.

Born about 1881 in Ohio. Died 17 November 1939 in Union County, Oregon (about 58 years, 10 months). Buried in Union Cemetery, Union County, Oregon. Married Arley Oliver Byfield 10 April 1905 in Jackson, Missouri.

1565.   **Fay Ora Byfield.** (Marion Josephus Byfield-3; Massia Byfield-2; Abraham H Byfield-1)

Son of Marion Josephus Byfield and Susan Angeline Biers. Born 15 September 1879 in Leroy, Coffey, Kansas. Died 29 March 1953 in Great Falls, Cascade County, Montana (73 years, 6 months). Buried in Shelby, Toole County, Montana. Married Gertrude Alice Rathbun 1933 in Ada County, Idaho.

Spouse: Gertrude Alice Rathbun.

Daughter of Clarence Eugene Rathbun and Fannie C Stewart. Born about 1895 in Montana. Died _____ in _____. Married Fay Ora Byfield 1933 in Ada County, Idaho.

Children of Gertrude Alice Rathbun and Fay Ora Byfield

+ 15651 i.   John R Byfield. Born 8 September 1934 in Idaho. Died 8 June 2010 in Mount Vernon, Skagit, Washington.

15652 ii.   Robert M Byfield. Born 21 December 1936 in Idaho. Died 25 January 1980 in Washington.

1571.   **William Melvin Allen.** (Louisa Byfield-3; Massia Byfield-2; Abraham H Byfield-1)

Son of Calvin L Allen and Louisa Byfield. Born 10 October 1865 in Coffey County, Kansas. Died _____ in _____. Married Arilla May Taylor 1890 in _____.

Spouse: Arilla May Taylor.

Born 4 May 1870 in Illinois. Died 22 July 1940 in Salem Township, Knox County, Illinois (70 years, 2 months). Married William Melvin Allen 1890 in _____.

Children of Arilla May Taylor and William Melvin Allen

+ 15711 i.   Roy Otis Allen. Born 25 October 1891 in Union Town, Illinois. Died 14 March 1966 in Farmington, Fulton, Illinois.

+ 15712 ii.   Clyde Valentine Allen. Born 18 October 1896 in Knox County, Illinois. Died _____ in _____.

+ 15713 iii.   Lillian M Allen. Born February 1898 in Illinois. Died _____ in _____.

+ 15714 iv.   Bruce Allen. Born about 1902 in Illinois. Died _____ in _____.

+ 15715 v.   Cecil Allen. Born 1903 in Illinois. Died 11 January 1953 in Douglas, Clark County, Illinois.

1572.   **James M Allen.** (Louisa Byfield-3; Massia Byfield-2; Abraham H Byfield-1)

Son of Calvin L Allen and Louisa Byfield. Born 24 October 1867 in Illinois. Died 26 November 1954 in _____ (87 years, 1 month). Married Nancy Ann Bennett 15 December 1897 in Hancock, Hancock County, Illinois.

Spouse: Nancy Ann Bennett.

Born 27 July 1878 in Missouri. Died 15 April 1966 in Rochelle, Ogle County, Illinois, of America (87 years, 8 months). Married James M Allen 15 December 1897 in Hancock, Hancock County, Illinois.

Children of Nancy Ann Bennett and James M Allen

15721 i.   Roy Norman Allen. Born 9 February 1899 in Illinois. Died 17 January 1943 in _____.

15722 ii.   Alis Lamine Allen. Born 2 January 1902 in Illinois. Died 14 November 1986 in Saint Petersburg, Pinellas County, Florida.

15723 iii.   Avis Irlene Allen. Born 2 January 1902 in Illinois. Died 31 March 1993 in De Kalb, De Kalb County, Illinois.

15724 iv.   Dorothy Vivian Allen. Born 26 April 1905 in Warsaw, Hancock County, Illinois. Died 22 November 1997 in West Chester, Chester County, Pennsylvania.

15725 v.   Una Belle Allen. Born 26 December 1906 in Illinois. Died 12 September 1980 in Rockford, Winnebago, Illinois.

15726 vi.   James Jefferson Allen. Born 8 February 1909 in Illinois. Died 16 August 1995 in Rochelle, Ogle County, Illinois.

1573.   **Clara M Allen.** (Louisa Byfield-3; Massia Byfield-2; Abraham H

Byfield-1)

Daughter of Calvin L Allen and Louisa Byfield. Born October 1871 in Illinois. Died _____ in _____. Married Lewis E Stephens 1890 in _____.

Spouse: Lewis E Stephens.

Son of Edward Stephens and Eliza Fisher. Born May 1866 in Iowa. Died _____ in _____. Married Clara M Allen 1890 in _____.

Children of Clara M Allen and Lewis E Stephens

15731 i.   Guy Evart Stevens. Born 14 April 1890 in Iowa. Died _____ in _____.

+ 15732 ii.   Esther Ethel Stephens. Born December 1896 in Iowa. Died _____ in _____.

15733 iii.   Paul E Stephens. Born May 1899 in Iowa. Died _____ in _____.

1574.   **John Franklin Allen.** (Louisa Byfield-3; Massia Byfield-2; Abraham H Byfield-1)

Son of Calvin L Allen and Louisa Byfield. Born about 1874 in Illinois. Died _____ in _____.

1575.   **Edwin T Allen.** (Louisa Byfield-3; Massia Byfield-2; Abraham H Byfield-1)

Son of Calvin L Allen and Louisa Byfield. Born 25 July 1877 in Illinois. Died 1931 in Union County, Iowa, (53 years, 5 months). Buried at Cromwell Cemetery, Union County, Iowa. Married Florence Belle Moreland _____ in _____.

Married: Florence Belle Moreland.

Daughter of Charles H Moreland and Mary Jane Murray. Born December 1877 in Woodford County, Illinois. Died 1959 in

Cromwell, Union, Iowa (81 years, 1 month). Married Edwin T Allen _____ in _____.

Children of Florence Belle Moreland and Edwin T Allen

15751 i.   Grace Allen. Born 1914 in Iowa. Died _____ in _____.

1576.   **Freddie Allen.** (Louisa Byfield-3; Massia Byfield-2; Abraham H Byfield-1)

Son of Calvin L Allen and Louisa Byfield. Born 25 July 1877 in Fulton County, Illinois. Died before 1920 in _____ (less than 42 years, 5 months). Married Carrie Margaret Chapman 29 August 1898 in _____.

Spouse: Carrie Margaret Chapman.

Daughter of Andrew 'Andy' Spitzer Chapman and Alice Scott. Born 1 April 1881 in Iowa. Died 21 February 1966 in Saint Louis, Missouri (84 years, 10 months). Married Freddie Allen 29 August 1898 in _____.

Children of Carrie Margaret Chapman and Freddie Allen

15761 i.   Amos Leroy Allen. Born 29 July 1899 in Nevinville, Adams County, Iowa. Died 15 October 1899 in Nevinville, Adams County, Iowa.

15762 ii.   Lloyd Allen. Born 8 March 1901 in Iowa. Died _____ in _____.

+ 15763 iii.   Acel Ray Allen. Born 7 April 1903 in Richland, Adair County, Iowa. Died _____ in _____.

15764 iv.   Goldia 'Goldie' May Allen. Born 4 August 1908 in Iowa. Died 1 January 1938 in Saint Louis, Saint Louis County, Missouri.

15765 v.   Alice May Allen. Born 15 June 1910 in Adair County, Iowa. Died _____ in _____.

15766 vi.   Floyd Allen. Born about 1913 in Summit, Adair County, Iowa. Died _____ in _____.

1577.   **Henry Allen.** (Louisa Byfield-3; Massia Byfield-2; Abraham H

Byfield-1)

Son of Calvin L Allen and Louisa Byfield. Born about 1880 in Illinois. Died _____ in _____.

1578.   **Lora Allen.** (Louisa Byfield-3; Massia Byfield-2; Abraham H Byfield-1)

Son of Calvin L Allen and Louisa Byfield. Twin to Cora Allen. Born 21 January 1882 in Illinois. Died 7 February 1965 in Missouri. Buried in Kirkwood, Saint Louis County, Missouri. Married Mae Means 15 September 1908 in Council Bluffs, Pottawattamie County, Iowa.

Spouse: Mae Means.

Daughter of Ensign K Means and Clara Hoffmaster. Born 16 November 1887 in LaCrosse, Kansas. Died 20 December 1961 in Webster Groves, Saint Louis County, Missouri (74 years, 1 month). Married Lora Allen 15 September 1908 in Council Bluffs, Pottawattamie County, Iowa.

Children of Mae Means and Lora Allen

+ 15781 i.   Gerald D Allen. Born 3 October 1909 in Iowa. Died 16 September 1965 in San Diego.

15782 ii.   Vivian Darlene Allen. Born about 1916 in Iowa. Died _____ in _____.

15783 iii.   Lyle E Allen. Born about 1918 in Iowa. Died _____ in _____.

15784 iv.   Leroy Merle Allen. Born 1 June 1921 in Shenandoah, Page Co, Iowa. Died 12 September 1976 in Saint Louis, Saint Louis City, Missouri.

1579.   **Cora F Allen.** (Louisa Byfield-3; Massia Byfield-2; Abraham H Byfield-1)

Daughter of Calvin L Allen and Louisa Byfield. Born 21 January 1882 in Illinois. Twin sister of Lora Allen. Died _____ in _____. Married Jerry M Benedict 1 January 1903 in Union

Township, Adams County, Iowa. Married Robert William Jones about 1923 in _____ .

Spouse: Jerry M Benedict.

Son of William F Benedict and Mary Powers. Born 1876 in Iowa. Died _____ in _____ . Married Cora F Allen 1 January 1903 in Union Township, Adams County, Iowa.

Children of Cora F Allen and Jerry M Benedict

15791 i.   Loraine Benedict. Born 1907 in Iowa. Died _____ in _____ .

Spouse: Robert William Jones.

Son of William Jones and Emma Dorthy Hilgemeyer. Born 14 April 1894 in Collinsville, Illinois. Died 4 March 1946 in Granite City, Madison, Illinois (51 years, 10 months). Buried 7 March 1946 in Collinsville, Madison County, Illinois. Married Ruth Irene Waymoth _____ in _____ . Also married Cora F Allen about 1923 in _____ .

157A.   **Earl Alva Allen.** (Louisa Byfield-3; Massia Byfield-2; Abraham H Byfield-1)

Son of Calvin L Allen and Louisa Byfield. Born 3 April 1884 in Illinois. Died _____ in _____ . Married Clara Josephine Johnson _____ in _____ . Lived in Shenandoah, Iowa most of his life.

Married: Clara Josephine Johnson.

Daughter of Oscar Johnson and Lena Anderson. Born December 1887 in Iowa. Died _____ in _____ . Married Earl Alva Allen _____ in _____ .

Children of Clara Josephine Johnson and Earl Alva Allen

+ 157A1 i.   Dorothy Dorene Allen. Born 26 January 1907 in Iowa. Died 17 December 1974 in Shenandoah, Page County, Iowa.

157B. **Mabel Grace Allen.** (Louisa Byfield-3; Massia Byfield-2; Abraham H Byfield-1)

Daughter of Calvin L Allen and Louisa Byfield. Born 3 March 1888 in Cass, Iowa. Died 26 March 1942 in _____ (54 years, 23 days). Married Earnest G Johnson _____ in _____. Mabel and her husband, Earnest, lived in Shenandoah, Iowa.

Married: Earnest G Johnson.

Son of Oscar Johnson and Lena Anderson. Born 20 January 1879 in Sweden. Died _____ in _____. Married Mabel Grace Allen _____ in _____.

Mabel Grace Allen

Children of Mabel Grace Allen and Earnest G Johnson

157B1 i.   Opal L Johnson. Born 1907 in Iowa. Died _____ in _____.

157B2 ii.   Paul Johnson. Born about 1912 in Iowa. Died _____ in _____.

1581. **Eva J Byfield.** (Milton Cass Byfield-3; Massia Byfield-2; Abraham H Byfield-1)

Daughter of Milton Cass Byfield and Hannah Elizabeth Randall. Born 1872 in Kansas. Died 1906 in Dade County, Missouri, (34 years). Married George A Culver 30 May 1888 in Barry, Missouri.

Spouse: George A Culver.

Born 12 August 1867 in Noble, Noble County, Indiana. Died 18 March 1915 in Greenfield, Dade County, Missouri, (47 years, 7 months). Married Eva J Byfield 30 May 1888 in Barry, Missouri.

Children of Eva J Byfield and George A Culver

15811 i.   James Harrison Culver. Born 30 October 1888 in Greenville, Dade County, Missouri. Died 21 February 1936 in Jerome, Jerome County, Idaho.

+ 15812 ii.   Dora Ella Culver. Born 14 August 1890 in Missouri. Died December 1977 in Miller, Lawrence County, Missouri.

+ 15813 iii. Leonard Milton Culver. Born 5 June 1894 in Dade County, Missouri. Died 17 September 1969 in Greenfield, Dade County, Missouri.

15814 iv.   Mary Elizabeth 'Bessie' Culver. Born 24 October 1896 in Center, Dade County, Missouri. Died 23 November 1983 in Morganton, Burke County, North Carolina.

+ 15815 v.   Charles Henry Culver. Born 15 June 1899 in Greenfield, Dade County, Missouri. Died 27 August 1972 in Bakersfield, Kern County, California.

15816 vi.   Alva Culver. Born about 1902 in Center, Dade County, Missouri. Died _____ in _____ .

1582.   **James L Byfield.** (Milton Cass Byfield-3; Massia Byfield-2; Abraham H Byfield-1)

Son of Milton Cass Byfield and Hannah Elizabeth Randall. Born 9 January 1873 in Missouri. Died 7 January 1908 in Dade County, Missouri (34 years, 11 months). Married Nora Elaine Smith 1893 in Greenfield, Dade County, Missouri.

Spouse: Nora Elaine Smith.

Daughter of Augusta Smith and Elizabeth Hicks. Born 13 July 1873 in Hamilton County, Illinois. Died 22 October 1940 in Goldencity, Barton, Missouri (67 years, 3 months). Married James L Byfield 1893 in Greenfield, Dade County, Missouri. Also married Robert E Gilliland 24 September 1914 in Dade County, Missouri.

Children of Nora Elaine Smith and James L Byfield

15821 i.   Bertha May Byfield. Born August 1896 in Missouri. Died _____ in _____ .

+ 15822 ii.   William Leslie Byfield. Born 4 December 1898 in Greenfield, Dade County, Missouri. Died 8 July 1977 in Inola, Rogers County, Oklahoma.

+ 15823 iii. Orville Byfield. Born about 1901 in Missouri. Died 6 June 1964 in San Bernardino, San Bernardino County, California.

15824 iv.   Edgar Byfield. Born 15 December 1905 in Missouri. Died 15 October

1958 in Fresno, Fresno, California.

15825 v.   James Leeman Byfield. Born 7 May 1908 in Missouri. Died 18 March 1957 in Fresno, Fresno, California.

1583.   **Mary Louise Byfield.** (Milton Cass Byfield-3; Massia Byfield-2; Abraham H Byfield-1)

Daughter of Milton Cass Byfield and Hannah Elizabeth Randall. Born about 1876 in Missouri. Died 14 December 1887 in Louisburg Twp, Montgomery County, Kansas (about 11 years, 11 months). Buried 15 December 1887 in Shady Grove Cemetery, Montgomery, Kansas.

1584.   **Flora Ann Byfield.** (Milton Cass Byfield-3; Massia Byfield-2; Abraham H Byfield-1)

Daughter of Milton Cass Byfield and Hannah Elizabeth Randall. Born 28 February 1879 in Greenfield, Dade County, Missouri. Died 29 June 1949 in Joplin, Newton County, Missouri, (70 years, 4 months). Buried in Joplin, Jasper County, Missouri. Married William Eugene Owens 26 December 1897 in Dade County, Missouri.   Flora and her husband lived around Joplin, Missouri.

Spouse: William Eugene Owens.

Born 14 July 1876 in Illinois. Died 19 December 1941 in Joplin, Jasper County, Missouri (65 years, 5 months). Buried in Joplin, Jasper County, Missouri. Married Flora Ann Byfield 26 December 1897 in Dade County, Missouri.

Children of Flora Ann Byfield and William Eugene Owens

+ 15841 i.   Crystal E Owens. Born 14 June 1898 in Missouri. Died 18 August 1971 in Joplin, Jasper County, Missouri.

1585.   **Melton Otis Albert Byfield.** (Milton Cass Byfield-3; Massia Byfield-2; Abraham H Byfield-1)

Son of Milton Cass Byfield and Hannah Elizabeth Randall. Born 22 February 1891 in Greenfield, Dade County, Missouri. Died 17 January 1954 in Fort Gibson, Muskogee County, Oklahoma, (62 years, 10 months). Buried in Three Rivers Cemetery, Okay, Wagoner County, Oklahoma. Married Jenny Lasater 9 March 1913 in Fort Gibson, Muskogee County, Oklahoma.

Spouse: Jenny Lasater.

Daughter of Thomas Lasater and Annie Eliza Graham. Born 17 February 1896 in Oklahoma. Died 2 May 1966 in Okay, Wagoner County, Oklahoma (70 years, 2 months). Buried in Three Rivers Cemetery, Okay, Wagoner County, Oklahoma. Married Melton Otis Albert Byfield 9 March 1913 in Fort Gibson, Muskogee County, Oklahoma.

Children of Jenny Lasater and Melton Otis Albert Byfield

15851 i. Annie Elizabeth Byfield. Born 6 April 1913 in Inola, Rogers County, Oklahoma. Died 29 January 1974 in Grants Pass, Josephine County, Oregon.

+ 15852 ii. Odie Jean Byfield. Born 11 February 1915 in Inola, Rogers County, Oklahoma. Died 7 January 1994 in Tulsa, Tulsa County, Oklahoma.

15853 iii. Thomas Otis Albert Byfield. Born 5 February 1916 in Inola, Rogers County, Oklahoma. Died 20 March 1971 in Klamath Falls, Klamath County, Oregon.

15854 iv. Emma Byfield. Born 29 March 1919 in Fort Gibson, Muskogee County, Oklahoma. Died 19 April 1935 in Wagoner County, Oklahoma.

15855 v. William Lee Byfield. Born 8 June 1921 in Inola, Rogers County, Oklahoma. Died 8 January 2007 in Fort Gibson, Muskogee County, Oklahoma.

15856 vi. Frances Virginia Byfield. Born about 1923 in Oklahoma. Died _____ in _____.

+ 15857 vii. Elsie Marie Byfield. Born 24 April 1925 in Inola, Rogers County, Oklahoma. Died 2 August 1979 in Muskogee, Oklahoma.

15858 viii. Ella Mae Byfield. Born 9 May 1927 in Oklahoma. Died 6 May 2009 in Okay, Wagoner County, Oklahoma.

+ 15859 ix. Pauline B 'Shorty' Byfield. Born 26 December 1930 in Inola, Rogers County, Oklahoma. Died 26 January 2009 in Muskogee, Oklahoma.

1585A x. Florene Byfield. Born about 1931 in Oklahoma. Died _____ in _____.

+ 1585B xi. Charles Henry 'Buck' Byfield. Born 15 July 1933 in Inola, Rogers County, Oklahoma. Died 25 April 2011 in Tahlequah, Cherokee County,

Oklahoma.

1585C xii.   James Russel Byfield. Born 1 June 1935 in Oklahoma. Died _____ in _____.

1585D xiii.   Allen Lee Byfield. Born 10 May 1938 in Oklahoma. Died _____ in _____.

+ 1585E xiv. David Lester Byfield. Born 9 May 1940 in Muskogee County, Oklahoma. Died 13 March 2009 in Cherokee County, Oklahoma.

Grandchildren of Andrew G Byfield

1611. **Arthur E Wells.** (Catherine Byfield-3; Andrew G Byfield-2; Abraham H Byfield-1)

Arthur E was born about 1852 in Indiana. He was the son of William A Wells and Catherine Byfield.

1612. **John Wells.** (Catherine Byfield-3; Andrew G Byfield-2; Abraham H Byfield-1)

John was born about 1854 in Indiana. He was the son of William A Wells and Catherine Byfield.

1613. **Cyrus A Wells.** (Catherine Byfield-3; Andrew G Byfield-2; Abraham H Byfield-1)

Cyrus A was born about 1856 in Indiana. He was the son of William A Wells and Catherine Byfield. He married Anna M Franzee on 1 January 1906 in Marion County, Indiana.

Spouse: Anna M Franzee.

Anna M was born in 1880 in Indiana. She was the daughter of William S Franzee and Randall. She married Cyrus A Wells on 1 January 1906 in Marion County, Indiana. She also married Lourding.

1614. **Mary Wells.** (Catherine Byfield-3; Andrew G Byfield-2; Abraham H Byfield-1)

Mary was born about 1860 in Indiana. She was the daughter of William A Wells and Catherine Byfield.

1615. **James M Wells.** (Catherine Byfield-3; Andrew G Byfield-2; Abraham H Byfield-1)

James M was born about 1862 in Indiana. He was the son of William A Wells and Catherine Byfield. He married Hattie E Jones on 16 December 1899 in Marion County, Indiana.

Spouse: Hattie E Jones.

Hattie E was born in 1870 in Indiana. She was the daughter of Elijah Jones and Owens. She married James M Wells on 16 December 1899 in Marion County, Indiana. She also married Mahlon Wells on 10 October 1887 in Jackson, Indiana.

1616.   **Rebecca Jennie Wells.** (Catherine Byfield-3; Andrew G Byfield-2; Abraham H Byfield-1)

Rebecca Jennie was born about 1869 in Indiana. She was the daughter of William A Wells and Catherine Byfield. She married Alfred R Perdue on 2 April 1889 in Indianapolis, Marion County, Indiana.

Spouse: Alfred R Perdue.

Alfred R was born in 1868. He married Rebecca Jennie Wells on 2 April 1889 in Indianapolis, Marion County, Indiana.

1621.   **Lucinda Byfield.** (Frederick W Byfield-3; Andrew G Byfield-2; Abraham H Byfield-1)

Lucinda was born on 8 December 1851 in Decatur County, Indiana. She died on 1 January 1852 in Decatur County, Indiana at the age of 24 days. She was buried in Decatur County, Indiana. She was the daughter of Frederick W Byfield and Nancy Jane Thorp.

1622.   **James H Byfield.** (Frederick W Byfield-3; Andrew G Byfield-2; Abraham H Byfield-1)

James H was born on 27 May 1853 in Decatur County, Indiana. He died on 5 June 1928 in Pocahontas, Bond County, Illinois at the age of 75 years, 9 days. He was buried on 7 June 1928 in Greenville, Bond County, Illinois. He was the son of Frederick W Byfield and Nancy Jane Thorp. He married Martha A Bouilon in 1888.

Spouse: Martha A Bouilon.

Martha A was born on 9 April 1870 in Shoal Creek Township, Illinois. She died on 19 January 1938 in Pocahontas, Bond County, Illinois at the age of 67 years, 9 months. She married James H Byfield in 1888.

Children of Martha A Bouilon and James H Byfield

16221 i.   Ethel Eunice Byfield. Ethel Eunice was born in October 1889 in Illinois.

+ 16222 ii.   Katie L Byfield. Katie L was born in October 1889 in Illinois.

16223 iii.   May J Byfield. May J was born in 1898 in Illinois.

1623.   **William A Byfield.** (Frederick W Byfield-3; Andrew G Byfield-2; Abraham H Byfield-1)

William A was born on 7 January 1857 in Decatur County, Indiana. He died on 7 October 1859 in Decatur County, Indiana at the age of 2 years, 9 months. He was buried in Decatur County, Indiana. He was the son of Frederick W Byfield and Nancy Jane Thorp.

1624.   **Flora B Byfield.** (Frederick W Byfield-3; Andrew G Byfield-2; Abraham H Byfield-1)

Flora B was born on 10 October 1861 in Decatur County, Indiana. She died on 28 December 1911 in Winfield, Cowley County, Kansas at the age of 50 years, 2 months. She was the daughter of Frederick W Byfield and Nancy Jane Thorp. She married Isaiah 'Ira' Holmes 7 April 1886 in Arkansas City, Kansas.

Spouse: Isaiah 'Ira' Holmes.

Isaiah 'Ira' was born 29 July 1862 in Congress, Wayne County, Ohio. He died 22 January 1933 in Los Angeles, California. He married Flora B Byfield 7 April 1886 in Arkansas City, Kansas.

Children of Flora B Byfield and Isaiah 'Ira' Holmes

16241 i.   Karl Byfield Holmes. Karl Byfield was born 21 January 1887 in Winfield, Cowley County, Kansas. He died 8 December 1893 in Pratt, Pratt, Kansas.

16242 ii.   Edith Gertrude Holmes. Edith Gertrude was born 18 July 1888 in Pratt, Pratt, Kansas. She died 15 December 1918 in Kansas City, Wyandotte County, Kansas.

16243 iii.   Chester Isaiah 'Chet' 'Sherlock' Holmes. Chester Isaiah 'Chet' 'Sherlock' was born 1 April 1895 in Pratt, Pratt, Kansas. He died 9 August 1971 in Sioux City, Clay, Iowa.

16244 iv.   Edna Ernestine Holmes. Edna Ernestine was born 9 February 1897 in Wellington, Sumner County, Kansas or Pratt County, Kansas. She died 13

February 1901 in Pratt, Pratt, Kansas.

16245 v.   Elma Josephine Holmes. Elma Josephine was born 2 July 1902 in Pratt, Pratt, Kansas or Arkansas City, Cowley County, Kansas. She died 26 or 16 May 1982 in Lakewood, Los Angeles County, California.

1625.   **Ida Mae Byfield.** (Frederick W Byfield-3; Andrew G Byfield-2; Abraham H Byfield-1)

Ida Mae was born on 15 July 1863 in Indiana. She died on 14 April 1916 in Bond County, Illinois at the age of 52 years, 8 months. She was buried in Mulberry Grove, Bond County, Illinois. She was the daughter of Frederick W Byfield and Nancy Jane Thorp. She married John W Parkinson on 14 June 1883 in Fayette County, Illinois.

Spouse: John W Parkinson.

John W was born in January 1849 in Indiana. He died on 14 December 1914 in Saint Elmo, Fayette County, Illinois at the age of 65 years, 11 months. He married Ida Mae Byfield on 14 June 1883 in Fayette County, Illinois.

Children of Ida Mae Byfield and John W Parkinson

16251 i.   Pearl Laurel Lewis C Parkinson. Pearl Laurel Lewis C was born on 2 March 1884 in Illinois. He died on 3 August 1944 in Gambier, Knox County, Ohio.

+ 16252 ii.   Charles M Parkinson. Charles M was born in October 1887 in Indiana.

+ 16253 iii.   Fred J Parkinson. Fred J was born in September 1889 in Illinois.

16254 iv.   Arthur Parkinson. Arthur was born in September 1891 in Illinois.

16255 v.   Frank H Parkinson. Frank H was born in October 1895 in Illinois.

1626.   **John W Byfield.** (Frederick W Byfield-3; Andrew G Byfield-2; Abraham H Byfield-1)

John W was born on 22 July 1867 in Decatur County, Indiana. He died on 10 April 1912 in Shamrock, Wheeler County, Texas at the age of 44 years, 8 months. He was the son of Frederick W Byfield and Nancy Jane Thorp. He married Lela McGill on 1 September 1895 in Oklahoma Indian Territory. He also married Margaret Lucas Cornett on 18 February 1905 in Minco, Grady County, Oklahoma.

Spouse: Lela McGill.

Lela was born on 2 April 1875 in Indian Territory, Oklahoma. She died on 9 October 1946 in Oklahoma, at the age of 71 years, 6 months. She married John W Byfield on 1 September 1895 in Indian Territory.

Children of Lela McGill and John W Byfield

+ 16261 i.　　Elsie Bell Byfield. Elsie Bell was born on 2 September 1896 in Tishomingo, Johnson County, (Oklahoma) Indian Territory. She died on 23 November 1990 in Purcell, McClain, Oklahoma.

Spouse: Margaret Lucas Cornett.

Margaret Lucas was born on 16 January 1868 in Clay County, Kentucky. She died on 29 July 1949 in Norman, Cleveland County, Oklahoma at the age of 81 years, 6 months. She married John W Byfield on 18 February 1905 in Minco, Grady County, Oklahoma.

Children of Margaret Lucas Cornett and John W Byfield

16262 i.　　Johnie R Byfield. Johnie R was born on 14 November 1906 in Oklahoma. He died on 15 March 1995 in Lexington, Cleveland County, Oklahoma.

16263 ii.　　Maggie J Byfield. Maggie J was born on 13 October 1908 in Oklahoma. She died on 10 January 2000 in Norman, Cleveland County, Oklahoma.

1627.　**Minnie Byfield.** (Frederick W Byfield-3; Andrew G Byfield-2; Abraham H Byfield-1)

Minnie was born about 1870 in Indiana. She was the daughter of Frederick W Byfield and Nancy Jane Thorp.

1628.　**Rhoda I Byfield.** (Frederick W Byfield-3; Andrew G Byfield-2; Abraham H Byfield-1)

Rhoda I was born on 12 November 1892 in Sorento, Bond County, Illinois. She was the daughter of Frederick W Byfield and Tabitha Jane 'Bessie' Thacker. She married John Price. She also married Eyman.

Spouse: Eyman.

He married Rhoda I Byfield.

Children of Rhoda I Byfield and Eyman

16281 i. Willard L Eyman. Willard L was born 7 December 1910 in Illinois. He died 28 December 1994 in Austin, Travis County, Texas.

Spouse: John Price.

John was born about 1871 in Illinois. He married Rhoda I Byfield.

Children of Rhoda I Byfield and John Price

16282 ii. Grace Price. Grace was born about 1919 in Illinois.

1629. **Frederick Byfield.** (Frederick W Byfield-3; Andrew G Byfield-2; Abraham H Byfield-1)

Frederick was born about 1879 in Cottonwood Grove, Bond County, Illinois. He was the son of Frederick W Byfield and Elizabeth Elmore Hubbard.

1641. **Martha Weatherington.** (Susan Elizabeth Byfield-3; Andrew G Byfield-2; Abraham H Byfield-1)

Martha was born in 1861 in Indiana. She was the daughter of Samuel S Wetherington and Susan Elizabeth Byfield.

1642. **Mary Ellen Weatherington.** (Susan Elizabeth Byfield-3; Andrew G Byfield-2; Abraham H Byfield-1)

Mary Ellen was born on 28 November 1863 in Graham, Jefferson County, Indiana. She died on 24 September 1943 in Phillipsburg, Laclede County, Missouri at the age of 79 years, 9 months. She was buried in Phillipsburg, Laclede County, Missouri. She was the daughter of Samuel S Wetherington and Susan Elizabeth Byfield. She married Thomas Jefferson Stokes on 27 March 1885 in Laclede County, Missouri.

Spouse: Thomas Jefferson Stokes.

Thomas Jefferson was born on 6 November 1857 in Tennessee. He died on 23 March 1925 in Laclede County, Missouri at the age of 67 years, 4 months. He married Mary Ellen Weatherington on 27 March 1885 in Laclede County, Missouri.

Children of Mary Ellen Weatherington and Thomas Jefferson Stokes

16421 i.   Elsie M Stokes. Elsie M was born on 9 October 1885 in Missouri. She died on 25 February 1976 in Laclede County, Missouri.

16422 ii.   E Aretas Stokes. E Aretas was born in December 1887 in Missouri. He died in 1903 in Laclede County, Missouri.

16423 iii.   Amzel Stokes. Amzel was born in July 1889 in Missouri.

16424 iv.   Ongole Stokes. Ongole was born on 3 March 1891 in Missouri. He died on 7 March 1951 in Laclede County, Missouri.

16425 v.   Amie Stokes. Amie was born in June 1893 in Missouri.

16426 vi.   Elda C Stokes. Elda C was born in November 1894 in Missouri.

16427 vii.   Tressa V Stokes. Tressa V was born in March 1897 in Missouri.

16428 viii.   Thomas Leslie Stokes. Thomas Leslie was born in April 1899 in Missouri. He died in 1903 in Laclede County, Missouri.

16429 ix.   Hildred Lola Stokes. Hildred Lola was born on 19 April 1901 in Missouri. She died on 30 September 1927 in Laclede County, Missouri.

1642A x.   Virgil W Stokes. Virgil W was born in 1902 in Missouri.

1642B xi.   Doris E Stokes. Doris E was born in 1905 in Missouri.

1643.   **John Weatherington.** (Susan Elizabeth Byfield-3; Andrew G Byfield-2; Abraham H Byfield-1)

John was born in 1867 in Graham, Jefferson County, Indiana. He was the son of Samuel S Wetherington and Susan Elizabeth Byfield.

1644.   **Sarah Adaline Weatherington.** (Susan Elizabeth Byfield-3; Andrew G Byfield-2; Abraham H Byfield-1)

Sarah Adaline was born 26 Sept 1870 in Indiana. She died on 18 June 1934 in Todd, Kentucky. She was the daughter of Samuel S Wetherington and Susan Elizabeth Byfield. She married Nathaniel G Benton on 27 January 1889 in Laclede County, Missouri.

Spouse: Nathaniel G Benton.

Nathaniel G was born in July 1841 in Missouri. He married Sarah

Adaline Weatherington on 27 January 1889 in Laclede County, Missouri.

Children of Sarah Adaline Weatherington and Nathaniel G Benton

16441 i.   Walter Benton. Walter was born in March 1883 in Missouri.

16442 ii.   Effie Benton. Effie was born in January 1886 in Missouri.

16443 iii.   Sylva Benton. Sylva was born in October 1889 in Arkansas.

16444 iv.   Ruby Benton. Ruby was born in December 1890 in Arkansas.

16445 v.   Lawrence Benton. Lawrence was born in September 1892 in Arkansas.

16446 vi.   Robert H Benton. Robert H was born in 1893 in Arkansas.

16447 vii.   Burney Benton. Burney was born in November 1894 in Texas.

16448 viii.   Dick Benton. Dick was born in June 1897 in Texas.

16449 ix.   Ola Benton. Ola was born in 1901 in Texas.

1644A x.   Bessie Benton. Bessie was born in 1903 in Texas.

1644B xi.   Frank Benton. Frank was born in 1905 in Missouri.

1651.   **John Andrew Miller.** (Martha P Byfield-3; Andrew G Byfield-2; Abraham H Byfield-1)

John Andrew was born on 16 April 1868 in Indiana. He died on 11 May 1936 in Jefferson, Kentucky at the age of 68 years, 25 days. He was the son of Joshua Miller and Martha P Byfield. He married Gertie C in 1889.

Spouse: Gertie C.

Gertie C was born in November 1869 in Ohio. She married John Andrew Miller in 1889.

Children of Gertie C and John Andrew Miller

16511 i.   Maude Miller. Maude was born in April 1890 in Indiana.

1661.   **Anna Byfield.** (James M Byfield-3; Andrew G Byfield-2; Abraham H Byfield-1)

Anna was born on 11 December 1869 in Jefferson County, Indiana. She died on 4 May 1936 in East Saint Louis, Saint Clair County,

Illinois at the age of 66 years, 4 months. She was buried on 6 May 1936 in Belleville, Saint Clair County, Illinois. She was the daughter of James M Byfield and Mahala Robinson. She married Charles A Schirmer in 1898.

Spouse: Charles A Schirmer.

Charles A was born in September 1867 in Illinois. He married Anna Byfield in 1898.

Children of Anna Byfield and Charles A Schirmer

16611 i.   Carl G Schirmer. Carl G was born in June 1892 in Missouri.

16612 ii.   Ruby E Schirmer. Ruby E was born in January 1899 in Illinois.

16613 iii.   William A Schirmer. William A was born about 1902 in Illinois.

16614 iv.   Robert Schirmer. Robert was born about 1905 in Illinois.

16615 v.   Elmer M Schirmer. Elmer M was born about 1910 in Illinois.

1662.   **James Edward Byfield.** (James M Byfield-3; Andrew G Byfield-2; Abraham H Byfield-1)

James Edward was born about 1870 in Indiana. He died on 12 July 1941 in Wood River, Madison, Ill at the age of about 71 years, 6 months. He was buried on 14 July 1941 in Wood River, Madison County, Illinois. He was the son of James M Byfield and Mahala Robinson.

1663.   **Mary Byfield.** (James M Byfield-3; Andrew G Byfield-2; Abraham H Byfield-1)

Mary was born in September 1872 in Indiana. She was the daughter of James M Byfield and Mahala Robinson.

1664.   **Elizabeth L Byfield.** (James M Byfield-3; Andrew G Byfield-2; Abraham H Byfield-1)

Elizabeth L was born in August 1874 in Madison, Jefferson County, Indiana. She died on 23 May 1937 in Chicago, Cook County, Illinois at the age of 62 years, 9 months. She was the daughter of James M Byfield and Mahala Robinson. She married William W Hurley on 22 April 1903 in East Saint Louis, Saint Clair County, Illinois.

Spouse: William W Hurley.

William W was born in 1879 in Illinois. He died on 2 January 1941 in Greenville, Bond County, Illinois at the age of 62 years, 1 day. He married Elizabeth L Byfield on 22 April 1903 in East Saint Louis, Saint Clair County, Illinois.

Children of Elizabeth L Byfield and William W Hurley

16641 i.   Esther L Hurley. Esther L was born on 9 May 1904 in Illinois. She died on 29 October 1990 in Los Angeles.

16642 ii.   Ivan Walter Hurley. Ivan Walter was born on 24 May 1905 in Illinois. He died on 18 June 1946 in Norton, Wayne County, Michigan.

16643 iii.   Nelson Jerald Hurley. Nelson Jerald was born about 1907 in Illinois.

16644 iv.   Mona L Hurley. Mona L was born on 15 March 1908 in Illinois. She died on 15 April 1929 in Rapid City, Rock Island County, Illinois.

16645 v.   Waldo W Hurley. Waldo W was born on 31 May 1910 in Illinois. He died on 24 August 1992 in Thermopolis, Hot Springs County, Wyoming.

16646 vi.   Ruth V Hurley. Ruth V was born about 1911 in Illinois.

16647 vii.   Glenn B Hurley. Glenn B was born about 1913 in Illinois.

16648 viii. Minetta C Hurley. Minetta C was born about 1915 in Illinois.

16649 ix.   Eldon V I Hurley. Eldon V I was born about 1916 in Illinois. He died on 9 July 1996 in Des Moines, Polk County, Iowa.

1665.   **Jeannette Paulina Byfield.** (James M Byfield-3; Andrew G Byfield-2; Abraham H Byfield-1)

Jeannette Paulina was born on 23 November 1876 in Indiana. She died on 22 November 1967 in Spokane, Spokane County, Washington of America at the age of 90 years, 11 months. She was the daughter of James M Byfield and Mahala Robinson. She married Oliver M Benton.

Spouse: Oliver M Benton.

Oliver M was born about 1873 in Missouri. He married Jeannette Paulina Byfield.

Children of Jeannette Paulina Byfield and Oliver M Benton

16651 i.   Margie M Benton. Margie M was born about 1916 in Nebraska.

1666.   **Rose Emma Byfield.** (James M Byfield-3; Andrew G Byfield-2; Abraham H Byfield-1)

Rose Emma was born on 11 May 1878 in Jennings County, Indiana. She died in March 1965 at the age of 86 years, 9 months. She was buried in Melba, Canyon County, Idaho. She was the daughter of James M Byfield and Mahala Robinson. She married John Emory Grover in 1916.

Spouse: John Emory Grover.

John Emory was born on 25 September 1870 in Illinois. He died on 19 July 1942 in Canyon, Idaho at the age of 71 years, 9 months. He was the son of John Emery Grover and Catharine L Kessler. He married Rose Emma Byfield in 1916.

Children of Rose Emma Byfield and John Emory Grover

16661 i.   Alice K Grover. Alice K was born about 1917 in Idaho.

1667.   **John Mathew Byfield.** (James M Byfield-3; Andrew G Byfield-2; Abraham H Byfield-1)

John Mathew was born on 24 October 1880 in Indiana. He died on 28 July 1929 in Spokane, Spokane County, Washington at the age of 48 years, 9 months. He was buried in Bonners Ferry, Boundary County, Idaho. He was the son of James M Byfield and Mahala Robinson.

1668.   **Albert Cleveland Byfield.** (James M Byfield-3; Andrew G Byfield-2; Abraham H Byfield-1)

Albert Cleveland was born on 9 March 1884 in Illinois. He died in 1954 at the age of 69 years, 9 months. He was buried in Bonners Ferry, Boundary County, Idaho. He was the son of James M Byfield and Mahala Robinson.

1669.   **Lillian Francis Byfield.** (James M Byfield-3; Andrew G Byfield-2; Abraham H Byfield-1)

Lillian Francis was born in 1887 in Indiana. She was the daughter of James M Byfield and Mahala Robinson. She married William Herbert Burton in 1913 in Greenville, Bond County, Illinois.

Spouse: William Herbert Burton.

William Herbert was born in May 1879 in Missouri. He was the son of Herbert Clark Burton and Mary L Edwards. He married Lillian Francis Byfield in 1913 in Greenville, Bond County, Illinois.

16B1.   **Willford Dallas Spencer.** (Mary Alvoretta Byfield-3; Andrew G Byfield-2; Abraham H Byfield-1)

Willford Dallas was born on 20 October 1877 in Jennings County, Indiana. He died on 6 July 1961 in Indianapolis, Marion County, Indiana at the age of 83 years, 8 months. He was buried in Indianapolis, Marion County, Indiana. He was the son of James H Spencer and Mary Alvoretta Byfield. He married Alma Onetta.

Spouse: Alma Onetta.

Alma Onetta was born about 1898 in Indiana. She died 25 July 1970 in Indianapolis, Marion County, Indiana. She married Willford Dallas Spencer.

16B2.   **Edgar John Spencer.** (Mary Alvoretta Byfield-3; Andrew G Byfield-2; Abraham H Byfield-1)

Edgar John was born on 15 January 1880 in Jennings County, Indiana. He died in November 1954 in Indianapolis, Marion County, Indiana at the age of 74 years, 9 months. He was the son of James H Spencer and Mary Alvoretta Byfield. He married Agnes A.

Spouse: Agnes A.

Agnes A was born about 1896 in Indiana. She married Edgar John Spencer.

16E1.   **Alford E McGuire.** (Rose Emma Lucinda Byfield-3; Andrew G Byfield-2; Abraham H Byfield-1)

Alford E was born on 2 July 1889 in Jennings County, Indiana. He died on 23 October 1889 in Jennings County, Indiana at the age of 3 months, 21 days. He was buried in Jennings County, Indiana. He was the son of John Elmer McGuire and Rose Emma Lucinda Byfield.

16E2.   **Walter McGuire.** (Rose Emma Lucinda Byfield-3; Andrew G Byfield-2; Abraham H Byfield-1)

Walter was born on 29 March 1890 in Paris Crossing, Jennings County, Indiana. He died on 19 August 1963 in Philadelphia, Philadelphia County, Pennsylvania at the age of 73 years, 4 months. He was buried in Philadelphia County, Pennsylvania. He was the son of John Elmer McGuire and Rose Emma Lucinda Byfield. He married Anna C Kellerman on 25 March 1914 in Jennings County, Indiana.

Spouse: Anna C Kellerman.

Anna C was born on 20 January 1890 in Philadelphia, Philadelphia County, Pennsylvania. She was the daughter of Kellerman and Anna. She married Walter McGuire on 25 March 1914 in Jennings County, Indiana.

16E3.   **Hazel McGuire.** (Rose Emma Lucinda Byfield-3; Andrew G Byfield-2; Abraham H Byfield-1)

Hazel was born on 12 October 1895 in Jefferson County, Indiana. She died 16 April 1972 in Jennings County, Indiana. She was buried in Vernon, Jennings County, Indiana. She was the daughter of John Elmer McGuire and Rose Emma Lucinda Byfield. She married Lavern W Wainscott on 12 October 1921 in Jefferson County, Indiana.

Spouse: Lavern W Wainscott.

Lavern W was born on 10 March 1899 in North Vernon, Jennings County, Indiana. He died in July 1978 in Commiskey, Jennings County, Indiana of America at the age of 79 years, 3 months. He married Hazel McGuire on 12 October 1921 in Jefferson County, Indiana.

GRANDCHILDREN OF VINCENT BYFIELD

1711. **Melvina 'Mellie' R Stephens.** (Ann Maria Byfield-3; Vincent Byfield-2; Abraham H Byfield-1)

Melvina 'Mellie' R was born on 6 December 1856 in Madison, Jefferson County, Indiana. She died on 30 May 1932 in Cincinnati, Hamilton County, Ohio at the age of 75 years, 5 months. She was the daughter of Henry Stephens and Ann Maria Byfield.

1712. **John W Stephens.** (Ann Maria Byfield-3; Vincent Byfield-2; Abraham H Byfield-1)

John W was born about 1859 in Indiana. He was the son of Henry Stephens and Ann Maria Byfield.

1713. **Joseph G Stephens.** (Ann Maria Byfield-3; Vincent Byfield-2; Abraham H Byfield-1)

Joseph G was born about 1862 in Indiana. He died on 14 January 1888 in Jefferson County Indiana at the age of about 26 years, 13 days. He was buried in Madison, Jefferson County, Indiana. He was the son of Henry Stephens and Ann Maria Byfield.

1714. **Adelaide Stephens.** (Ann Maria Byfield-3; Vincent Byfield-2; Abraham H Byfield-1)

Adelaide was born about 1865 in Indiana. She died on 19 November 1886 in Jefferson County Indiana at the age of about 21 years, 10 months. She was buried in Madison, Jefferson County, Indiana. She was the daughter of Henry Stephens and Ann Maria Byfield.

1715. **Frank Stephens.** (Ann Maria Byfield-3; Vincent Byfield-2; Abraham H Byfield-1)

Frank was born about 1867 in Indiana. He died 28 January 1894 in Jefferson County, Indiana. He was buried in Madison, Jefferson County, Indiana. He was the son of Henry Stephens and Ann Maria Byfield.

1716.   **Delos Stephens.** (Ann Maria Byfield-3; Vincent Byfield-2; Abraham H Byfield-1)

Delos was born about 1871 in Indiana. He died on 10 May 1895 in Jefferson County Indiana at the age of about 24 years, 4 months. He was buried in Madison, Jefferson County, Indiana. He was the son of Henry Stephens and Ann Maria Byfield.

1717.   **Fannie Stephens.** (Ann Maria Byfield-3; Vincent Byfield-2; Abraham H Byfield-1)

Fannie was born on 28 March 1872 in Indiana. She died on 29 June 1912 in Cincinnati, Hamilton County, Ohio at the age of 40 years, 3 months. She was the daughter of Henry Stephens and Ann Maria Byfield.

1731.   **Charles Howard Byfield.** (Vinson Delas Byfield-3; Vincent Byfield-2; Abraham H Byfield-1)

Charles Howard was born on 23 May 1873 in Kentucky. He died in May 1935 in Marion County, Indiana at the age of 61 years, 11 months. He was buried in Indianapolis, Marion County, Indiana. He was the son of Vinson Delas Byfield and Rebecca Turner Johnson. He married Lina E Livingstone on 18 July 1894.

Spouse: Lina E Livingstone.

Lina E was born in 1874 in Indiana. She married Charles Howard Byfield on 18 July 1894.

Children of Lina E Livingstone and Charles Howard Byfield

+ 17311 i.   Margeret K Byfield. Margeret K was born on 17 June 1897 in Marion County, Indiana. She died on 10 December 1980 in Dayton, Montgomery, Ohio.

17312 ii.   Charles H Byfield. Charles H was born on 24 May 1908 in Indiana. He died on 20 April 1997 in Indianapolis, Indiana.

17313 iii.   Lionel E Byfield. Lionel E was born 7 December 1909 in Indiana. He died 3 March 1981 in Indianapolis, Marion County, Indiana.

17314 iv.   Elizabeth B Byfield. Elizabeth B was born on 26 June 1914 in Indiana.

1732. **Delila Elizabeth Byfield.** (Vinson Delas Byfield-3; Vincent Byfield-2; Abraham H Byfield-1)

Delila Elizabeth was born on 2 January 1875 in Indiana. She died on 6 May 1950 in Bethel, Clermont, Ohio at the age of 75 years, 4 months. She was the daughter of Vinson Delas Byfield and Rebecca Turner Johnson. She married George Clifford Anderson on 27 October 1897 in Marion County, Indiana.

Spouse: George Clifford Anderson.

George Clifford was born on 3 August 1873 in Ohio. He was the son of George Anderson. He married Delila Elizabeth Byfield on 27 October 1897 in Marion County, Indiana.

Children of Delila Elizabeth Byfield and George Clifford Anderson

+ 17321 i.   Harry Virgil Anderson. Harry Virgil was born on 19 March 1899 in Batavia, Clermont County, Ohio. He died in 1956 in Brown County, Ohio.

17322 ii.   Leona P Anderson. Leona P was born on 23 October 1901 in Clermont County, Ohio.

17323 iii.   Grace E Anderson. Grace E was born in 1905 in Clermont County, Ohio.

1733. **Helen Malinda Byfield.** (Vinson Delas Byfield-3; Vincent Byfield-2; Abraham H Byfield-1)

Helen Malinda was born on 11 August 1879 in Indiana. She died on 8 October 1949 in Los Angeles County, California at the age of 70 years, 1 month. She was the daughter of Vinson Delas Byfield and Rebecca Turner Johnson. She married Harry Bridwell on 22 July 1901 in Madison.

Spouse: Harry Bridwell.

Harry Bridwell was born about 1880 in Indiana. He married Helen Malinda Byfield on 22 July 1901 in Madison.

Children of Helen Malinda Byfield and Harry Bridwell

+ 17331 i.   Sarah A Bridwell. Sarah A was born about 1903 in Indiana.

+ 17332 ii.   Howard W Bridwell. Howard W was born on 7 September 1905 in Indianapolis, Marion County, Indiana. He died on 6 February 1970 in

Cleveland, Cuyahoga County, Ohio.

17333 iii.   Nellie Bridwell. Nellie was born about 1908 in Indiana.

17334 iv.   Harry Vincent Bridwell. Harry Vincent was born on 15 July 1912 in Indiana. He died on 25 February 1992 in San Bernardino, California.

17335 v.   John R 'Jack' Bridwell. John R 'Jack' was born on 21 May 1915 in Indianapolis, Marion County, Indiana. He died on 17 February 2008 in Upland, San Bernardino County, California.

1734.   Harriet B 'Hattie' Byfield. (Vinson Delas Byfield-3; Vincent Byfield-2; Abraham H Byfield-1)

Harriet B 'Hattie' was born on 27 August 1882 in Marion County, Indiana. She died on 12 August 1930 in Indianapolis, Marion County, Indiana at the age of 47 years, 11 months. She was buried in Indianapolis, Marion County, Indiana. She was the daughter of Vinson Delas Byfield and Rebecca Turner Johnson. She married John William Whitaker on 11 October 1916 in Marion County, Indiana.

Spouse: John William Whitaker.

John William was born on 10 October 1883 in Indianapolis, Marion County, Indiana. He died on 4 May 1964 in Indianapolis, Marion County, Indiana at the age of 80 years, 6 months. He was the son of Anna Whiteker. He married Harriet B 'Hattie' Byfield on 11 October 1916 in Marion County, Indiana.

1735.   Florence J Byfield. (Vinson Delas Byfield-3; Vincent Byfield-2; Abraham H Byfield-1)

Florence J was born on 22 July 1884 in Indianapolis, Marion County, Indiana. She died on 2 June 1964 in Los Angeles, Los Angeles County, California at the age of 79 years, 10 months. She was the daughter of Vinson Delas Byfield and Rebecca Turner Johnson.

1741.   Charles Davis. (Elizabeth D 'Lizzie' Byfield-3; Vincent Byfield-2; Abraham H Byfield-1)

Charles was born in 1866 in Indiana. He was the son of William B Davis and Elizabeth D 'Lizzie' Byfield.

GRANDCHILDREN OF ELIZA ANN BYFIELD

1811. **James Samuel Downs.** (George Washington Downs-3; Eliza Ann Byfield-2; Abraham H Byfield-1)

James Samuel was born on 30 November 1854 in Indiana. He died on 27 January 1937 in Yuma, Yuma, Arizona at the age of 82 years, 1 month. He was the son of George Washington Downs and Lenora Marie Byram.

1812. **Sarah Jane Downs.** (George Washington Downs-3; Eliza Ann Byfield-2; Abraham H Byfield-1)

Sarah Jane was born on 26 August 1856 in Logansport, Jennings County, Indiana. She died on 18 August 1938 at the age of 81 years, 11 months. She was the daughter of George Washington Downs and Lenora Marie Byram.

1813. **William Riley Downs.** (George Washington Downs-3; Eliza Ann Byfield-2; Abraham H Byfield-1)

William Riley was born on 23 April 1858 in Indiana. He died in 1939 at the age of 80 years, 8 months. He was the son of George Washington Downs and Lenora Marie Byram.

1814. **John Wesley Downs.** (George Washington Downs-3; Eliza Ann Byfield-2; Abraham H Byfield-1)

John Wesley was born on 11 August 1859 in Indiana. He died on 29 November 1860 in Indiana at the age of 1 year, 3 months. He was the son of George Washington Downs and Lenora Marie Byram.

1815. **Hannah Belle Downs.** (George Washington Downs-3; Eliza Ann Byfield-2; Abraham H Byfield-1)

Hannah Belle was born on 30 November 1860 in Vernon, Hancock County, Indiana. She died on 13 August 1943 in Pontiac, Oakland County, Michigan at the age of 82 years, 8 months. She was the daughter of George Washington Downs and Lenora Marie Byram.

1816.   **Elizabeth Alice Downs.** (George Washington Downs-3; Eliza Ann Byfield-2; Abraham H Byfield-1)

Elizabeth Alice was born on 16 February 1866 in Indiana. She died on 30 July 1889 at the age of 23 years, 5 months. She was the daughter of George Washington Downs and Lenora Marie Byram.

1817.   **George Elmer Downs.** (George Washington Downs-3; Eliza Ann Byfield-2; Abraham H Byfield-1)

George Elmer was born on 17 June 1872 in Michigan. He died on 18 February 1935 in Reed City, Osceola, County Michigan at the age of 62 years, 8 months. He was the son of George Washington Downs and Lenora Marie Byram.

1818.   **Henry Ansel Downs.** (George Washington Downs-3; Eliza Ann Byfield-2; Abraham H Byfield-1)

Henry Ansel was born on 25 December 1875 in Michigan. He died on 11 October 1876 in Michigan at the age of 9 months, 17 days. He was the son of George Washington Downs and Lenora Marie Byram.

1819.   **Vincent A Downs.** (George Washington Downs-3; Eliza Ann Byfield-2; Abraham H Byfield-1)

Vincent A was born on 14 April 1877 in Michigan. He died on 26 December 1916 in Port Huron, Saint Clair County, Michigan at the age of 39 years, 8 months. He was the son of George Washington Downs and Lenora Marie Byram.

181A.   **Anna Belle Downs.** (George Washington Downs-3; Eliza Ann Byfield-2; Abraham H Byfield-1)

Anna Belle was born on 22 May 1878 in Michigan. She died on 26 February 1937 at the age of 58 years, 9 months. She was the daughter of George Washington Downs and Lenora Marie Byram.

1821.   **Ann Eliza Smith.** (Rebecca A Downs-3; Eliza Ann Byfield-2; Abraham H Byfield-1)

Ann Eliza was born about 1854 in Indiana. She was the daughter of

Nelson Smith and Rebecca A Downs. She married Samuel B Stokely on 8 May 1870 in Marion County, Illinois.

Spouse: Samuel B Stokely.

He married Ann Eliza Smith on 8 May 1870 in Marion County, Illinois.

1822. **Thomas C Smith.** (Rebecca A Downs-3; Eliza Ann Byfield-2; Abraham H Byfield-1)

Thomas C was born about 1856 in Indiana. He was the son of Nelson Smith and Rebecca A Downs.

1823. **James C Smith.** (Rebecca A Downs-3; Eliza Ann Byfield-2; Abraham H Byfield-1)

James C was born about 1859 in Indiana. He was the son of Nelson Smith and Rebecca A Downs.

1824. **Lydia J Smith.** (Rebecca A Downs-3; Eliza Ann Byfield-2; Abraham H Byfield-1)

Lydia J was born about 1862 in Indiana. She was the daughter of Nelson Smith and Rebecca A Downs.

1825. **Jennie S Smith.** (Rebecca A Downs-3; Eliza Ann Byfield-2; Abraham H Byfield-1)

Jennie S was born about 1865 in Illinois. She was the daughter of Nelson Smith and Rebecca A Downs.

1826. **Samuel S Smith.** (Rebecca A Downs-3; Eliza Ann Byfield-2; Abraham H Byfield-1)

Samuel S was born about 1869 in Illinois. He was the son of Nelson Smith and Rebecca A Downs.

1831. **Rebecca Ann Downs.** (James Andrew Downs-3; Eliza Ann Byfield-2; Abraham H Byfield-1)

Rebecca Ann was born in 1862 in Jefferson County, Indiana. She was the daughter of James Andrew Downs and Sarah Jane Perry.

Appendix A

NEWSPAPER ACCOUNTS OF THE MURDER TRIAL OF IVY LESTER REYNOLDS

The Indianapolis Star, 14 November 1914

"OTHER" WOMAN IN MURDER CASE

Prosecutor Declares State Will Show Connersville Man Wrote Many Love Letters Before Wife's Sudden Death.

SECOND WEDDING IN 11 DAYS

Friend Said to Have Received Mail as Go-Between to Be Witness—Postal Inspectors to Aid Prosecution.

[Special to The Indianapolis Star.]

CONNERSVILLE, Ind., Nov. 13.—After a grind of two and a half days a jury was sworn this afternoon to try Ivy L. Reynolds, 38 years old, Spanish-American war officer and former postal clerk, charged with administering cyanide of potassium to his late wife, Mrs. Elizabeth Reynolds, 34 years old, whose death occurred suddenly Feb. 16 last.

Immediately after the jury was impaneled Prosecutor Frank M. Edwards began his opening statement. The prosecutor explained how the "other woman" entered the case. The alleged other woman is Reynold's present wife, formerly Miss Dora Gerber of Morenci, Mich., whom he married eleven days after his first wife's death.

The state expects to show, he said, that Reynolds became acquainted with the girl by mail and that on Nov. 21, 1913, he sent her money to meet him at Toledo, O. The state's attorney asserted that witnesses will testify that Reynolds and the girl met at that place and stayed two days in a hotel, being registered as Mr. and Mrs. Ivy L. Reynolds. Otto Billau of Connersville will testify for the state in this connection, it is said.

Letters to Be Shown.

Letters will play an important part in the case. The state alleges Reynolds began a voluminous correspondence with Miss Gerber after the Toledo trip, some of the letters, it is said, expressing infatuation for the girl and his determination to make her his wife. Miss Gerber is said to have received three letters from Reynolds in a single day a week before Mrs. Reynolds's death.

Miss Marie Huston of Morenci, Mich., the girl in whose care Reynolds is said to have addressed his letters to Miss Gerber, is here and will testify for the state. The state declares Miss Huston received a letter from the defendant after he was in jail, in which he beseeched her to offer false testimony.

W. C. Ela of Indianapolis and J. C. Garrighus of Evansville, United States postal inspectors, appeared this morning among the attorneys for the state. These men figured prominently in the investigation of Reynolds's record, which was followed by his dismissal from the postoffice.

Jurors Are All Farmers.

More than 100 talesmen were examined. Strong opposition to capital punishment was the cause of the dismissal of more than half of this number. The jurymen, all farmers of Fayette County, are Charles A. Corbin, Albert E. Goble, Herman L. Adams, William H. Kidd, Martin Bilby, Train Pike, Robert W. Henry, George Pryfogle, Ernest Maurer, Oliver McGraw, Walter Heck and Thomas H. Bell.

Reynolds showed no emotion as Prosecutor Edwards made his opening statement. He converses with his attorneys, laughs at times and expresses a firm belief that he will be freed. He made shorthand notes of the opening statement and was apparently deeply interested in all of the charges.

The present Mrs. Reynolds and the defendant's five small children have been constant attendants since the opening day of the trial. The court room was packed. Mrs. Reynolds is attracting much attention. She is calm and talks much with her husband and his attorneys. She laughed when the prosecutor made serious charges against her.

The Indianapolis Star 17 November 1914

REYNOLDS CHEERFUL DURING MURDER TRIAL

Connersville Man Little Affected by Testimony of State Witnesses, Who Assert First Wife Was Neglected.

[Special to The Indianapolis Star.]

CONNERSVILLE, Ind., Nov. 16.—Ivy L. Reynolds, 38 years old, former postal clerk, on trial here, charged with poisoning his late wife, Mrs. Elizabeth Reynolds, was apparently cheerful when he entered the court room today. He kissed his young wife and children and waved a greeting to friends as the day's proceedings began.

Mrs. Harvey Skeens, a half sister of the first Mrs. Reynolds, was the first witness called by the state. Her testimony occupied half of the afternoon and dealt principally with the home life of Reynolds and his first wife. She testified that Reynolds had frequently betrayed strong irritation toward his wife, called her ignorant and crazy and once, Mrs. Skeens said, attempted to slap her.

Neglect of Wife Charged.

Mrs. Skeens told the court that the defendant had neglected his wife, leaving her alone for days when she was dangerously ill. On the day of the funeral, the witness testified, Reynolds said to his wife's mother, Mrs. Louise Watkins of Shelbyville, "Oh! Louise, I didn't take your girl away from you." Reynolds remarked, Mrs. Skeens testified, on the day after his wife's death, that he was well nigh crazed with the sense of his position, that he was finding difficulty in finding a housekeeper and that they need not be surprised if he was married within a week.

Mrs. Walter Maher testified that she and her husband visited the Reynolds home one night and that Reynolds pulled the lapel of his coat back, looked at a portrait and said, "Oh, you dear little black-headed doll." The witness said Mrs. Elizabeth Reynolds heard her husband's statement. The state contends the "black-headed doll" was Dora Gerber, the present Mrs. Reynolds, whom Reynolds married eleven days after his first wife died.

The Indianapolis Star, 21 November 1914

STORY OF DOCTOR SHAKES REYNOLDS

Accused Man Shows First Signs of Emotion When Physician Describes Conditions Surrounding First Wife's Death.

UNCERTAIN REGARDING CAUSE

Witness Asserts Woman's Sudden Collapse Caused Surprise and Admits Possible Error in Hasty Diagnosis.

[Special to The Indianapolis Star.]

CONNERSVILLE, Ind., Nov. 20.—Dr. B. R. Smith, who attended the late Mrs. Elizabeth Reynolds during her illness last February and who was present at her death, was the principal witness for the state in the Ivy L. Reynolds murder trial today. Reynolds, who has maintained his composure during the nine days' grind of the trial, shewed his first signs of emotion today when the physician and others described the deathbed scene.

Dr. Smith testified that he called at the Reynolds home on Friday, on Saturday and twice on Sunday before Mrs. Reynolds's death on Monday. On these visits, the doctor testified, he found the woman's condition apparently growing better. She did not seem to be depressed, he said, and he found no reason why she should be discouraged or contemplate suicide.

Surprised by Condition.

The doctor testified that he told the woman she could leave her bed the next morning. He was called to the Reynolds home on the following morning, Monday, Feb. 16. The physician said he found Mrs. Reynolds senseless, with her body rigid and presenting the superficial symptoms of death from cerebral hemorrhage. That condition, the physician testified, surprised him. He was so surprised that he suggested to others that Mrs. Reynolds acted as though she had "taken something."

Dr. Smith said Mrs. Reynolds died within an hour after his arrival and that he was persuaded from what he had heard since that his diagnosis of rupture of brain blood vessels was in error and that, had he been allowed to observe all the symptoms more closely, his diagnosis would have been quite different.

The state inquired how closely the symptoms of cyanide of potassium poisoning resembled those of brain hemorrhage. Dr. Smith answered with caution. He explained that he had not had much opportunity to see the effects of cyanide of potassium on the human body. He was asked how long a capsule filled with the poison would lie in the stomach before death resulted. The physician replied that it varied so greatly that he could not give a satisfactory answer.

Tells of Reported Cruelty.

Mrs. Carrie Theders testified that when she nursed the late Mrs. Reynolds through a severe illness several years ago she found a serious bruise on Mrs. Reynolds's body, at the place where she seemed to be suffering the most pain. She testified that it was rumored that Reynolds had kicked his wife in the side, which was the direct cause of her illness. The patient had explained her illness, but the witness was not allowed to testify to Mrs. Reynolds's explanation, as the defendant was not present when his wife talked to Mrs. Chapman. She testified, however, that Reynolds come to her home and asked whether she had heard his wife's illness resulted from kicks he gave her.

Mrs. Philip Adams, a neighbor of the Reynoldses, testified that she had known the defendant to leave his wife alone when she was alarmingly ill. Glen Zell related how he once telephoned to Reynolds at Indianapolis, where he was attending a celebration, telling him to come home at once, as his wife was not expected to live. The husband promised to come immediately, but, witnesses testified, he did not reach Connersville until after midnight.

John Franklin, a Connersville insurance man, testified that he rode to Hamilton, O., with Reynolds a year ago. The witness said Reynolds told him that he had met a Cuban girl during his army service and that he still corresponded with her. Reynolds said his little daughter Batiste was named for the dark-skinned maiden. The witness alleged that Reynolds mentioned a newer friend, a Michigan girl, with whom he was corresponding. As they left the train in Hamilton, the witness asserted, Reynolds said, "For God's sake, don't say anything about seeing me. I am supposed to be on my way to Cicero."

The Indianapolis Star, 24 November 1914

WIFE COLLAPSES IN MURDER TRIAL

Young Woman's Nerves Give Way After Identifying Telegram From Reynolds Which Led to Hasty Second Marriage.

DEFENSE TO OPEN TODAY

Postoffice Inspector's Testimony That Different Letters Were Written on Same Typewriter Concludes State's Case.

[Special to The Indianapolis Star.]

CONNERSVILLE, Ind., Nov. 24.—The state brought its case to an end in the Ivy L. Reynolds murder trial this afternoon, after thirteen days consumed in presenting sensational evidence in an effort to prove the former postoffice clerk poisoned his first wife, who died last February.

Mrs. Dora Gerber Reynolds, the man's present wife, was again summoned by the state. She was almost ill from the nervous strain and the prosecution recognized that her position was a trying one. She pleaded that she felt unable to testify, but the state assured her that the examination would be brief.

She answered the attorney's question in a shaky voice and identified certain letters she had received from her husband and admitted the genuineness of telegrams sent her by Reynolds soon after his first wife's death.

Identifies Telegrams.

She was shown a telegram which Reynolds sent her, the language of which was clouded. She replied that it was intended as a question whether she would marry Reynolds and come to Connersville. At that point her overwrought nerves gave away and the witness asked that she might be excused. The young wife collapsed as they conducted her from the stand.

Postal Inspectors Ela of Evansville and Garaghus of Indianapolis testified that they were experienced in handwriting and typewriting. They examined the letter which the defendant wrote in answer to their charges and letters which Miss Mary Watkins of Shelbyville received just before Mrs. Reynolds died.

Declare Same Machine Used.

The inspectors asserted that these letters were all written on the same typewriter. The letters to Miss Watkins stated that Mrs. Elizabeth Reynolds was very ill and that her condition was growing rapidly worse.

Volney Caldwell, a local postoffice employe, testified that Reynolds had absented himself from the postoffice parts of certain days, including the dates of the alleged trip to Toledo, O.

Among other witnesses who testified regarding the defendant's handwriting were P. H. Kensler, a banker, James Clifton and Emil Holmes.

When the state rested the jury was dismissed for the day, as one of the members was slightly ill. David W. McKee, attorney for the defense, presented the usual motion to instruct the jury to find the defendant not guilty. It is expected that the outline of the defense to the jury will be made tomorrow morning.

The Indianapolis Star, 28 November 1914

REYNOLDS IS SET FREE.

Court Instructs for Acquittal, Reversing Earlier Ruling.

CONNERSVILLE, Ind, Nov 27—Ivy L. Reynolds, 38 years old, former post-office clerk, who was charged with poisoning his first wife Mrs Elizabeth Reynolds, was set free this morning when Judge George L Gray reversed his previous ruling on the motion to instruct the jury to find the defendant not guilty Court convened at 9 o clock with the understanding that the evidence for the defense would be heard and that the case should go to the jury

The judge arrived an hour later and announced that he had sustained the motion formally made by David W Mc Kee, counsel for the defense The action was a surprise to the state s attorneys, who had been informed Wednesday afternoon that the case would be allowed to proceed

The jury was instructed by the court to bring in a verdict of acquittal

Reynolds burst into tears when the verdict was read He kissed his young wife and hugged his five children by the first wife Reynolds married a second time eleven days after the death of the first Mrs Reynolds

Judge Gray's ruling has caused much comment, even among those who believed the defendant innocent There was no demonstration of approval on the part of the audience A few of the jurors shook hands with Reynolds and the others moved away, not waiting for an opportunity to do so In a long speech Judge Gray made it clear that he considered the state s case weak Attorney Leland H Stanford told Judge Gray that he had underestimated the state s case The attorney contended that he had never prosecuted a case with stronger circumstantial evidence and where a motive was so plainly shown

Appendix B

BESSIE BYFIELD SUICIDE

The Indianapolis Star – 3 May 1915

GOES TO GOTHAM TO END HER LIFE

Miss Bessie Byfield of Indianapolis Leaves Note Saying She Could Not Commit Suicide Among Loved Ones.

ACCIDENT BELIEVED CAUSE

Young Woman, Who Disappeared Friday, Had Suffered Violent Headaches After Being Hit by Golf Ball.

[Special to The Indianapolis Star.]

NEW YORK, May 2.—Because she could not bear to kill herself at home, among those who loved her, Miss Bessie Byfield, daughter of Mrs. Jessie Byfield, 1729 North Illinois street, Indianapolis, took a train to New York, went to the Park Avenue Hotel and committed suicide early this morning by taking poison. She was found about 1 o'clock this afternoon, when a chambermaid entered the room. Dr. A. B. Moore, 121 East Thirty-eighth street, was called and declared that the woman had been dead several hours.

Leaves Letter to Mother.

Miss Byfield left two letters, one addressed to her mother and the other to her sister, both in Indianapolis, in which she explained why she had come to New York to die. She asked that her body be cremated.

According to the story told at the hotel, Miss Byfield came there late Saturday night, having with her only some hand baggage. She engaged a room and gave the clerk $10 with the request it be deposited for her and then went to her room.

The body was taken to the undertaking rooms of Charles Plowright, 144 Lexington avenue, awaiting instructions from Indianapolis.

SUICIDE CAUSE NOT KNOWN.

Blow on Head by Golf Ball Believed to Have Led to Act.

Miss Bessie Byfield, who died in New York yesterday after taking poison, disappeared from Indianapolis mysteriously Friday morning when she was thought by her family to be downtown, and a search had been instituted when the message of her death came from New York. Her relatives are utterly unable to account for her suicide, as she was of a very happy disposition, and the only theory is that of mental derangement, caused probably by a blow on the back of the head suffered a week ago, when she was hit by a golf ball while on the links. From that time on she complained frequently of severe headaches and inability to sleep and the last word from her was a telephone message to a friend Friday morning, after she had left home, in which she complained of a violent headache.

Miss Byfield, who was about 32 years old, was the youngest daughter of Mrs. Jessie Byfield and is survived by her mother, one sister, Miss Emma Byfield, and three brothers, A. D. Byfield and Charles Byfield of Indianapolis and Harry Byfield of California.

Arrangements were made last night to return the body to Indianapolis.

Appendix C

GAVIN PAYNE'S ARTICLE ABOUT HIS GRANDFATHER

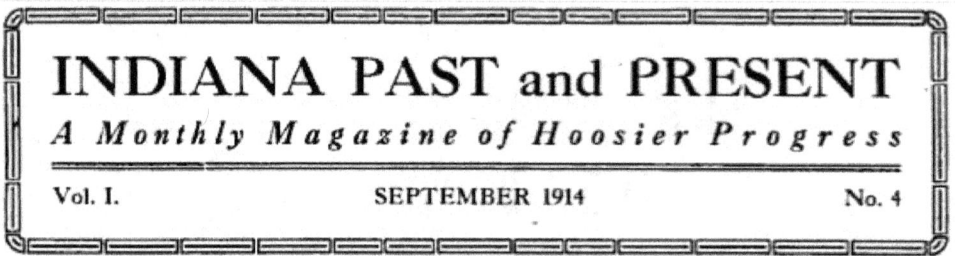

INDIANA PAST and PRESENT
A Monthly Magazine of Hoosier Progress

Vol. I.   SEPTEMBER 1914   No. 4

FIRST GOOD ROAD BUILDER
IN INDIANA
By GAVIN L. PAYNE

The State of Indiana possessed, up to the time of the World's Fair at Chicago, a relic, which would have been of particular interest now, in light of the wide movement for a good roads system. This was the first wooden plow used in road building in the State. It was a very substantial implement, and showed signs of unusually good workmanship, notwithstanding it was a home-made affair of pioneer days. Horatio Byfield, of Jefferson county, was the maker and the user of this big plow, which turned up the soil for roads north of Madison about the year 1816, or in the spring in 1817. Mr. Byfield had come down the Ohio river on a flatboat at the opening of the new State, and after first inspecting land in Clark county, settled in Jefferson county, where he entered a homestead south of Dupont and built his log cabin. In the early thirties, he supplanted the old log cabin with a pretentious two-story brick house, which is still standing. His land holding increased to three hundred acres, and in ante-bellum days, the old Byfield place was a scene of much hospitality. Mr. Byfield was one of the original advocates of internal improvements, and he lent a practical hand by building this plow and making a road to Madison. The old plow was stored away in the big barn until

the late William Wesley Woollen, formerly City Controller of Indianapolis, who knew the Byfield family intimately, discovered it and presented it to the State Museum, where the plow, properly placarded, reposed for many years. In 1893, it was taken to the Indiana building at the Chicago World's Fair, as an interesting feature of that exhibit, and from there it carelessly disappeared. A theory is that in the chill autumn days, vandals took the old plow and fed the fireplace with it.

Mr. Byfield was a well-known character in southern Indiana. It was related of him in a sketch by Mr. Woollen that in one famine year, Mr. Byfield's fine farm yielded corn abundantly and he was offered extravagant cash prices for it by buyers from along the river. Instead of selling, he distributed his entire crop among his neighbors for miles around, taking their two and three year plain notes for the corn. In this wise much distress was averted and the neighborhood had corn for seeding. The late Wm. H. English and Mr. Byfield were friends and when Mr. English came to Indianapolis and made realty investments that enabled him to accumulate several millions before he died, he urged Mr. Byfield to sell his

large farm and come to the capital city. Mr. Byfield, however, after a trip to the new capital, could see few possibilities to the place.

Of Mr. Byfield's large family, but two are living, Mrs. Mary B. Payne and Whitcomb Byfield, of Indianapolis. Among his grandchildren are Gavin L.

Payne, of Indianapolis, and Charles Byfield, assistant postmaster at Indianapolis.

The old Byfield farm is now in the family of ex-Senator W. A. Guthrie, and still standing on the old place is a tract of the original forest, to which the axe is even yet a stranger.

Appendix D

THE BYFIELD CEMETERY

In 1988, the Indiana Department of Natural Resources, recorded the Byfield Cemetery in it's inventory of historic sites. At that time they noted:

> *Hilltop cemetery is originally believed to have contained at least 50 stones. A former owner bull-dozed all but this one large marker which can be seen from the road. This stone has the names of 7 Byfield family members on it.*

The location given for the cemetery is on the west side of State Road 7, near the location of the Byfield Farm. Approximately 3/10 mile off the road. Although the researchers from the Department of Natural Resources were told that the cemetery had originally contained at least 50 stones, the WPA, in their listing from the 1930s, found only about 15 stones. Many stones were removed in the 1960s. In 2012 the large central stone was still standing but no other sign of the cemetery remains.[28]

The land that included the Byfield Farm and the Byfield Cemetery was originally bought from the government by Jesse Spann around 1816. Spann was a Revolutionary War veteran from Carolina. He moved his family to Kentucky and then to Indiana. He purchased 320 acres on either side of Big Creek. Jesse Spann's daughter, Elizabeth, is the first burial recorded.

I've found no record of the date that Horatio Byfield bought the land from Jesse Spann. Horatio built the brick farmhouse there in the 1820s. There is no record of a Byfield burial in the cemetery until 1846.

The following information is from a transcription found on the GenWeb genealogy web pages.

```
Jefferson County: Byfield Graves
Sat, 11/15/2008 - 6:49pm — Ruth Hoggatt
Byfield Graves
Lancaster Township
Section 28 - 5 - 9
```

> *Section 28 of the Lancaster Township is mostly on the west side of Big Creek but, a small portion covers some of the Horatio Byfield farm on the east side. The Byfield family cemetery was near the river.*

```
Transcription by Ruth Hoggatt.
```

> *Ruth probably transcribed this from the WPA cemetery transcription done around 1930.*

```
Byfield (one large stone)
, Daniel Sep 11 1823 - Nov 2 1850
```

> *Daniel Byfield was the first child of Horatio Byfield and Jennette Griffith.*

```
, Willis, s/o D. & M. Byfield, Dec 4 1848 - Jul 5
1850
```

> *Willis Byfield was the son of Daniel Byfield and Martha Baldwin.*

---

28 I would like to know what happened to the original stones that were removed by some farmer. Were they just shoved off to the edge of the field where they may still be found?

, Horatio Aug 29 1796 - Aug 20 1859

This is Horatio Byfield, second child of Abraham Byfield and Patience Corbin. The cemetery is on land that was part of Horatio's farm.

, Patience, w/o Abraham, d. Apr 14 1888, in her 63rd yr

Patience Corbin was the wife of Abraham Byfield and the mother of Horatio.

, Jennet, w/o Horatio Byfield, d. Aug 30 1869, age 61 yr

Jennet Griffith was the wife of Horatio Byfield. In her will she left the farm to her son Horatio.

, Alford Mar 15 1825 - Oct 7 1846

Alford Byfield was the second child of Horatio Byfield and Jennet Griffith.

, James, s/o A. & N., Aug 21 1844 - Feb 10 1847

James Byfield was the first child of Alford Byfield and Nancy Graham.

Byfield, small stones with names of
Horatio, Daniel, Willis, James, Alford & Patience.

Conway, Whitcomb B., s/o William & E., Jan 10 1860 - Mar 12 1863

Whitcomb B Conway was the first child of William Conway and Emily Byfield. Emily was the eighth child of Horatio Byfield and Jennet Griffith.

Polasky, John, d. Sep 28 1867, age 27 yrs

John Polasky was the first husband of Catherine (Kate) Byfield. She later married Judge Thomas Woolen.

Reynolds, Levi B., s/o W.S. & H., Sep 12 1849 - Jan 31 1851

Levi B Reynolds was the first child of William Simeon Reynolds and Henrietta Byfield. Henrietta was the third child of Horatio Byfield and Jennet Griffith.

, Jeanette, d/o W.S. & H., Aug 3 1852 - Sep 12 1853

Jeanette Reynolds was the second child of William Simeon Reynolds and

Henrietta Byfield.

Storey, Elizabeth Spann, consort of Thomas J.,
Apr 15 1806 - Feb 20 1825, age 18y 10m 5d
an infant d/o Thos. J. & E.S., died Apr 5 1826, age
11 mos.

Elizabeth Spann was the daughter of Jesse Spann who was the original owner of the land that later became the Byfield Farm. She married Thomas J Storey in 1822 and died a few years later. An infant daughter of Elizabeth and Thomas is also buried here. Horatio Byfield would have probably owned this land by the time Elizabeth died in 1825.

The first Byfield burial recorded here is Alford in 1846.

Walker, Tanner, s/o T.T. & E. Walker, Sep 13 1864,
age 9m 11d

Tanner Walker was the first child of Thomas T Walker and Elva Byfield. Elva was the ninth child of Horatio Byfield and Jennet Griffith.

Appendix E

NEWSPAPER ACCOUNTS OF THE BYFIELD — CHANDLER SCANDAL

"BUNK," SAYS HE—BUT THE BYFIELDS FILE SUITS FOR $125,000 AGAINST CANDLER

MRS. SARAH BYFIELD and INSETS, WALTER CANDLER (LEFT) AND CLYDE K. BYFIELD (RIGHT).

By NEA Service

Atlanta, Ga., Aug. 22.—"Bunk and frameup," says Walter T. Candler, son of Georgia's Coca Cola king and vice president of a local bank, in answer to suits for $125,000 filed against him by Clyde K. Byfield, an auto dealer, and Sarah Byfield, his wife.

But the Byfields insist the money should be paid them, and have filed suits for the amount, alleging Candler attempted to attack Mrs. Byfield in her stateroom on the liner Berengaria, en route to France.

Clyde and Sarah passport application photograph

Walter Candler, Whose Trouble With the Byfields Followed the Mid-Ocean Champagne Party.

Lima News, 17 September 1922:

Clyde K. Byfield, manager of an automobile company in Atlanta, also was interested in race horses. He had married Sarah Gillespie, and, although she was the daughter of a city detective, she was pretty and vivacious and did not find it particularly difficult to "crash" Atlanta society, including the race-horse set led by Walter Candler and his wife.

Mrs. Byfield posed as a cigarette girl at one of the Lullwater fetes. She and her husband were invited to the Walter Candler home. They chummed together frequently. When Walter Candler decided to sail for Europe this Summer he offered to pay the expenses of Mr. and Mrs. Byfield if they would go along. Mrs. Byfield, he said, could look after the children, as Mrs. Candler was going to visit her parents in California.

The Byfields, Candler and the Candler children sailed on the same boat. They returned on different vessels. And scarcely had Candler reached Atlanta again when he filed suit against Clyde Byfield to stop him from collecting on a note for $20,500 Candler had signed!

Said Walter Candler in substance: "The Byfields held me up. There was a champagne party our last night on board going across. I was intoxicated and don't know exactly how it happened that I got in Mrs. Byfield's stateroom. Byfield crashed in the door and demanded $25,000. He hit me and I hit him. I was dazed and submitted to his demand. I gave him a check for $25,000. In Paris I took it back in exchange for $2,000 cash and a note for $20,500. It was blackmail."

"That's false!" replied Byfield. "The last night on board there was a champagne supper, but nobody was drunk. I heard Mrs. Byfield crying out from her stateroom. I rushed in to find her struggling with Candler. I did my best to kill him with my bare hands. Afterward he came to me of his own accord, cringing and cowardly, and offered me the money. I took it because I was afraid he would leave me stranded in Europe. The letter I signed exonerating him of misconduct was false."

While these charges and counter-charges were being hurled the report came from California that Mrs. Candler was on her way to Honolulu and would sue for divorce. Then she cabled that she would stand by her husband. To add to the mixup, Mrs. Byfield sued Walter Candler for $100,000, claiming he injured her and bloodied her face. "If anybody bloodied her face," replied Candler, "it was her husband. He gave her a terrific beating."

Behind this maze of alleged blackmail, champagne parties, fights and rumored divorce actions looms the slight figure of Asa Candler, Walter's father. What, asks Atlanta, does he think of this scandal? Or is he too much occupied with his own engagement tangle to think? Will he marry the New Orleans divorcee in spite of his family? Is he happy with his millions?

RETRIAL OF HER SUIT AGAINST CANDLER HEIR

By Associated Press.

ATLANTA, Ga., Dec. 15.—Mrs. Clyde Byfield was Monday granted a new trial in her suit for $100,000 damages against Walter Candler, growing from an alleged attack on the steamship Berengaria two years ago. The Georgia Court of Appeals reversed the finding of a DeKalb County jury which found a verdict for Candler.

San Antonio Express, 16 DEC 1924

Alphabetical Index

Illustration Index

www.ingramcontent.com/pod-product-compliance
Lightning Source LLC
Chambersburg PA
CBHW052032280526
45791CB00010B/2941